# The

# Eucharistic Heart of Jesus

## Readings for the Month of June

From the Writings of

Father A. Tesniere, S. S. S.

## Nihil Obstat

LUDOVICUS ESTEVENON, S.S.S.

*Superior Generalis.*

Rome, March 25, 1908.

## Nihil Obstat

REMIGIUS LAFORT, S.T.L.

*Censor Librorum.*

## Imprimatur

✠ JOANNES M. FARLEY, D.D.

*Archiepiscopus Neo-Ebor.*

New York, April 4, 1908.

# APPROBATION

THE Month of the Eucharistic Heart of Jesus will be cordially welcomed by all devout Catholics who desire to respond to Our Lord's appeal at Paray-le-Monial for adoration and frequent Communion. The Sacred Heart and the Eucharist can never be disassociated. Devotion toward the one increases love for the other.

These pious thoughts will help souls to know the Heart of Our Saviour better and, consequently, will foster love for the Sacred Humanity of Jesus Christ residing in the Most Blessed Sacrament. We gladly give our approval to this little book, for we feel sure it will enable the Faithful to spend the thirty days of June in close communion with the Eucharistic Heart of Christ.

*J. Card. Gibbons*

# PREFACE

THE month of June contains two feasts which appeal in a special manner to all devout souls. They are the feasts of Corpus Christi and the Sacred Heart. One is the complement of the other. The revelation of the Divine Master to St. Juliana of Liège in the thirteenth century received its crowning glory at Paray-le-Monial nearly five hundred years after. Since then the two feasts seem to breathe the same spirit, until now devotion to the Sacred Heart practically means an ardent love for the Blessed Sacrament.

Our Holy Founder, Père Eymard, advises all earnest adorers to have one book on the Blessed Sacrament, which they shall read carefully during the month of June. He says this close study and concentration of thought is the most powerful means of imbibing a deep Eucharistic spirit.

It is in order to supply the Faithful with such a book that the following pages have been culled from the prolific writings of

# Preface.

Reverend Albert Tesnière, S.S.S.  His is an able pen whence flow thoughts thoroughly impregnated with the spirit of his venerable Founder.  Every meditation is in the form of the four ends of Sacrifice, a method of prayer which has now become identified with Père Eymard and his Society, the Fathers of the Most Blessed Sacrament.

Being a profound theologian, Père Tesnière has given the Eucharist long and deep study.  He makes the soul realize that only in the tiny white Host can she find on earth the Sacred Humanity of Our Saviour.  The Sacred Heart is the vital organ of that Humanity in His Eucharistic, as It was in His mortal life.  When Jesus appeared to Blessed Margaret Mary, He raised the veils of the Sacred Species, and revealed to the lowly Visitandine His Heart throbbing and longing for our love.  " Behold the Heart that has so loved men ! "

The dominant tone of all the wonderful revelations at Paray-le-Monial is an appeal from the Man-God for more fervent adoration and frequent Communion.  They are the means by which souls can alleviate His " ardent thirst to be loved by men in the

## Preface.

Sacrament of His love." Pictures and statues are representations that appeal to the senses, but only in the Eucharist can be found here on earth the Divine Original.

We trust that, by faithfully using these beautiful thoughts of Père Tesnière, pious souls may spend a month all perfumed with the Eucharistic spirit and that, at the close of June's thirty days of grace, they may find themselves nearer and dearer to the great Heart of our Eucharistic Lord.

S.S.S.

# THE MONTH OF JUNE

His Holiness of happy memory, Pope Pius IX, by a Decree of the Sacred Congregation of Indulgences, May 8, 1873, granted to all the Faithful who, during the month of June, either in public or in private, shall with at least a contrite heart say some special prayers or perform some pious acts in honor of the Most Sacred Heart of Jesus: AN INDULGENCE OF SEVEN YEARS AND SEVEN QUARANTINES once a day.

A Plenary Indulgence on any day of the month, provided that, being truly penitent after confession and Communion, they shall visit some church or public oratory, and there pray devoutly for the intention of His Holiness.

## NEW INDULGENCES FOR THE MONTH OF THE SACRED HEART.

His Holiness Pius X, adding to the favors of his predecessors, has granted exceptional Indulgences, which will rejoice all friends of the Heart of Jesus. To extend the devotion of the Month of the Sacred Heart,

## The Month of June.

His Holiness was requested to grant the following Indulgences:

1. A PLENARY INDULGENCE *toties quoties* (as often as) applicable to the souls in purgatory, on June 30th, in churches in which the Month of the Sacred Heart shall have been solemnly celebrated;

2. The privilege of the Gregorian altar *ad instar,* at the Mass on June 30th, for the preachers of the Month of the Sacred Heart and the rectors of churches in which this devotion shall have been solemnly celebrated;

3. For all who propagate this holy devotion, an Indulgence of 500 days to be gained for every work done to propagate it or to have it more solemnly celebrated; a *Plenary Indulgence* for the Communions made in the *Month of June.* All these Indulgences applicable to the souls in purgatory.

From an audience with His Holiness, August 8, 1906.

ALOYSIUS CARD. TRIPEPI, *Pref.*
*of the Cong. of Indulgences and Relics.*
*Pro-Pref. of the Cong. of Rites.*

## PROMISES OF OUR LORD JESUS CHRIST TO BLESSED MARGARET MARY ALACOQUE IN FAVOR OF THOSE DEVOTED TO HIS SACRED HEART.

1. I will give them all the graces necessary for their state of life.

2. I will establish peace in their families.

3. I will console them in all their afflictions.

4. I will be their assured refuge in life, and more especially at death.

5. I will pour out abundant benedictions on all their undertakings.

6. Sinners shall find in My Heart the source and infinite ocean of mercy.

7. Tepid souls shall become fervent.

8. Fervent souls shall advance rapidly to great perfection.

9. I will bless the house in which the image of My Sacred Heart shall be exposed and honored.

10. I will give to priests the gift of moving the most hardened hearts.

11. Persons who propagate this devotion shall have their names inscribed in My Heart, never to be effaced from it.

12. I promise thee, in the excess of the

## Promises of Our Lord.

mercy of My Heart, that Its all-powerful love will grant to all those who receive Communion on the First Friday of every month, for nine consecutive months, the grace of final penitence, and that they shall not die under My displeasure, nor without receiving the Sacraments, and My Heart shall be their secure refuge at that last hour.

# DAILY PRAYERS FOR THE MONTH OF JUNE

## AN OFFERING.

My loving Jesus, I give Thee my heart, and I consecrate myself wholly to Thee out of the grateful love I bear Thee, and as reparation for all my unfaithfulness! With Thy help, I purpose never again to sin.

(*Indulgence,* 100 *days once a day.*)

(Plenary Indulgence once a month if the prayer be said before a picture of the Sacred Heart, on the usual conditions, confession and Communion, and prayers for the Sovereign Pontiff's intentions.)

" Eucharistic Heart of Jesus, have mercy on us ! "

(*Indulgence of* 300 *days, toties quoties.*)

## THE PRAYER OF ST. GERTRUDE TO THE SACRED HEART.

Hail, O Sacred Heart of Jesus, living and quickening source of eternal life, infinite treasury of the Divinity, burning furnace of divine love! Thou art my refuge and my sanctuary. O my amiable Saviour, consume my heart with that burning fire with which Thine is ever inflamed! Pour down on my soul those graces that flow from Thy love, and let my heart be so united to Thine that our wills may be one, and mine in all things conformed to Thine. May Thine be the standard and rule of my desires and actions! *Amen.*

### PETITIONS TO THE SACRED HEART.

O God, who, out of Thy immense love, hast given to the Faithful the Sacred Heart of Thy dear Son, Our Lord, as the object of their tender affections, grant, we beseech Thee, that we may so love and honor this pledge of Thy love on earth that by It we may merit to love both Thee and Thy gift, and be eternally loved by Thee and this most blessed Heart in heaven, through the same Jesus Christ Our Lord, Thy Son, who liveth and reigneth with Thee in the unity of the Holy Ghost, one God, world without end! *Amen.*

### AN ACT OF CONSECRATION AND REPARATION TO THE SACRED HEART.

O Sacred Heart of Jesus, my Saviour and my God, deign to receive me among the number of Thy adorers, notwithstanding my unworthiness! Humbly prostrate before Thee, I adore Thee with all the powers of my soul. I consecrate them forever to Thee with all my thoughts, words, and actions, in grateful acknowledgment for my redemption, but more particularly for Thy love in always dwelling with us in the Most Adorable and Most Blessed Sacrament of the Altar. Why cannot I, O Sacred Heart, by my adorations and those of my associates, repair all the outrages Thou hast ever received, and that Thou wilt continue to receive till the end of time? Why cannot I offer Thee as much love and glory as Thou dost render to Thy Eternal Father? Do Thou repair all my faults. Be my Protector, my Strength, my Asylum at the hour of my death!

I ask the same for all poor sinners, for all in affliction, for the agonizing, and for all mankind that none may lose the fruits of the Precious Blood Thou didst shed upon the Cross. May it be applied to the souls in purgatory, also! This is my request, and I shall continue to make it until my last breath. *Amen.*

# LITANY OF THE SACRED HEART

Lord, have mercy on us. *Christ, have mercy on us.*

Lord, have mercy on us.

Christ, hear us. *Christ, graciously hear us.*

God, the Father of Heaven,

God, the Son, Redeemer of the world,

God, the Holy Ghost,

Holy Trinity, one God,

Heart of Jesus, Son of the Eternal Father,

Heart of Jesus, formed by the Holy Ghost in the womb of the Virgin Mother,

Heart of Jesus, substantially united to the Word of God,

Heart of Jesus, of infinite Majesty,

Heart of Jesus, sacred temple of God,

Heart of Jesus, tabernacle of the Most High,

Heart of Jesus, house of God and gate of heaven,

Heart of Jesus, burning furnace of charity,

Heart of Jesus, abode of justice and love,

*Have mercy on us.*

# Litany of the Sacred Heart.

Heart of Jesus, full of goodness and love,

Heart of Jesus, abyss of all virtues,

Heart of Jesus, most worthy of all praise,

Heart of Jesus, king and centre of all hearts,

Heart of Jesus, in whom are all the treasures of wisdom and knowledge.

Heart of Jesus, in whom dwells the fulness of Divinity,

Heart of Jesus, in whom the Father was well pleased,

Heart of Jesus, of whose fulness we have all received,

Heart of Jesus, desire of the everlasting hills,

Heart of Jesus, patient and most merciful,

Heart of Jesus, enriching all who invoke Thee,

Heart of Jesus, fountain of life and holiness,

Heart of Jesus, propitiation for our sins,

Heart of Jesus, loaded down with opprobrium,

Heart of Jesus, bruised for our offences,

*Have mercy on us.*

# Litany of the Sacred Heart.

Heart of Jesus, obedient unto death,
Heart of Jesus, pierced with a lance,
Heart of Jesus, source of all consolation,
Heart of Jesus, our life and resurrection,
Heart of Jesus, our peace and reconciliation,
Heart of Jesus, victim for sin,
Heart of Jesus, salvation of those who trust in Thee,
Heart of Jesus, hope of those who die in Thee,
Heart of Jesus, delight of all the saints,

*Have mercy on us.*

Lamb of God, who takest away the sins of the world, spare us, O Lord.
Lamb of God, who takest away the sins of the world, graciously hear us, O Lord.
Lamb of God, who takest away the sins of the world, have mercy on us.

*V* Jesus, meek and humble of Heart.
*R.* Make our hearts like unto Thine.

### Let us pray.

O almighty and eternal God, look upon the Heart of Thy dearly beloved Son, and upon the praise and satisfaction He offers Thee in the name of sinners and for those

## *Litany of the Sacred Heart.*

who seek Thy mercy. Be Thou appeased, and grant us pardon in the name of the same Jesus Christ, Thy Son, who liveth and reigneth with Thee in the unity of the Holy Ghost, world without end. *Amen.*

# PRAYER TO OUR LADY OF THE MOST BLESSED SACRAMENT

O Virgin Mary, OUR LADY OF THE MOST BLESSED SACRAMENT, who art the glory of Christians, the joy of the Universal Church, and the hope of the world, pray for us! Stir up in all the Faithful devotion to the Most Holy Eucharist, that they may render themselves worthy to communicate every day.

*An Indulgence of 300 days each time for the recital of this prayer to Our Lady of the Most Blessed Sacrament.*

S. CARD. CRETONI, Praef.
January, 23, 1907.

## INVOCATION TO OUR LADY OF THE MOST BLESSED SACRAMENT.

Our Lady of the Most Blessed Sacrament, pray for us!

*300 days' Indulgence, when said before the Most Blessed Sacrament exposed.*

PIUS PP. X.
December 30, 1905.

# CONTENTS

# Contents

# First Day.

SUBJECT.—The Revelation of the Sacred Heart, viewed as a whole, comprehends: first, the manifestation properly so called of the adorable Heart; secondly, Its serious and sorrowful complaints; thirdly, Its desires and demands; fourthly, Its magnificent promises.

We shall gather them from the writings of Blessed Margaret Mary and present them to our readers. These words, coming forth from the mouth of the Saviour under the impulse of the various sentiments of His Heart, are too eloquent to have need of lengthy commentaries. It suffices to recall them in order to rouse in turn lively feelings of adoration, thanksgiving, reparation, and petition.

## ADORATION.

### THE MANIFESTATION OF THE SACRED HEART.

" Once, when the Blessed Sacrament was exposed, and I felt my soul abyssed in extraordinary recollection of all its powers and

**1**

senses, my sweet Master Jesus Christ presented Himself before me all shining with glory, His five Wounds brilliant as suns; from every part of His Sacred Humanity radiated flames, but above all from the region of the Heart, which resembled a furnace. Opening His breast, He showed me His all-loving and amiable Heart, the living source of these flames. It was then that He discovered to me the inexplicable wonders of His pure love, and to what an excess He had carried it for the love of mankind.        ."

This first manifestation, in which the Sacred Heart discovers Itself in Its double object: the Heart of flesh beating in the breast of a true Man, and the infinite love with which Christ loved us and still loves us, is followed up by a manifestation still more brilliant and significant.

" Being before the Blessed Sacrament one day in the octave of Corpus Christi, disclosing to me His Divine Heart, the Saviour said to me:  ' Behold this Heart which has so loved men that It has spared nothing even to exhausting and consuming Itself in order to show Its love.' "

" Behold this Heart!"—He shows It there under the veils of the Eucharist, which He has miraculously withdrawn in order to appear to the Blessed Sister. He shows It living and beating in His open breast, the source of the Blood that flows in His veins, the motor of the life that animates Him. He shows It loving, the organ of the affections of His soul, the sensible symbol of His spiritual love of God and man and, as we shall soon see It, offended at the coldness of men and longing to be loved.

It is truly the Heart of Jesus, insepa-- rable from the Humanity of which It is one of the essential organs, inseparable from the Person of the Word who deifies It substantially, inseparable from the Sacrament whose sign alone can permit the Christ of glory to remain really here below.

Let us adore the reality of Its double nature, the divine and the human. Let us adore the reality of Its life and love. Let us adore Its real and abiding Presence in the Eucharistic Christ. May our adoration and homage, the profession of our faith and love, pour themselves out at the foot of the altar, before the tabernacle which has guarded It since the evening of the Last

Supper and which will guard It till the last evening of the world!

### THANKSGIVING.

#### THE PROMISES OF THE SACRED HEART.

The Promises with which it pleased Our Lord to accompany the Revelation of His Heart are magnificent as this manifestation itself, which He calls "the last effort of His love." Some regard the universal Church and the whole world; others are addressed to special classes and show that the Divine Heart is as delicate and attentive as It is generous and magnificent.

The general Promises are so large and so powerful that we may say that the Revelation of the Sacred Heart is a new effusion of inexhaustible love equal, at least, to that spread abroad by the Word on coming into this world, or to that of the Spirit of Love and Life on the days of Pentecost. "For," said the Saviour to the Blessed Sister, "My Heart is so passionately in love with men that, not being able to contain in Itself the flames of Its burning charity, It must of necessity allow them to burst forth. It must reveal Itself to them in order to enrich them with the precious treasures I have shown thee and which contain all the sanctifying graces necessary to snatch them from the abyss of perdition."

It might seem that, after Calvary and the Eucharist, Christ could do nothing more for us, since He had given His life and was constantly renewing that gift in a perpetual Sacrifice and in a Food repeated every day: " *In finem dilexit.* " But in the Eucharist there is a Heart swelling with love, with unmeasured reserves of love accumulated for ages. On the day of Its Revelation, it burst forth anew: " For my Saviour gave me to understand that the great desire He experienced to be perfectly loved by men had led Him to form a design of manifesting His Heart, and of giving in these last ages this final effort of His love, by proposing to them an object and a means so calculated to win them to love Him, and love Him most truly."

The momentum of this effort opens to the world, now old and decrepit, " all the treasures of love. mercy, grace, sanctification, and salvation that It contains, that whoever will render to It and procure for It all the honor and love possible, may be enriched with a profusion of the divine treasures of which It is the fruitful and ever plentiful source."

The devotion to the Sacred Heart is a repetition of the work of Redemption in modern times, the apparition of a new Mediator coming to reconcile to God the world which the great apostasy of naturalism has separated from Him. " My Saviour gave me to understand," says Blessed Margaret Mary, " that His Sacred Heart is the Holy of Holies, and that He willed It to be known in our day in order to be a new Mediator between God and men ; for He is all-powerful to procure their peace by turning away the chastisements that our sins have drawn upon us and by obtaining for us mercy." " What a happiness for you," she wrote to a fellow-laborer, " and for all who contribute to make the Sacred Heart known ! They secure for themselves thereby the eternal friendship and benediction of that lovable Heart."

The Promises to all who confidently recur to the Sacred Heart are not less rich nor numerous, for It is the open source of all grace, the unfathomable ocean of all good. We shall recall some of these Promises enumerated by the Blessed Sister in a letter to Père Rollin:

" Why can I not recount all that I know of this sweet devotion to the Sacred Heart of Jesus? Why can I not discover to the whole world the treasures of grace which Jesus Christ encloses in His adorable Heart and which He intends to pour forth profusely upon them who practise this devotion? Yes, I say confidently if we knew how agreeable this devotion is to Jesus Christ, there is not a Christian, how little soever his love for this sweet Saviour, who would not at once practise it.

" Try, above all, to make religious persons embrace it. for they will derive from it so much help that no other means will be necessary to restore first fervor in Communities even the least regular, and to lead to the height of perfection those that already live in the most exact regularity.

" My Divine Saviour has made me understand that they who labor at the salvation of souls shall acquire the art of touching the most hardened hearts and of laboring with marvellous success, if they themselves are deeply penetrated with a tender devotion toward His Sacred Heart.

" As for seculars, they will find by means of this amiable devotion all the aid necessary for their state, namely, peace in their family, help in their labors, the blessing of Heaven on their undertakings, consolation in their trials. It is, indeed, in this Sacred Heart that they will find a refuge during their whole life and chiefly at the hour of death. Ah, how sweet it is to die after having had a constant devotion to the Heart of Him who is to be our Judge! "

Who does not feel himself reanimated and encouraged to labor and combat, to support trials, to confront suffering, when sustained by such promises? And who could fail to have, according to the words of Blessed Margaret Mary, " a grateful love for Jesus Christ such as is that which is shown Him by the devotion to His Sacred Heart? "

### REPARATION.

#### THE COMPLAINTS OF THE SACRED HEART.

Some are general, and others particular; but all are full of that deep and bitter sadness that springs from the disappointment of one who, having made many and great advances, has a right to expect reasonable returns, and yet receives them not.

"Behold this Heart that has so loved men," said the Saviour, sensitive and justly jealous of His love; and He added sadly: "And in return, I receive for the most part only ingratitude by their irreverence and sacrileges, by the coldness and contempt they have for me in this Sacrament of Love!"

As the manifestation showed the adorable Heart in the Sacrament, revealing the Presence, the life, the love of the Christ in that inert symbol, so does He complain of the insults that wound Him in the Eucharist, as much by cold and contemptuous abstention from It as by irreverent and sacrilegious reception of It. If we consider one by one the outrages of which this loving Heart complains, we shall be filled with contrition for our own shortcomings and compassion for the Adorable Victim of human ingratitude. Again He complains of "receiving only ingratitude and forgetfulness from those that He has loved even to excess," and He adds: "That is much more sensible to Me than all I endured in My Passion. If they would render Me some return of love, I should look upon all I have done for them as little and I should, if that were possible, do still more. But they meet My eagerness to do them good with coldness and rebuffs."

Lastly, comes this moan of anguish, which caused Blessed Margaret Mary insupportable grief: "I thirst, but with a thirst so ardent to be loved by men in the Most Blessed Sacrament that I am consumed by it. I find no one who tries to meet My desire, who tries to slake My thirst by making Me some return for My love!"

Having given utterance to His complaints against "the most part" of men who despise and outrage Him, the Divine Master specifies His grief respecting some particular classes of individuals. He mentions those whom He loved more, whom He called to His own immediate service, and whom He loved with a love of predilection, loading them with the most excellent gifts. They are His priests, religious, consecrated virgins, persons who make profession of piety, and whose infidelity is most injurious to Him. And He said: "What is still more grievous to Me is that there are hearts consecrated to Me who treat Me thus!"

On another occasion, He said: "My chosen people persecute Me in secret and irritate My justice. But I will expose their secret sins by striking chastisements, for I will sift them in the sieve of My sanctity in order to separate them from My well-beloved." "Showing me then His loving Heart all torn and transpierced with blows, He said to me: 'Behold the wounds I have received from My chosen people. Others are satisfied with striking My Body, but they attack My Heart which has never ceased to love them.'

"One day after Holy Communion, my Saviour presented Himself to me, torn and disfigured, as the *Ecce Homo.* He said: 'I find no one willing to give Me shelter in this suffering and sorrowful state!' This sight filled me with so lively sorrow that death would have been a thousand times sweeter to me than to see my Saviour in such a condition. He said to me: 'If thou didst know who it is that put me in such a state, thy sorrow would be much greater! Five souls consecrated to My service have treated Me as thou dost see!'

"One day after Holy Communion, He showed me a frightful crown formed of nineteen very sharp thorns which pierced His divine head. The sight filled me with such sorrow that I could express my sympathy only by tears. He told me that He had come to look for me that I might draw out these thorns for Him, which had been forced in by an unfaithful spouse. ' She pierced Me with as many thorns as she preferred herself to Me by her pride.' "

From the multitudes, from His friends and spouses, from all ranks of Christian society, He receives but ingratitude, indifference, and outrage. " And that is more deeply felt by Him than all that He endured in His Passion! " Not that Jesus suffers physically or morally. He has entered into His glory and He can no longer suffer. But when still passible, He foresaw all these injuries, and endured all their sorrow and humiliation. At present He still experiences injuries, but in the manner of a God, without any diminution of His beatific joy, without any alteration of His immortal life. But that certainly does not lessen the culpability of our offences, which surely strike and attack Him, and it imposes upon every one of us contrition, penitence, and reparation; for who has not contributed his share of bitterness by his forgetfulness, irreverence, and perhaps sacrilegious betrayals of this Heart of the Divine Friend, so preventing and so faithful?

### PETITION.

### THE DESIRES AND DEMANDS OF THE SACRED HEART.

In the first Revelation of His Heart, on the feast of St. John the Evangelist, Blessed Margaret Mary says: "The Divine Heart was represented to me on a throne of fire and flames, shooting out rays on all sides, more brilliant than the sun, and transparent as crystal. The wound that It had received upon the cross was plainly to be seen. A crown of thorns encircled the Divine Heart, which was surmounted by a cross. It was presented to me with these words: 'I thirst ardently to be loved and honored by men in the Blessed Sacrament!'"

In another place she writes: "The Sacred Heart wishes to establish Its reign. He said to me: 'I will reign!'"

"He desires to enter with pomp and magnificence into the palaces of princes and kings, to be honored therein as much as He was outraged, despised, and humiliated during His Passion. He wishes to receive as much pleasure from beholding the great ones of the earth abased and humbled before Him as He once felt bitterness at seeing Himself annihilated at their feet. Here are the words that I heard on this subject: ' Make known to the eldest son of My Sacred Heart that I wish him to consecrate himself to My adorable Heart which desires to triumph over his and, by his intervention, over those of the great ones of the earth. It wishes to reign in their palaces, to be painted on their standards, and engraven on their arms, thus to render them victorious over all their enemies and those of Holy Church.' "

The Divine Master now makes His desires more specific, and transforms them into formal demands akin to commandments. He preludes them by this striking supplication: " Do thou, at least, give Me the satisfaction of supplying for their ingratitude as far as thou art able! "

" When I represented to Him my impotence, He replied to me: ' Well, then, behold wherewith to supply for all that is wanting to thee!' and at that moment the

Divine Heart opened, and there shot forth a flame so ardent that, thinking I should be consumed, I begged Him to have pity on my weakness. ' I will be thy strength,' He said to me, ' fear nothing. But be attentive to what I ask of thee for the accomplishment of My designs:

" ' First, thou shalt receive Me in the Most Blessed Sacrament as often as obedience will permit, whatever mortification and humiliation it may bring upon thee.'

" ' Secondly, thou shalt communicate the first Friday of every month.'

" ' Thirdly, every night between Thursday and Friday, thou shalt rise between eleven and twelve to keep Me company in that prayer which I then offered to My Father, and I shall make thee share in the mortal sadness that I willed to suffer in the Garden of Olives. Thou shalt prostrate, thy face on the ground, as much to appease the divine wrath by imploring mercy for sinners as to assuage the bitterness that I felt from the abandonment of My Apostles, which forced from Me the reproach that they could not watch one hour with Me.'

" ' Fourthly, I demand of thee that the first Friday after the octave of Corpus

Christi be dedicated as a special feast to honor My Heart, by communicating on that day and making to It an Act of Reparation to repair the indignities It has received during the time It was exposed on the altars.' "

Private homages, public honors, more frequent Communions, more prolonged attendance near His Tabernacle in one same prayer, public reparation and compensation —these are the demands of the Sacred Heart.

Jesus insists on this point of reparation by telling Blessed Margaret Mary to offer herself with Him as a victim for sinners, and to accept the chastisement due their sins in order to obtain for them mercy.

" It is true, My daughter, that My love has made every sacrifice for men without their making Me any return.  But at least do thou afford Me the satisfaction of supplying, as far as thou art able, for their ingratitude by the merits of My Sacred Heart.  For that purpose, I wish to give thee My Heart.  But first of all, I seek for this Heart a victim that will sacrifice self as a host of immolation for the accomplishment of My designs."

Our Lord demands these reparations for

secret sinners: " My justice is irritated and ready to punish secret sinners by manifest chastisements if they do not penance. I wish to make thee know when My justice will be ready to deal its blows upon those criminal heads. It will be when thou wilt feel the weight of My sanctity upon thee. Thou oughtest then to raise thy heart and hands to heaven by prayers and good works, to present Me continually to My Father as a victim of love immolated for the sins of the world, and place Me as a rampart between the divine justice and sinners in order to obtain My mercy."

Jesus demanded, above all, reparation for the time in which sin abounds, namely, the Carnival. " During the time of the Carnival, Our Lord presented Himself to me under the form of an *Ecce Homo* laden with His Cross and all covered with wounds and bruises. His adorable Blood was flowing on all sides, and He said to me with a voice painfully sad: ' Will no one have pity on Me, compassionate and share My sorrow in the pitiable state to which sinners have reduced Me, especially at present? '

" I presented myself to Him and prostrated at His sacred feet with tears and groans. He laid His heavy Cross upon my shoulders. Feeling myself weighed down by it, I began to understand better the malice and gravity of sin. I detested it so strongly in my heart that I would have preferred a thousand times to cast myself into hell than voluntarily to commit one."

The reparation that Jesus demanded so earnestly of Blessed Margaret Mary, the adorable Heart expects from all Christians who pretend to love Him, for to repair is to love, and not to repair is not to love. Blessed Margaret Mary says: " The Sacred Heart demands souls reparatrix, who will give Him love for love and who will most humbly implore pardon of God for all the injuries done Him. By means of this Divine Heart, it will belong but to us to satisfy Divine Justice."

Let us sincerely ask strength for this, and let us generously resolve to " fill up in our body what is wanting to the Passion " of His Heart.

Pray for an increase of adorers of our Eucharistic Lord.

May the Eucharistic Heart of Jesus be blessed !

(50 *days' Indulgence.*)

# Second Day.

The universal primacy belonging to Our Lord Jesus Christ by every title, and which ought to be accorded Him by the worship of heaven and earth, is magnificently pictured by St. Paul the Apostle in the following words: " Giving thanks to God the Father, who hath made us worthy to be partakers of the lot of the saints in light. Who hath delivered us from the power of darkness, and hath translated us into the kingdom of the Son of His love, in whom we have redemption through His Blood, the remission of sins: who is the image of the invisible God, the first-born of every creature: for in Him were all things created in heaven and on earth, visible and invisible, whether thrones or dominations, or principalities, or powers: all things were created by Him and in Him: and He is before all, and by Him all things consist. And He is the Head of the body, the Church, who is in the beginning, the first-

19

born from the dead, that in all things He
may hold the primacy: *Ut sit in omnibus
ipse primatum tenens;* because in Him it
hath well pleased the Father that all fulness should dwell: *Quia in ipso complacuit
omnen plenitudinem inhabitare* " (1).

What St. Paul says of Christ, let us say
of His Heart deified by the hypostatic
union.   That Heart is the symbol of the life,
of the love, and of the sufferings of Jesus.
All primacy belongs to Him by right. We
ought, then, in very truth, to give Him
everywhere the first place, since the plenitude of all perfection, divine and human, resides in Him.

### ADORATION.

To the Heart of the Son of God made
Man belongs the Primacy of being, of dignity, and of excellence.   We ought to give
Him the first place in our love, our worship,
and our life.

In the adorable compound of the Word
Incarnate, the Sacred Heart of Jesus occupies the first place, because It is, at least
as the symbol, the sanctuary in which resides His Divinity, the principle of His

—————

(1) Coloss. i, 12-19.

divine and human life, the furnace of His love, the source of His virtues, the sublime strength which made Him embrace and support all the sufferings of His Passion and even death itself, the treasure-house of all the gifts of grace and of the living Gift of Himself in the Eucharist. That Heart is, in fine, the cause of His own glory, and the eternal centre of the glory of the elect.

The Heart of Jesus is the love of Jesus. Is not love the good *par excellence,* the good infinite in itself? *Deus charitas est,* and the cause of all the good that has ever been created in the world of nature and of grace. *Charitate perpetua dilexi te, ideo attraxi te miserans.* Père Eymard wrote: "The Eucharistic Heart of Jesus is the end of the Incarnation, the Redemption, and of the Eucharist Itself, because It is the consummation of love!" May It hold the first place in our love, also, in our worship, and in our life!

May It hold the first place in our love, by our esteeming It above everything else, by our preferring It to everything else! Let us make in our heart a dwelling-place reserved absolutely for It alone, which It may possess without division. Let us in Its regard practice as perfectly as possible the First Commandment, "loving It with our whole mind, with our whole heart, with our .whole soul, with all our will, and all our strength."

May It hold the first place in our worship in such a way that all our religion, all our devotions, whether toward Mary, toward the Passion, even toward the Eucharist, may end in the adorable Heart which gave us Mary and His Blood, and which ceases not to give us His Sacrament!

May It hold the first place in our life in such a way that It may possess, inspire, conduct, correct, and sanctify our whole interior! Let us make profession of depending on It in everything, and of doing nothing but to serve and please It, of being devoted and consecrated to It, immolated to It without power of withdrawal. This is the adoration that the Primacy of Its unique excellence, Its sovereign dignity, Its supreme authority demands for It. It is thus that It will reign over us.

Blessed Margaret Mary tells us: "The Sacred Heart wishes to establish Its reign, and It has said to me, 'I shall reign! I shall reign in spite of Satan and of all those that Satan excites in opposition to It. Satan and his adherents shall be confused!' The adorable Heart of Jesus wishes to establish in all hearts the reign of Its pure love, by proposing to Christians in these last ages the object and the means most proper to engage them to love It, and to love It solidly. This is what It has given Its unworthy slave to understand. May all, then, yield to It! May all be submissive, may all obey Its divine love! This is the most earnest desire that the adorable Heart has given me "(1).

#### THANKSGIVING.

The Sacred Heart possesses and exercises in our behalf the Primacy of goodness and love. It desires to hold the first place in our gratitude.

The creature having no right over God, no debt to demand, it is evident that all the gifts and favors of nature, of grace, and of glory flow from the altogether free, spontaneous, and gratuitous love of God. God has so loved the world as to give it His

---

(1) Vie et Oeuvres de la Bienheureuse Marguerite-Marie Alacoque, publication du monastère de la Visitation de Paray-le-Monial.—Poussielque, Paris.

only Son.   The Son so loved men as to deliver Himself to death to ransom them. He
has so loved His own who are still on earth
as to go to the extreme limit of love by
making Himself their never-failing food;
and He will hereafter love them so much
that He will give Himself to them without
measure or end in the communication of
His glory and beatitude:  *" Propter nimiam
charitatem suam, qua dilexit nos!"* (1)

How could it be possible that all goods
and gifts and delicate attentions, all lights
and helps and support, all consolations and
victories, all hopes and tenderness and joys
would not be ours with the gift of Himself,
which Jesus makes so generously and multiplies so abundantly?  *" Quomodo non etiam
cum illo omnia nobis donavit?"* (2)

But this eternal love of God, which gave
to us the Word at Bethlehem,—this love of
the Word Incarnate, which gave to us the
Christ of Calvary, which still gives us the
Christ of the Altar with all His gifts, is the
Sacred Heart.   When revealing It to the
modern world, Jesus says in an outburst of
tenderness:   " Behold this Heart which has

---

(1) Ephes. ii, 4-6.
(2) Rom. viii, 32.

so loved men that It has spared nothing, even exhausting and consuming Itself in order to testify to them Its love!" Every good thing, then, comes to us from that Heart, and it is thus that It exercises the Primacy of love and benevolence.

In return for all this love, the Sacred Heart longs to hold the first place in our gratitude. To satisfy that most legitimate desire, all the thanksgiving of our heart should incessantly mount toward It; all Its benefits should be for us an occasion for proclaiming to It our thanks. For life, health, and temporal goods, for our Christian vocation, grace, preservation from evil, victory over temptation, pardon of sin, for faith and love, for every act of virtue and for the success of our labors, we owe that dear Heart thanks. For the Holy Mass and Communion, for the great protection of the abiding Presence of Jesus in the tabernacle, for the never-failing assistance of our guardian angels, for the maternal love of Mary, our Mother, and the devoted vigilance of the Holy Church, we owe heartfelt thanks. For these and all other benefits, our hearts should spring up to the Sacred Heart, devoting itself to It in humble, faithful gratitude—gratitude that knows no bounds, that is never satisfied but that is constantly seeking to express itself still more.  Yes, our gratitude should lead us to abandon ourseves blindly to Its ever-benevolent guidance, which is always aiming at our welfare, no matter what It may permit to befall us.

" Jesus Christ made known to me," says His blessed confidante, Margaret Marv " that He wished by solid devotion to His Divine Heart, to gather an infinite number of faithful servants, of perfect friends, and of children truly grateful." And she adds · " It is certain that there is no one in the world who would not experience all kinds of favors from Heaven if he had for Jesus Christ a grateful love such as is testified to Him by devotion to His Sacred Heart."

### REPARATION.

The Sacred Heart claims the Primacy of suffering endured for redemption from sin. This prerogative gives It the right to possess the first place in the compassion of our heart and in our contrition for sin.

When in spite of all the sin of mankind and the irreparable misfortunes with which they inundated the world, the Son of God enjoyed undiminished plenitude of happiness in the bosom of the Father, His love for us urged Him to assume the responsibility of our prevarication together with its rigorous chastisement. Having taken for that end the possible condition of guilty man condemned to suffering and death, He took upon Himself all our sins and bore them on His shoulders even to the Cross, that He might wash away their stains in His own Blood and destroy their guilt by His death. All humiliations and ignominies, ail sorrows of mind and heart, all sufferings that bruise and wounds that tear the body, He has taken upon Himself. He has embraced them, He has delivered Himself up to them. He has been wounded, devoured, consumed by them. He has suffered in His own Person more than all men in the world ever endured. He has suffered the greatest possible torments. He endured them in all their horror, in all their keenness, without the least alleviation. He suffered them freely and voluntarily. He sanctified them, He rendered them fruitful by His perfect virtues and infinite merits. He threw into them, above all, His love, all His love for

His Father in order to avenge Him, to satisfy Him, and all His love for man in order to save him. And His Heart, open upon the Cross and always open on the altar, the first Inspirer of this design, the principal Instrument of this work, proclaims Its Primacy in His redemptory suffering: " Come and see whether there be sorrow like unto My sorrow!" *Virum dolorum!* He was *the* Man of sorrows. He exhausted in Himself the reality of every suffering: *Scientem infirmatem.* Jesus is the only one who knew how to render sorrow holy, vivifying, victorious, and glorious. He is the only Repairer of God's glory, the only Redeemer of all mankind: *Si posuerit pro peccato animam suam, videbit semen longævum* (1).

Thus does Jesus with good right claim the first place in the compassionate love of our heart, the first place in the contrition and penitence which we ought to conceive for our sins, and in the implacable hatred with which we ought to pursue sin. Has He not a right, He who, for love of us, suffered more to restore us to the life of grace

(1)   Is. liii, 10.

than our mother did in giving us birth,—
has He not a right to behold our heart consecrated to compassionating Him, to consoling Him with all the tenderness and pity
that they possess? He demands, He seeks,
He implores this consolation from His redeemed: *Sustinui qui simul contristaretur
et qui consolaretur* (1). " Do thou,
at least," did He say to Blessed Margaret
Mary, " do thou endeavor to comfort Me by
making Me some return ! " Ah ! let us, too,
weep over Him as over the Being the most
beloved and the most to be pitied, our only
Well-Beloved.

Let us arm ourselves against sin with love
for Him who was its innicent Victim. We
conceive true sorrow, generous and victorious hatred for evil only in proportion as
we see in sin the cause of all the sufferings
and death of the Just One *par excellence,*
and comprehend that the malice of sin is as
great as the Passion of Jesus, that is to say
infinite. Let us, then, pursue it to the death
in ourselves and in souls, wherever it makes
ravages, hourly crucifying, even with in-
creasing hatred, if that were possible, its

---

(1) Ps. lxviii, 21.

innocent Victim. We shall punish it by works of penance generously embraced. We shall expiate it by courageously accepting the pains and sufferings sent us by Almighty God.

Disclosing the abyss of His unfathomable bitterness, Jesus said: "What I endure from their ingratitude is more painful to Me than all I endured in My Passion!" "And He asked me," says Blessed Margaret Mary, "whether I would not stay by Him on the Cross, telling me that I ought to groan, to weep with Him incessantly to obtain mercy, that sin might not reach its height, and that God would pardon sinners through the love He bears this amiable Heart." The generous daughter replied: "O my Saviour, discharge upon me all Thy anger, efface me from the Book of Life, rather than the loss of those souls that have cost Thee so dear!"

### PETITION.

Prayer supposes two essential things: the bountiful liberality of God, from whom alone can come to the creature all kinds of benefits necessary for furthering him on to the infinite good, which is eternal happiness; and the power of intercession, which moves that liberality and inclines Him to grant us His gifts. The Sacred Heart here, again, possesses and exercises a double Primacy, that of beneficent goodness, and that of all-powerful mediation.

Heart of the Son of God, the sum total of all goodness, It is the ocean of all created goods, which flow from this inexhaustible source. It is " from the treasury of this Divine Heart," infinitely good, that are ceaselessly brought forth " all good things both old and new." It glories in being prodigal and magnificent when invoked with confidence. " You have never asked anything of Me. Ask, then, and you shall receive ; for, Amen, I say to you, if you abide in Me, if you continue to pray lovingly to Me, whatever you demand, shall be granted you."

Heart of man deified, It is the Heart of the Priest infinitely pure and loving, always pleasing to the Father, always heard by Him. It is the Heart of the Sacred Victim who has purchased with His Blood all kinds of benefits for redeemed man.

Heart of Man victorious, It has received by a new title of conquest the full possession and sovereign dispensation of all riches for men now become Its happy subjects. By all these titles, It is the perfect and all-powerful Mediator, the only Mediator by right, through whom we are sure of being heard and of having our prayers granted.

It is for this reason that Jesus wishes to possess the first place in our confidence, our hopes, and our prayers. It is to Him, above all other mediators, however powerful or benevolent they may be, that we must make known our desires, raise our eyes, and extend our hands. It is to Him that we must discover the shocking state of our wants, our miseries, our wounds, how deep soever they may be, however incurable they may appear. It is by Him, by His intercession as universal and eternal High Priest, by His indefatigable pleading as our almighty Advocate, that all our requests must ascend. If our confidence wavers, if our prayers hesitate, Jesus has no longer in our hearts the undisputed and incontestable Primacy that He ought always to hold there.

Is not the Sacred Heart the Heart of the merciful Priest, compassionating all our needs, because It has Itself experienced them? of the faithful Priest, who has burdened Himself with all our interests, and who stands before God, always interceding for us? of the eternal Priest, in fine, who, upon our earthly altars as on that of glory, never ceases to offer His Sacrifice of infinite value for our salvation? " It is by Him, O Lord, Thou dost always create, sanctify, quicken, bless, and give us all these good things—*Per quem haec omnia semper bona creas, sanctificas, vivificas benedicis et praestas nobis"* (1).

Let us, then, seconded by the saints and their Queen, go straight to the Sacred Heart. Let us implore It and always, in every conjecture and for everything, pray by It. Let us invoke It for ourselves and our brethren, for the whole world, the world of the living and that of the dead. It has charge of all, and It is sufficient for all. Blessed Margaret Mary, Its confidante, writes: " Our Lord gave me to understand that His Heart is the Saint of saints, the Saint of love, that He wishes It to be known in our day that It may be the Mediator between God and men, for It is all-powerful to procure us peace and mercy, by turning away the chastisements which our sins have attracted."

---

(1) Canon of the Mass.

*Est ante omnes, ipse caput*                    *qui*
*est principium  .          primogenitus:*  O
Sacred Heart, whom I adore in Thy hidden
Presence, and yet so living and so loving in
the Blessed Sacrament, Thou art above all
things, the Head, the Principle, the First-
born of all hearts!  To Thee in my heart,
in all hearts, be the first place, the Primacy,
recognized, loved, adored, obeyed, forever
established and forever invoked: *Ut sit
ipse in omnibus primatum tenens.*

Pray for an increase of devotion among
the Faithful toward the Eucharistic Heart
of Jesus.

May the Eucharistic Heart of Jesus be
blessed.

(50 *days' Indulgence.*)

# Third Day.

## A CALL TO ADORE THE EUCHARISTIC HEART.

*" Come, let us praise the Lord with joy, let us joyfully sing to God, our Saviour. Let us come before His presence with thanksgiving, and make a joyful noise to Him with psalms; for the Lord is a great God, and a great King above all gods. For in His hands are all the ends of the earth, and the heights of the mountains are His. For the sea is His, and He made it, and His hands formed the dry land."* (*Ps. xciv.*)

### ADORATION.

This Psalm, as its text expresses and as commentators agree, is a call to prayer, an invitation to divine worship. The Church has chosen it for the " Invitatory " of her Breviary, by which she daily exhorts her sacred ministers in the name of the Faithful to acquit themselves toward God of the chief duty of public praise. Adoration of the Most Blessed Sacrament is one of the forms of worship and praise. This Psalm contains, then, the call of the Holy Spirit, who inspired it, to all Christians to come before the real and merciful Presence of God on our altars, there to render their homage of adoration, praise, and prayer.

Logically analyzed, this Psalm contains: a pressing exhortation to come and adore the Lord in His temple; an enumeration of His titles to our adoration, which create for us so many duties on that point; the indication of a certain number of acts which our adoration ought to comprise; and, lastly, the very grave penalty fulminated by the Lord against an absolute refusal to adore Him. From this we may justly fear that negligence to adore Him as much and as well as He has a right to expect of us individually, will not go without its punishment.

*"Venite!"* Come, says the Holy Ghost by the mouth of the Psalmist, hasten! no hesitation, no delay! Leave your couch, go out of your dwelling, discontinue your labor, interrupt your wordly conversations, quit every other occupation, in order to fulfil the great work of prayer! That is the principal duty of life, the only duty absolutely necessary, under one form or another, in a de-

gree more or less great, but from which no one, in whatever place, in whatever state he may live, can be entirely dispensed. It is the chief end of the rational creature, for prayer constitutes the personal service of God, and man is created, above all else, to praise and serve God. *"Venite!"*

Come in the morning to consecrate your day to God. Come in the morning before your daily occupations have engrossed your attention and your time, and thus secure to God His share, for He ought always to come first. Come in the evening to finish your day in Him who is to be the eternal end of your life, and to submit all its actions to Him who will on the last day judge them without appeal. Come even at night, because the night belongs to Him as well as the day. Come to sanctify it by the part of it that you will offer to Him in sacrifice, and by the salutary repose He permits you to take during it. Come, then, come from all sides. Hasten! *"Venite!"*

*"Let us come before His presence!"* Let us seek the Face of the Lord, and let us come into His Presence, for His Face, His adorable Countenance, or His Presence, are one and the same holy and desirable reality.

What! is it necessary to leave the place in which we are in order to seek the Face of the Lord when there is question of adoring and praising Him? Is not God present everywhere? Is not every one of us very near to Him, so that we " are, we live, and we move in Him? " Is it not easy to discover Him, to bless Him, under the features of all creatures, whose first reason for existing is to manifest by reflection His beauty, His power, and His goodness? Certainly, this universal Presence of God in nature is very real. It is the attribute of His immensity, which contains all things; of His all-seeing eye, whose glance penetrates everywhere; and of His power, which maintains and animates every being. This Presence wills to be recognized and adored by reason, respected by submission to the order that It establishes, and by flight from sin which disturbs It. It wills to be served by the right use of all the goods It has created, and loved through gratitude for the benefits of which It is the generous dispenser. Viewed in the light of supernatural revelation, It demands the faith, hope, love, and praise of the heart, as well as that of the lips.

But because It is necessary and invisible in Itself, It testifies on the part of God less love for man, and It is to him less accessible and less favorable than certain other forms of presence, by which God has willed to reveal Himself to His privileged creature and enter into relations with him. Such, for instance, is the supernatural, but altogether spiritual, presence by which God in the Trinity of His Persons, dwells in the soul justified by grace; such, also, was the Presence, partly sensible, by which He willed to abide in the Ark of the Covenant, and later in the Temple of Jerusalem. "I shall be there all days in the midst of My people," He said. "My eyes will be open, My ears attentive, and My Heart ready to receive the petition of all that come to pray to Me therein." The throne of this merciful Presence was called the "propitiatory," that is, the place chosen by God to draw near to His people, to receive their religious homage, both public and private, and to grant them help. Now, it was to that Temple, to the foot of that altar, that the Psalmist exhorted the adorers of the true God to go seek His ever-helpful Presence and to find

His ever-benevolent Countenance. *" Let us come before His presence!"*

### THANKSGIVING.

This presence, however, is symbolical and the signs that reveal this " Face " of God are foreign to Him. Ah! Lord, if Thou wouldst only take a human face, animated by a human soul, whose glance could divine the affections of our heart, and whose lips could express the thoughts of our mind! If Thou wouldst take a face like our own, which we could see, could recognize with our eyes, and could not forget when out of sight! If Thou wouldst take a human face that would at the same time be a divine Face, because Thy divine Face, that is, Thy eternal nature, would shine through its features, and because one of Thy Divine Persons had formed it and united it to Himself to make of it His own countenance forever! Lord, how the whole earth would then long for Thy Face, and with what eagerness Thy people would seek Thy Presence, now become human, though remaining all divine! *" Vultum tuum desiderat universa terra!"*

Ah! Thou hast heard this longing, O

good God, and hast satisfied this need of
earth! And we have seen the Word made
Flesh dwelling among us, full of grace and
truth, showing us "in the goodness, the
amenity, and the smile of Our Lord Jesus
Christ, all that there is in Thee of love and
mercy for men!" And Thy human Presence, which the world began to enjoy at
Bethlehem, Thou didst not withdraw from
it even when the time had come for Thee
to transfer It to the right hand of the
Father, there to receive Its glorious recompense. But simply hiding Its splendor by
the sacramental veil, Thou remainest with
us always God made Man in the Eucharistic
tabernacles everywhere multiplied. It is in
them Thou dost await our religious homage due to Thy Divinity and Humanity. It
is in them that we must seek Thee if we
would freely pray to Thee with confidence
and love, since there it is that, remaining
our Lord and our God, Thou art at the same
time our Father and our Pastor, our Priest
and our Brother, like unto ourselves!

"*Venite, præoccupemus faciem ejus!*
Come, then, all! Hasten to the Presence
of the Lord and adore Him!"

### REPARATION.

The Psalmist enumerates a certain number of reasons very capable of leading souls to adore God, the meditation of which in His holy Presence should send up from our heart to His throne acts of adoration and canticles of praise.

First, " The Lord is a great God and a great King above all gods: *Quoniam Deus magnus, et Rex magnus super omnes deos."* The Psalmist here proclaims the essential excellence of the Divine Being, which puts Him in a rank absolutely apart and infinitely above all created beings.  His is by nature infinite, and the *only* infinite,—infinite in being, infinite in perfection, infinite in action, infinite in power, infinite in duration. He transcends all created beings—the kings of the earth, the demons (whom men, dazzled by their power, call gods), and even the angels, those gods created to serve the one only great Lord and God.  To Him, therefore, on account of this incommunicable excellence, give the adoration that belongs but to Him alone.  To Him the praise that He alone deserves, in which every creature should disappear and be annihilated, since He alone exists of Himself and alone has a right to be: *"Quoniam Deus magnus Dominus et Rex magnus super omnes deos!"*

Again, this great God, who exists of Himself, is the Creator of all that is, both on land and on sea. His power and immensity have hollowed out the fathomless abysses of the ocean. The strength and skill of His hands have consolidated the continents and fashioned the wonders that cover them: *"Quoniam ipsius est mare, et ipse fecit illud; et siccam manus ejus formaverunt*—For the sea is His, and He made it, and His hands formed the dry land." And because these mighty wonders of creation with all that they contain, are born of His thought and exist but by His will, they belong to Him by right. If man is allowed to enjoy them, it is because it pleased the great God to create them for his use and happiness. *"Quoniam ipsius est mare!"*

The sole Creator of all that exists, having of His own free will called them forth from the abyss of His being, He is their absolute Master and Sovereign Ruler. However extended the frontiers of His vast empire, one, as they are, with the universe itself, He tranquilly holds them in His hand, which knows no weariness in governing them: "*Quia in manu ejus sunt omnes fines terrae*—For in His hand are all the ends of the earth." However elevated the mountain summits, He rules them with all the dwellers upon them, in the might of His boundless authority: "*Et altitudines montium ipsius sunt*—And the heights of the mountains are His." The Roman psalter says that the Lord "sees under His feet the heights of the mountains—*Et altitudines montium ipse conspicit.*" It is again the idea of God's supreme dominion over all that He has created, with this difference, that things the highest, in the moral, as well as in the material world, dignities and royalty, ambition and domination, science and riches, power and pride,—all, all He regards with supreme disdain, as a grain of sand under His feet, and men who vaunt themselves on such things appear in His eyes like atoms scarcely emerged from nothingness: "*Et altitudines montium ipse conspicit!*"

Another title which God has to our homage, one which touches us very closely and which presses upon us with still greater weight, is that He has made us, that He is the Creator of man: "*Adoremus. Dominus qui fecit nos.*" It is He that made us, He, God in Three Persons, having conceived the idea before all ages and entertained the design in His eternal love: "*Qui fecit nos!*" It is He who made us with His divine hands, lovingly fashioning us with paternal care to His own image and likeness, not only by impressing His own intelligent and loving nature upon our intelligence and will, but by the supernatural communication of His own life in the gift of sanctifying grace, by the communication of His own knowledge in the gift of faith, and of His own love in the gift of divine charity: "*Ipse fecit nos!*" It is He who made us, masterpieces and kings of the world of nature by the perfection of our rational nature, children of His divine Paternity, brethren of Jesus, His first-born, and heirs of His glory by the entirely gratuitous adoption that He willed to make of us: "*Ipse fecit nos!*" Ah! what love on His side, and what magnificent gifts to us! What honor and greatness and glory for us in that this great God has willed to be our Creator and we are His creatures: "*Adoremus eum qui fecit nos!*"

PETITION.

But all this was not enough.   Having
made us, the great God willed to protect us
and lead us to our eternal destiny.   He constituted Himself " our God and our Father,
and we are become the people of His pasture
and the sheep of His hand:   " *Quia ipse est
Dominus Deus noster, nos autem populus
pascuae ejus et oves manus ejus.*"   It is the
touching and marvellous mystery of the paternal providence of God over His elect that
the Psalmist evokes in these words, and
which demands our grateful adoration. It
is His providence that disposes the sure
ways that lead to heaven, that makes us enter therein, conducting us by the hand.   It is
His providence that protects us and defends
us on those ways, that helps us with its suc-
cors, that arms and furnishes us with all
the means of salvation.   His providence it
is that feeds us with Divine Bread, which He
sends us every day from heaven, which contains, with all the virtue to sustain and develop our life, all the remedies to cure our
infirmities, and all the sweetness to console
and enliven: *"Nos populus pascuae ejus
et oves manus ejus!"*

Why, excepting by our pride, our malice, and ingratitude, our blindness and folly, are we become creatures turned against this Creator, subjects revolted against this Sovereign, ungrateful children toward this Father, and sheep escaped from the crook of this Shepherd? This is a monstrosity capable of casting earth and heaven into a state of stupor and indignation. It imposes upon us the obligation of adoring, by the sincere confession of our sins and by the bitter tears of our broken heart, the goodness and holiness, the justice and mercy of God: "*Ploremus ante Dominum*—Let us weep before the Lord!" This spontaneous and penitent avowal made here below before the merciful Face of the Lord, is alone capable of preserving us from the public accusation and eternal condemnation that we shall have to undergo before the irritated Face of the formidable Judge when He shall appear to judge all men: "*Præoccupemus faciem ejus in confessione*—Let us come before His Presence with thanksgiving!"

A last motive for adoration proposed by the Psalmist is: "God is our salvation—*Jubilemus Deo salutari nostro.*" As we owe Him adoration because He is our first principle, being our Creator and the source of all our goods, we owe it to Him, also, as to our last end, our necessary end, for whose service and advantage alone we were created. He is the supreme end dominating all our life, commanding and directing it, calling us, at last, to Himself to terminate our earthly career, as well as to judge us. All that is conformed to this end is good, all that is contrary to it is bad. Now, God, in His entirely gratuitous bounty, has willed to be Himself our last end, and that the possession of Him should constitute our supreme perfection, our supreme rest. Before that man should fall, God willed to sanctify him for his noble end; and after he had fallen, He willed to raise him up and redeem him from the eternal death which he had incurred. It is in this that God is our salvation: *" Jubilemus Deo salutari nostro —Let us rejoice in God, our Salvation! "* He is the object of our salvation, proposing Himself as our infinite recompense and eternal beatitude. He is the Agent of our salvation, having become incarnate and having died, thus acquiring all the merits, and disposing all the necessary means to enable us to reach salvation: *" Jubilemus Deo salutari nostro.''* By this title we owe to God the adoration of hope and that of prayer, demanding of Him insistently, and firmly expecting from Him alone, the helps of salvation faithfully to pursue our journey here below; the grace of final perseverance, which alone assures salvation; and lastly, the glory which puts the soul in the definitive possession of God. Let us, then, adore our Salvation and our Saviour and, as says the text of St. Jerome: "The unshaken rock of our salvation—*Jubilemus petrae Jesu nostro!"*

Pray that you may hunger for Holy Communion.

O Sacred Heart of Jesus, I confide in Thee.

(300 *days' Indulgence.*)

# Fourth Day.

*Come, let us adore and fall down, and
weep before the Lord that made us. For
He is the Lord, our God, and we are the
people of His pasture and the sheep of His
hand. Today if you shall hear His voice,
harden not your hearts, as in the provoca-
tion, according to the day of temptation in
the wilderness, where your fathers tempted
Me. They proved Me, and saw My works.
Forty long years was I offended with that
generation, and I said: These always err
in heart. And these men have not known
My ways; so I swore in My wrath that they
shall not enter into My rest. (Ps. xciv.)*

## ADORATION.

In this Psalm the Holy Spirit revea's
many reasons for adoring God in the sanctuaries consecrated to His Real and Personal Presence. He teaches, also, some of

50

the forms that may be lawfully used to express our homage of adoration.

*" Adoremus et procidamus."* This is the first act of adoration, exterior adoration: *Procidamus;* and of interior adoration: *Adoremus.* As soon as we appear before the Face of God, it is our duty to recognize Him, to salute Him by an exterior and public sign. And since His Presence is that of the Divine Majesty, before whom the angels constantly prostrate; since It is that of the risen Christ, before whom every knee should bow in heaven, on earth, and even in hell, we cannot do better than to bend our knees before Him and profoundly incline our head. This attitude is that of respect, of religion, of dependence, which is proper for the creature before his Creator, for the subject before his King, for the servant before his Lord, for the criminal in presence of his Judge whom he wishes to appease. *" Procidamus!* Let us fall down."

*" Adoremus!"* Interior adoration ought to accompany that of the body, and give to it a soul to render it true and spiritual, consequently, pleasing to God who, being spirit and truth, wishes that they who adore Him should do so in spirit and in truth. Adora-

tion should express man's nothingness in presence of the plenitude of the Divine Being, man's universal submission before the fulness of the sovereign rights of God, the gift of self to Him who is our principle and our end, by the sacrifice of everything that we are and of all that we possess to His holy will and good pleasure. " *Adoremus!* —Let us adore ! "

" *Exultemus Domino!*—Let us joyfully sing to the Lord ! " Let us be joyful, let us thrill with gladness, let our heart bound with joy when before the Lord ! Is not this worship of happiness, of joy, of thanksgiving, as rightful as it is necessary when God grants us the honor and, at the same time, the favor of admitting us to His Presence? Propriety, respect, good manners, are not sufficient, joy must shine forth. Do we not feel glad when gazing upon some marvellous beauty? when meeting some one whom we very much love? To behold one day His Face unveiled will be infinite blessedness, and to go into His eternal dwelling will be to plunge into an ocean of joy. Although the sacramental cloud that envelops His Presence extends its shadow over our heart to moderate the expression of our joy, the

sentiment of it should be neither less profound nor less lively. Like John the Bap-
tist, though beholding his God through the
immaculate cloud of Mary's womb, let us
tremble with happiness when the star of the
sanctuary announces to us that He is there.
" *Exultemus Domino!* "

" *Jubilemus Deo, et in psalmis jubilemus ei*
—Let us joyfully sing to God, and make a
joyful noise to Him with Psalms!" If the
heart is full of joy, of necessity it pours itself out in songs and canticles. Inward
speech is not sufficient for it, nor discreet
effusions, nor a moderate tone. It must cry
aloud its happiness. Besides, as songs are
one of the forms of homage rendered to
princes and victors, one of the features of
feasts and rejoicings among men, are canticles in which the voices are supported and
perfected by musical instruments. We
thus express our gratitude to God. It is by
hymns, in which admiration, love, en-
thusiasm break away from that calm range
of prose, that we celebrate in harmonious
rhythm and all the freedom of poetry His
perfections, His greatness, and the wonders
of His love: " *Et in psalmis, jubilemus
ei!* " Let us, then, sing to the Lord, min-

gling our voices with those of the choirs of monks and nuns who solemnize the praises of the liturgical Office! Let us sing to the Lord, uniting our acclamations with those that accompany the public Sacrifice, in which the Lamb gives to God transcendent praise by the voice of His Blood. If it is in private that we fulfil the duty of adoration, let us still sing, but in our hearts, as the angels chant around the altar, as did Cecilia on the day of her voluntary immolation to the love of the Divine Spouse: *" Et in psalmis jubilemus ei!"*

### THANKSGIVING.

*" Præoccupemus faciem ejus in confessione.    .    et ploremus ante Dominum!"* The confession(1), the avowal of our actual sins, of our past sins, of our passions, our defects, our ignorance; the sincere and humble avowal; the repeated ac-

---

(1) *" Praeoccupemus faciem ejus in confessione."—This verse may be understood in two ways: first, that we come before the Lord to praise Him; secondly, as the Prophet teaches, the confession of our own miseries may be mingled with the praise of God's mercy. The Fathers concur in this latter exposition. Bellarm., Com. Ps. xciv, 2.*

knowledgment, which implores pardon of
infinite Mercy ; the avowal which supplicates
Justice not to remember what the repentant
one has disavowed,—behold a necessary expression of adoration for every man who
appears before the thrice-holy God, for all
are by nature sinners, and he who says that
he is not, is, at St. John declares, a liar.
This humble confession wins for us the
favor of the God of truth, who " willingly
looks upon the contrite and humble heart,
while He repulses and sees only from afar
the proud." This confession is, also, a canticle, the canticle of our weakness, our
frailty, our misery, to the glory of the goodness, the longanimity, the patience, and the
Mercy of our Father: *" In confessione
jubilemus ei!"* This confession must be
completed by tears, those of the eyes or
those of the heart. They must be tears of
regret, of repentance. of true sorrow, the
sorrow of filial love, whose bitterness is
sweet, because it is demanded as an expiation, and whose value is precious before
God, because tears of contrition are the
blood of the soul immolated to God as a sacrifice for sin: *" Ploremus ante Dominum!"*
There are other sources of tears. They

may spring from compassion for the sufferings, the humiliations, and the abandonment of Jesus in His Passion. They may
be shed over the ingratitude, contempt, and
injuries of which He is the victim in the
Eucharist. They may be tears of charity
and zeal over the unhappy state of sinners
to obtain their conversion. They may be
tears of tender pity over the woes of the
Church, the Spouse of the Son of God, and
our Mother, combated by the furious hatred
of her enemies, and betrayed by her own
children. They may, also, be tears of desire, drawn forth by the pressure of a need
keenly felt, of succor ardently longed for.
Such tears intensify prayer. Lastly, joy,
too, has its tears to express its fulness, its
liveliness, its gratitude. Let them flow,
then, at the feet of the Lord. They honor
Him as a sacrificial libation, for they are an
effusion in which the soul itself flows out before its Saviour, and nowhere can they flow
with more security than under His eye, nor
give to him who sheds them more peace and
consolation: "*Ploremus ante Dominum!*—
Let us weep before the Lord!"

"*Hodie si vocem ejus audieritis, nolite
obdurare corda vestra*—Today if you shall

hear His voice, harden not your hearts." In these words we have the law of adoration and its sanction. The Royal Prophet, who had invited the Israelites to the adoration of the Lord, revealed to them the reasons for it and dictated various formulas for it. He now gives place to the Lord to proclaim in Person the obligation, which He will sanction by threatening the most terrible chastisement against the refractory, namely, the refusal to admit them into His eternal repose.

"Today, if you shall hear *My* voice, harden not your hearts as did your fathers in the desert, where they dared to tempt Me and provoke Me, but where I showed them My works," in wonders of power and goodness. "For the forty long years that I was with this people to conduct and protect them, they excited My anger by their offences and I saw that they always erred in heart. Their sons have not desired to know My ways, therefore, in My wrath I have sworn that they shall not enter into my rest: *Ut juravi in ira mea: si introibunt in requiem meam!*"

The voice of the Lord, awful and solemn, had, indeed, resounded on Sinai, in the noise of thunder and the terrors of light-

ning, and had uttered as the first commandment of the Law: "The Lord thy God
shalt thou adore and Him only shalt thou
serve." But the people, following their car-
nal instincts, prostrated before the altars of
the false gods that were honored among the
neighboring nations. On another occasion,
they made a golden calf out of the trinkets
of all the women of Israel and, offering it
incense, they solemnly adored it. The wrath
of the Lord was roused against these evil
doings, but the prayer of Moses appeased
Him. Then this too indulgent Father of a
people always too forgetful, to keep them
faithful, multiplied His miraculous benefits,
among them the manna falling every morning from heaven to feed them and the water
bursting from the rock at the touch of the
rod of Moses to quench their thirst. The
obstinacy and ingratitude of the people rendering useless the continuance of His goodness, the Lord condemned the whole guilty
generation to die in the desert and, consequently, never to enter the Promised Land,
the land of rest after their rude wanderings
of forty years. This land was an image of
the heavenly country in which God admits
His elect to a share in His eternal repose:

"*Si introibunt in requiem meam!*—They shall not enter into My rest!*"

REPARATION.

This is the literal and historical sense of the close of this Psalm. Its moral sense is, that it is a fundamental obligation of the natural law to adore God as reason shows Him. The first duty of the positive law is to adore God, who has revealed Himself in the Holy Scriptures; and the Son of God, the Restorer of the Law, proclaimed it anew in the Gospel in the presence of Satan, who had dared to demand adoration from Him:

*Vade, Satana! Scriptum est enim, Dominum Deum tuum adorabis et illi soli servies!*—Begone, Satan! for it is written, 'The Lord thy God thou shalt adore and Him only shalt thou serve!'"

Jesus came to seek upon earth adorers for God, His Father. He instructed them in all that can here below be known of His mysteries, in order that their adoration might be true, and He sanctified them interiorly that it should be interior and spiritual. He immolated Himself in sacrifice on the Cross that God might thus receive absolutely perfect adoration, and He instituted the public

and essential rite of adoration in the Sacrifice of His Flesh and Blood perpetually renewed.  He dictated the formula of prayer
which the Father always hears.  He set
the example of divine praise, whether by
publicly blessing His Father, or by reciting
the Psalms, which received new consecration in thus passing the lips of the Son of
God.  Spending whole nights in the adoration of God, He taught us to prolong in the
watch of interrupted repose, the sacred
praises, the contemplation of the divine
mysteries, and unwearying supplication.

Claiming for His Father divine honors,
He demands them for Himself, also, declar-
ing that He and the Father are one, and that
whoever sees Him sees the Father likewise.
The living Throne of God, who dwells in
Him personally, He has remained on earth
in the Most Blessed Sacrament, prescribing
to His Apostles and to all priests, their suc-
cessors, to adore Him by offering " in
memory of Him," that is, to Himself and
His honor, the Eucharistic Sacrifice offered
by Himself to the Divine Father.  He has
also ordained to the Faithful of all ages to
adore Him by eating His Flesh, which is to
believe in His Presence here below and to

profess their desire of living on It, food being the principle of life.

Such is the promulgation and the grand plan of the law of adoration by Christ, the Son of God. Who does not understand that it obliges in a supreme degree, and that whoever rejects it deserves to be forever excluded from the eternal peace promised by Jesus to those that believe in Him! "*Si introibunt in requiem meam."*

The Church, heiress of the legislative power of Jesus Christ and ordered by Him to reduce to positive precepts the institutions founded by His word and example, has ordained that the offering of the Sacrifice of the Mass shall be obligatory on certain days, and the participation of the Faithful in it by their personal presence also obligatory. She has, too, made it a law that sacramental participation in the Flesh of Christ, at least once a year, shall be obligatory. To withdraw one's self from either of these precepts of adoration, is to resist Jesus Christ and to exclude one's self from His rest: "*Si introibunt in requiem meam!"*

Providing for exterior adoration which His personal Presence calls for. Holy Church has consecrated to Him abodes which she desires should be as worthy as possible of His Majesty. She surrounds them with guarantees which secure their being exclusively devoted to His worship. She organizes in them ceremonies of religion and solemn pomp to honor Him and preserve for Him the fidelity of men, who have need of such means to rouse and express their faith. To support these sacred dwelling-places and the worship rendered in them to the Christ-God, she authorizes and encourages gifts and foundations which form the personal treasure of the Eucharistic King become poor for us. To lay a hand on these sacred abodes, to seize their treasures, to thwart this worship, are so many crimes against the law of adoration due to God and His Christ, which rouse their wrath and malediction: *"Si introibunt in requiem meam!"*

### PETITION.

Christ having snatched His Apostles from the servitude of the world in order to attach them to His service by prayer and the apostolate, the Church has imposed upon priests in their freely chosen vocation a certain amount of daily prayer and a recitation of the divine praise, from which they may not exempt themselves without violating a sacred obligation. Then follows separation from their Divine Master for eternity: " *Si introibunt requiem meam!* "

And all they who, by the religious vows or by private promises, have engaged to pay to God a tribute of prayer, of various forms or measure,—all henceforth, by a new title and in proportion to their engagements, come under the grand law of adoration. They cannot be voluntarily unfaithful to it without incurring the displeasure of God and, perhaps, His anger. If they do not always expose themselves to the chastisement of irrevocable privation of the divine rest, they certainly defer the possession of it. In the fiery prison, where desires and regrets are sharper than the bite of the most penetrating flames, they will discharge the debt of negligence to fulfil their duty of prayer: " *Si introibunt in requiem meam!* "

We implore you, then, in the name of the sovereign will of God, in the name of the divine institution of Jesus, in the name of His Presence here below and the desires of His Heart, as well as in view of the most sacred interests of your soul; in the name of your obligation to fulfil, of your needs to satisfy, of consolation to find, of peace to experience, and of even the joy that you shall taste, priests, religious men and women, priest-adorers, and you, also, aggregates of the Blessed Sacrament, all,— every time that you hear the voice of God, under the sound of the bell that calls you, or under the form of the hand marking on the dial the hour assigned you, harden not your hearts: *"Hodie si vocem Domini audieritis, nolite, obdurare corda vestra!* Today if you shall hear the voice of the Lord, harden not your hearts!"

May sensuality and the love of our own ease, may sloth and negligence oppress not our hearts to enervate and hinder us from promptly responding, without hesitation, without delay, to the duty of praise or adoration! May the dissipation of worldly conversations, or the too eager pursuit of what pleases render not our hearts so inconstant as to forget the homage promised to God and the satisfaction that He expects from it: *"Hodie si vocem Domini audieritis, nolite obdurare corda vestra!"*

It is the Creator who calls us to life. It is the Saviour who calls us to grace. It is the Supreme Remunerator who will one day call us to glory. It is He Himself who invites us today to adore and praise Him in the Sacrament of His beneficent Presence. Let us not do Him the injury, the wrong of remaining deaf to His voice, which makes known the tender love of His Heart: *"Hodie si vocem Domini audieritis, nolite obdurare corda vestra!"*

Ask Our Lord to increase your love for the Blessed Sacrament.

May the Eucharistic Heart of Jesus be blessed!

*(50 days' Indulgence.)*

# Fifth Day.

## THE HEART OF THE INFANT GOD.

THE state of the Incarnate Word in His infancy offers to us an important study, because it presents the first manifestation of the Man-God on this earth. It is sweet to contemplate, and it shows Him to us at the first dawn of life, which is always clothed with charms. The Heart of Christ, morally and physically, animates this phase of His life. To study Its state, Its functions, Its sentiments during this radiant springtime, which, however, is not undisturbed by storms, is the subject of this adoration. In it we shall set forth our duty to the Host of Christmas, in which the Heart that began to love and to redeem us at Bethlehem, continues Its love for us and confers upon us the fruits of Its first annihilations, Its first benefits, Its first sorrows and prayers.

Blessed Margaret Mary composed a canticle very simple in form, but vigorous in sense, full of sweet and tender love for the Infant of Bethlehem. We shall give it here in separate stanzas suited to the different parts of this adoration, in order to present our homage in union with this most perfect and pleasing adorer of the Sacred Heart.

*My turn near Him I've taken,*
*Sweet Babe, so oft forsaken;*
*May He my senses waken,*
  *To hear His voice divine!*
*My love shall here be plighted,*
*My heart to His united,*
*And from It flames be lighted,*
  *To burn the dross from mine.*

### ADORATION.

" This day is born to you a Saviour, who is Christ, the Lord, in the city of David. And this shall be a sign unto you. You shall find the infant wrapped in swaddling-clothes and laid in a manger." In these words did the angel announce to the shepherds on the mountain the great news of the birth of the Son of God become man.

Come, let us go to Bethlehem, to the House of Bread, the Eucharistic Tabernacle. Let us by faith raise the linens of the Sacred Species that cover the Infant God. Let us enter into His Heart, whose palpitations cause His breast to heave and send to

His gracious countenance the brilliant hues of His life-blood, as Mary lays Him in the crib.

It is the Heart of a victim, for it is the Heart of Him who, St. Paul says: " Emptied Himself, becoming obedient unto death, even to the death of the cross—*Exinanivit semetipsum, formam servi accipiens, et habitu inventus ut homo* "(1). The weakness of life just begun, its feebleness, dependence, poverty, silence, or its inarticulate wailing, its uncertain infantine gestures —all betoken life in its greatest impotence, existence emerging from the confines of nothingness: *Exinanivit semetipsum!*

But It is at the same time the Heart of a perfect man, of the most perfect of all men, of the Head of humanity from all time; for this Heart is, even under Its appearance of feebleness and in Its bonds of impotence, in full possession of intellectual and moral life, of supernatural and divine life in all their plenitude of intensity and interior action. The Beatific Vision fills It with light, love, holiness, power, and joy; and if It compresses in unfathomable depths the actual

_____

(1)   Philip. ii, 7.

joy of Its infinite gifts, It preserves the incontestable possession of them, It employs and utilizes their dominion. As It is, by virtue of the exquisite communications of the Divinity, the Head of all mankind, It rules and sanctifies them, and offers to God in their name the homage of a religion absolutely perfect and worthy of Him. Priest from the moment of the Incarnation, and the only Priest for eternity, It exercises Its sublime and necessary function for the Father's glory and the profit of the world: " *Ad Filium autem: Dilexisti justitiam et odisti iniquitatem: propterea unxit te Deus, Deus tuus, oleo exultationis prae participibus tuis*—But to the Son: Thou hast loved justice, and hated iniquity: therefore, God, Thy God, hath anointed thee with the oil of gladness above Thy fellows "(1).

But still more, it is the Heart of the only Son of God! Although formed of the substance of a woman and nourished with her milk, the Father recognizes in this Infant the Son who lives in Him from all eternity. He ceases not to say to Him in the annihilations of the Crib, as He said to Him in the

---

(1) Heb. i, 9.

splendor of His glory: "*Filius meus es tu, ego hodie genui te!*—Thou art my Son, this day have I begotten thee!" I am, I shall ever be His Father, He will always be My Son: "*Ego ero illi in Patrem, et ipse erit mihi in Filium*—I will be to Him a Father, and He shall be to me a Son"(1).

Let us adore all these states of the Heart of the Infant God. Every one of them is true, immense, infinite. Their harmonious whole makes of this Sacred Heart the adorable masterpiece of the wisdom, the power, and the love of God for us.

> *Eternal glory leaving,*
> *For our poor hearts retrieving,*
> *And triumph there achieving,*
>    *He makes in them His throne.*
> *To earth He comes a stranger,*
> *A Babe, His crib a manger,*
> *To rescue us from danger,*
>    *To claim us for His own.*

### THANKSGIVING.

Because It is personally united to the Eternal Word, of whom It is the true Heart, which union sanctifies It with the most per-

---

(1) Ibid. i, 5.

fect holiness, which is that of glory; because It is on that account the abode of predilection of the Most Holy Trinity, it cannot be but that the Heart of the Infant-God should be beatified in Its substance, clothed with definitive glory, filled with all the joys of the Vision, both for Itself and for all the members of which It is the supernatural Motor and the Furnace of life. But while for Himself miraculously suspending the sentiment of all these joys, in order to give Himself up wholly to suffering; thinking of us, and knowing that we could not possibly live without joy nor persevere in our aim at eternal happiness without some foretaste of it, He wills that His Heart should be a source of delight pouring into ours an abundant and inexhaustible stream: " *Haurietis aquas in gaudio de fontibus Salvatoris*—You shall draw waters with joy out of the Saviour's fountains " (1).

The angel announced it to the shepherds as the great joy come down from heaven: " *Evangelizo vobis gaudium magnum*—I bring you good tidings of great joy "(2).

---

(1)   Isaias xii, 3.
(2)   Luke ii, 10.

Great joy from His glance which rests upon them with recognition and satisfaction, from His mouth which smiles upon them, from His arms which twine around their neck, from His lips which tenderly kiss them, from His Heart which beats against theirs when He reposes on their bosom. Such are the effusions of joy that inundate Mary and Joseph. He is so truly the image and the sweetness of God that whoever beholds Him, whether in His Crib or in the Temple, as did Anna the prophetess, and the High-Priest Simeon, feels his soul cheered and dilated; he is ravished, he exults with joy: *"Benignitas apparuit Salvatoris nostri Dei*—When the goodness and kindness of God our Saviour appeared"(1).

Ah! it is because He is the personal Love of God, incarnated by pure love, in order to perform the work of love. Love presses Him and gushes from His Heart under every form. "For God so loved the world as to give His only-begotten Son—*Sic Deus dilexit mundum ut Filium suum unigenitum*

---

(1) Tit. iii, iv.

*daret"*(1). And this will of the Father's love hurries away His own, which yields itself up to it without reserve. Now, " The Father sent not His Son into the world to judge the world, but that the world may be saved by Him—*Non enim misit Deus Filium suum ut judicet mundum, sed ut mundis salvus fiat per ipsum"*(2). Let us, then, give thanks to God for the unspeakable gift of this Child who is our Saviour, who lies before us with all the graces of salvation, and who gives Himself to us for our everlasting gain: " *Gratias Deo super inenarrabili dono ejus!*—Thanks be to God for His unspeakable gift "(3).

*What joy, what peace and pleasure!*
*What bliss beyond all measure!*
*I find in Him, my Treasure,*
  *The Bridegroom of my soul!*
*My Portion! naught shall ever*
*My heart's affections sever*
*From Him—And sin?—Ah, never*
  *Shall it my will control!*

---

(1) John iii, 16.
(2) Ibid.
(3) II. Cor. ix, 15.

### REPARATION.

The wintry blast of this December night, which chills His members in spite of the swaddling-bands in which His Mother so carefully wraps Him, and the warm breath of the ox and the ass, more compassionate than the inhabitants of Bethlehem; the poverty of this abandoned stable to which the indifference of His fellow-citizens has relegated Him; the exile in a hostile coun- try to which He will soon have to submit; the tears that fall from His innocent eyes at sight of the painful visions that rise up in the distance; the horrible massacre of the children of Bethlehem and its neighborhood, which filled their mothers with inconsolable sorrow—all this proclaims her Child the victim announced to Mary by the angel " to save the world from its sins."

Although He had to wait thirty-three years before being immolated, before His sacrifice was exteriorly consummated, yet from His very birth the Infant-God was slain and sacrificed in His Heart. The de- cree of Divine Justice was that the salva- tion of guilty man, powerless to redeem himself, should be at the price of the death of an innocent man. When the will of God rejected all other sacrifices, the Word offered Himself, and He planted in the midst of His Heart this decree more penetrating than all the swords of immolation: "*Et legem tuam in medio Cordis mei—*And Thy law is in the midst of My Heart!" He desires only this will of His Father, and it is to accomplish it that He has become incarnate: "*Ecce venio ut faciam tuam voluntatem—*Behold, I come that I should do Thy will!" However terrible and bloody it may be, Jesus already accomplishes it by giving Himself up to it without a word of contradiction. "I will not restrain my lips: O Lord, Thou knowest it!"(1)

But in this fearful will to which, lying powerless in His Crib, He submits, there are all the unrecognized rights of God, of His goodness, His holiness, and His justice. There are, consequently, all the wrath, all the vengeance of God. There are all the sins, all the baseness of man, all the torments, the ignominy, the abandonment of the Passion. There are all the sorrows of His well-beloved Mother

(1) Ps. xxxix, 9.

and, lastly, for the damned the utter uselessness of His immense sufferings. Thus does this Child begin to experience in His Heart, even in the Crib, the frightful agony under the crushing weight of which He sweat blood in the Garden.

Yes, from this moment, although repressing the outward manifestation of it, " He began to grow sorrowful and to be sad— *Cœpit pavere et tædere, contristare et mœstus esse."* The grotto of Bethlehem is as inhospitable to Him as that of Gethsemani ; the Crib in which He is lying in His helplessness as hard as the wood of the Cross or the nails that fastened Him to it. From the first moment of His life on earth, He felt in His heart only sorrow and opprobrium : *" Improperium exspectavit Cor meum et miseriam!—*My Heart hath expected reproach and misery ! "(1)

It is particularly hard to see a child suffer. Its innocence and infantine charms call for joy and happiness without a care. Shall we not, then, pity the Infant-God who, later on, in the Sacrament, in which He continues His Passion as He anticipated

---

(1) Ps. lxviii, 27.

it at Bethlehem, showed to Blessed Margaret Mary " His Heart surrounded by a crown of thorns, a gaping wound in the centre, and surmounted by a Cross. He revealed to her that, from the first moment of His Incarnation, all His torments had been present before Him, and it was from that moment that the Cross had been, as it were, planted in His Heart. He told her that He accepted at that moment all the sorrows, all the humiliations that He was to suffer in His mortal life, and even the outrages to which His love for man would expose Him in the Blessed Sacrament till the end of the world."

*He sobs e'en in His sleeping,*
*Dear Babe, our coldness weeping;*
*His mother watch is keeping,*
*Nor can her grief repress.*
*Some portion of her sorrow,*
*Each day and each tomorrow,*
*From Mary let us borrow,*
*To comfort His distress.*

*How could I live without Him?*
*For heaven is all about Him.*
*Oh, never shall I doubt Him,*
*Though life be dark and cold!*

*But whereso'er He leadeth,*
*Where famished souls He feedeth,*
*Where on the Cross He bleedeth,*
*My station near Him hold.*

### PETITION.

It seems, indeed, that two graces, above all, are to be asked from the Heart of the Infant-God, because they flow directly from His state of infancy.  They are the precious grain that He produces from the straw on which He lies: first, personal sanctification, the grace, the spirit, the virtues of spiritual infancy;  and  secondly,  the  apostolate, zealous and devoted love for the salvation of little children.

In imitation of Eternal Wisdom, become silent and docile in the Babe of Bethlehem, of Almighty Power and Sovereignty become  submissive  and  dependent,  of Supreme Majesty voluntarily abased in extreme humility and the poorest of little ones, the grace of spiritual infancy is found in simplicity,  humility,  docility,  dependence, obedience, holy abandonment of mind, heart, and will.  These were the virtues that filled the Heart of the Infant-God.  Where is He more " meek and humble of heart " than in the Crib or in His exile in Egypt? in the arms of His Mother? or in the labors to which St. Joseph introduced Him? These virtues and this spirit are so important that for those who do not clothe themselves with them in order to become like little children, it is impossible to enter the kingdom of heaven. The Infant-God is the ideal child. Let us, then, keep His Heart constantly before our eyes, and supplicate Him to render ours like unto His.

Let us carry away from the contemplation of this Child of love the apostolic grace of devotedness and zeal for the salvation of little ones. He is full of love for them, since He embraces their state in order to render Himself supernaturally, divinely, lovable to all. He consecrates their weakness and innocence by His own, their poverty by His own, their dangers by those He Himself runs, their sufferings by His tears. It is in this state of infancy, become entirely like unto them, that He begins to attract them, that He wishes them to be allowed to come unto Him. Far from preventing them, their elders should help them to do so, should lead them to Him.

Satan and the world, whose murderous

hatred willed the death of Jesus, and who, in the person of Herod and his cruel ministers, procured the destruction of the children of Bethlehem, still continue the bloody persecution of these innocent souls, and, above all, by godless schools. These children, adopted by God in Baptism, baptized in the Blood of Jesus, sanctified by the presence of the Holy Spirit, pupils of the Church, and heirs of heaven, are taught by a godless education to ignore their Saviour. It teaches them to disown Christ, to despise the Church, and to have no care for their eternity. Godless education commits the great crime, the irremissible crime of " scandalizing the little ones." It does this by destroying the first germs of faith which they inherit from the crib, or even forestalling their reception by the apostasy into which the enemies of salvation entice the miserable parents. Woe to the world for all these scandals, but, above all, for scandalizing these little ones ! *" Qui scandaliza-verit unum de pusillis istis, expedit ei ut sus-pendatur mola asinaria in collo ejus et de-mergatur in profundum maris !*—He that shall scandalize one of these little ones that believe in Me, it were better for him that a mill-stone should be hanged about his neck, and that he should be drowned in the depth of the sea!"(1)

For the love of the adorable Eldest Brother of all little children, let us make in His Heart the resolution of devoting ourselves to their salvation. Let us do this, first, by furthering the Eucharistic education of even the tiniest, that is, by forming them from earliest infancy to piety toward the Blessed Sacrament, by speaking to them of It, by taking them before the Tabernacle, by teaching them to show It great respect, and above all, to pray to It with great confidence. Later on, let us do all in our power, both in the family circle and in catechetical instructions, to contribute to a good preparation for First Communion. Let us spread the practice of frequent, even daily Communion for all children after their First Communion. Lastly, let us devote ourselves to the propagation of Christian schools making pecuniary sacrifices for their foundation and support.

On Christmas day, 1685, Our Lord appeared to Blessed Margaret Mary. He

---

(1) Matt. xviii, 6.

showed her the pupils of the Visitation and her own young novices, grouped around her like little lambs, and as once to St. Peter, He said to her: " Feed My Lambs! "—The Sacred Heart repeats to each of us: " Lovest thou Me?—Feed my lambs! "

To please the Heart of the Infant-God, let us love and serve His little ones!

*He begs us with Him suffer,*
*For sinner and for scoffer,*
*With mind and heart to offer*
*Some generous sacrifice;*
*That with contrition rending*
*Our own soul for offending,*
*With justice, mercy blending,*
*May lead to Paradise.*

Say the prayer to Our Lady of the Most Blessed Sacrament for the increase of daily Communion among the Faithful.

Eucharistic Heart of Jesus, have pity on us!

(300 *days' Indulgence.*)

# Sixth Day.

## HEART OF JESUS, SON OF MARY.

SUBJECT.—We are about to adore the Heart of Jesus in Its relations with the Most Blessed Virgin. These relations are, first, those of the most perfect of sons with the most perfect of mothers; secondly, those founded on nature or filial love; thirdly, those springing from services or benefits rendered; fourthly, those arising from sufferings borne together; and fifthly, and lastly, those dependent upon mutual co-operation in the work of the world's salvation. They are, on the other side, first, the relations of the most loving of mothers with the most beloved of sons; relations of unparalleled love, expressed by the most worthy homage of adoration, thanksgiving, compassion, and prayer, offered without faltering by the Mother, and which filled the Heart of the Son with satisfaction and delight. All these relations are expressed in this grand invocation of the Litany of the Sacred Heart, short in words,

83

but in meaning infinite: *" Cor Jesu, Filii Virginis Matris!*—Heart of Jesus, Son of a Virgin Mother!"

### ADORATION.

*" Cor Jesu, Filii Virginis Matris, miserere nobis!"* Let us adore the Heart of the little Infant beating against the heart of His Mother, while she presses Him with joy in her tender and sheltering arms. This Infant is the true, the own Son of this Mother, formed of her blood and strengthened by her substance, born of her womb and nourished by her milk. After the Divine Sonship, which He received from His Father in eternity, nothing is truer, greater, more necessary to God and to the world, nor dearer to Jesus Himself than the human Sonship that He received in time from His Mother.

Thence spring the sacred and august relations which forever bind the Heart of this unique Son to this unique Mother. First, they are the bonds of nature: the bond of origin, which attaches the child to the mother as to the cause of its existence; the bond of blood which, flowing from the heart of the mother into that of the child, creates between them a kind of identity; and the bond of life preserved and increased by the nourishment received from the maternal bosom. Secondly, there are the moral bonds of the natural law which obliges the child to dependence upon and obedience to her who holds from the Creator the care of directing its infancy; which obliges it by gratitude toward her who, having given it life by exposing her own, surrounds it at every instant by her devoted care and solicitude. Lastly, the bonds of choice, of affection, of love, which attach the child to its mother by the qualities and virtues that it discovers in her, by their life in common, their mutual joys and sorrows, in which their hearts are dissolved in one same affection, which, by ennobling, strengthens all the other ties.

The Heart of the Infant God so much the more perfectly embraced all these sacred obligations toward His Mother, as it was to Mary alone, the unique principle of His human life, that He owed all that He had received. He loved those bonds so much the more ardently as Mary possessed in the highest degree all the qualities of motherhood, and fulfilled its duties without faltering. It was with all the strength, all the tenderness and delight of His Heart that He loved His Mother, gave Himself to her, obeyed and served her. With the same affections He still continues, and He will forever continue to serve her even in His glory, looking upon Himself as forever bound to her by the most profound filial piety.

But at the moment that, formed of the blood of His Mother, the Heart of Jesus began to be attached to her by this powerful love, the Heart of Mary, undergoing the natural law which was energized in her by the loving force of the Holy Spirit who effected her divine maternity, turned ardently to the living Fruit of her womb, gave herself up unreservedly to Him, attached herself to Him forever, and proclaimed that she was willing to become His Mother only that she might more perfectly be His servant: "*Ecce ancilla Domini!*—Behold the handmaid of the Lord!" From that moment she began to give Him, along with her maternal care, all the services of supernatural love, of religion, of adoration in spirit and in truth, of perfect praise, unreserved sacrifice, and perpetual immolation.

What her Well-Beloved was to her, she was to her Well-Beloved. They were inseparably united in the same love. It made them live one in the other, and joined them in one single Heart, the Heart of Jesus and Mary: "*Dilectus meus mihi, et ego illi—* My beloved to me and I to Him."

Let us, then, adore the filial piety which ceased not to dwell in the Heart of Jesus for His Mother by appropriating to ourselves all the love, all the devotedness of Mary for Jesus. This divine Mother desires that the Heart of her Son should be honored and loved. She declared it authoritatively in one of the revelations of the Sacred Heart. Blessed Margaret Mary says: "The sweet Heart of Jesus having appeared to me on a throne of flames, Its Wound radiating beams of light and heat, the Most Blessed Virgin, who was standing beside the adorable Heart, invited me in motherly words to approach. 'Come,' she said, 'draw near. I am going to make you the depository of the great Treasure which the divine Sun of Justice formed in the virginal earth of my heart, where It was hidden for nine months before being manifested to men. Behold this Divine Treasure whose tender love longs to enrich you by bestowing Itself upon you!'"

"*Cor Jesu, Filii Virginis Matris, miserere nobis!*"

### THANKSGIVING.

"*Cor Jesu, Filii Virginis Matris, miserere nobis!*" The generous love of the Sacred Heart in creating Mary immaculate and enriching her with all graces, in order to sanctify her and render her worthy to become His Mother, forms a new bond between the Sacred Heart and her. This unique love of the Incarnation by which He gives Himself to her as her Son is for her the plenitude of grace. Behold the infinite tenderness of His love for Mary!

This Blessed Mother, having given to Him human life that He might consecrate it to the service of His Father, the Blood with which He was to redeem the world, the faithful co-operation of prayer and devotedness in His work here on earth, the consolation of her sympathy in His sufferings, and her heroic participation in the pains of His death, a new source of love was opened in His Heart, and it constantly surged and flowed in glad waves toward the Heart of

Mary. It was the love of gratitude, that virtue so pleasing to Jesus. He rejoiced in it, gloried in it. He returned to Mary a hundredfold of happiness, glory, power in heaven and on earth for all that He had received from her. Hence, the perpetual effusion of His most magnificent gifts, blessings, thanksgivings, and praise: *" Ave, Maria, benedicta tu in mulieribus!"* Thou hast opened in my Heart an incurable wound of love, O My well-beloved! *" Vulnerasti cor meum, soror mea sponsa!—* Thou hast wounded My Heart, My sister, My spouse!"(1) " Come, come that I may crown thee in a triumph eternally renewed! *—Veni coronaberis, veni!"*

These flames of her Son's love enkindle in the Heart of Mary a sense of gratitude which becomes almost a torture, for if she herself has given anything, it was of the fruits that she had received, and what she has received will always be infinitely more than she has given. She fully understands the abundance, the price of the divine benefits. In her most pure gratitude she retains nothing for herself and, being incapable of

---

(1)   Cant. iv, 9.

egoism, her soul melts into thanksgiving. She is transformed into the living expression of praise, and she eternally chants to the Heart of her Son her canticle of gratitude: *"Magnificat anima mea Dominum, et exultavit spiritus meus in Deo salutari meo!*—My soul doth magnify the Lord, and my spirit hath rejoiced in God, my Saviour!"

It is only by uniting our thanksgivings to those of Mary, in order to purify them, to enliven them with love, that our duties of thanksgiving, and they are innumerable, infinite, since we have been infinitely loved, will be pleasing to Jesus. There is only one voice that charms and captivates His Heart: *"Sonet vox tua in auribus meis, vox enim tua dulcis*—Let thy voice sound in my ears, for thy voice is sweet"(1). There is only one voice that He still desires to hear, and that is the voice of His Mother: *"Quæ habitas in hortis, amici anscultant; fac me audire vocem tuam!*—Thou that dwellest in the gardens, the friends hearken. Make me hear thy voice!"(2)    That

---

(1) Cant. ii, 14.
(2) Cant. viii, 13.

voice of Mary, did we know how to make it sound upon our lips, will open to us the Heart of her Son, causing inexhaustible torrents of grace to fall upon the earth.

" Once," says Blessed Margaret Mary, " my Mother made me see the Sacred Heart of Jesus as a source of living water, whence it flowed gently by five canals.      ." Again, she says, " This Queen of goodness, speaking to the daughters of the Visitation, said: ' Not only should they enrich themselves from this inexhaustible Treasure, but still more should they distribute Its precious coin as far as they are able.    Let them give largely.    Let them enrich the whole world with It, fearing not that It will ever fail, for the more they will draw from It, **the** more It will have to give!' "

### REPARATION.

" *Cor Jesu, Filii Virginis Matris, miserere nobis!* "    Nothing more closely unites two beings than sorrow, whether one endures it for the love and service of the other or, struck by the same blow, they help each other to bear the burden together.    Their common grief is a millstone that grinds both hearts, their tears make an indestructible cement of the dust, and the wounds that are dug into their hearts, afford a retreat into which they flee, there to remain forever strictly united to each other. Thus it was with the common martyrdom of Jesus and Mary. It created between them new ties while rendering all others more intimate.

By virtue of the requirements of Divine Justice which demanded this supreme expiation, this Son, who would have wished to shield from all sorrow His faultless Mother, by her very innocence exempt from the law of suffering,—this Son so loving and so tender, must draw His Mother into the tempest of His Passion and deliver her to its fury by which He Himself was to be bruised and broken. She suffered only from His sufferings. He alone was her executioner and her martyrdom. He constituted all her pain, which was as great, immense, infinite as Himself! Mary, on her side, loved Jesus so much that, in spite of the martyrdom which she was to endure, she willed to follow Him in order to share His pains and opprobrium, to endure in her compassion the punishment of His Passion, to mingle her tears with His Blood and, by that faithful co-operation, to help

Him, to support Him, to relieve and indemnify Him as much as in her lay.

In this mutual combat, in which are united so much love and so much sorrow, Jesus attaches Himself to Mary by the sweetest ties of infinite tenderness, infinite pity, infinite compassion. To testify to her the feelings that pass all expression, He allows His Heart to be opened under her eyes. As she is standing nearer the Cross than all others, she receives in greater abundance the waves of Blood and grace that issue from It. She was the first to enter by her longing gaze, by her sorrow and love into that retreat to which Jesus attracted her, commanding her to abide therein forever, to exercise her sublime and maternal functions of consoler of her only Son and of reparatrix for all her other children.

From that moment Mary's ministry of reparation near the Sacred Heart was crowned with success, for it was to her intercession that the Good Thief owed his pardon; the centurion, the soldiers, and the crowds that were converted, the contrition and faith which made them strike their breast, saying, " Indeed, this was the Son of God ! "

Mary continues her intercession all through the ages, as we learn from the following vision of Blessed Margaret Mary:

" One day, on the feast of the Visitation, I was before the Most Blessed Sacrament, asking of God some special grace for our Institute. But I found the Divine Goodness inflexible to my prayer. He addressed to me the words: ' Say no more to Me about it. They turn a deaf ear to My Voice; they are destroying the foundation of the edifice ! '—But the Most Blessed Virgin, assuming our interests with her Divine Son, now so irritated, prostrated before Him, saying to Him these tender words: ' Exercise upon me Thy just wrath. These are the daughters of my heart. I shall be to them a shield to receive the blows which Thou wilt deal out to them.' —Then the Divine Saviour, assuming a sweet and gentle expression, said to her: ' My Mother, it is for thee to distribute My grace as seems good to thee. I am ready for love of thee to endure the abuse that they make of it.    .    If their interests are dearer to thee than Mine, thou canst arrest the course of My justice.' But the Queen of goodness and of love more than maternal, replied: 'I ask for delay only till the feast of the Presentation. Until that time I shall spare neither care nor trouble to render Thy graces victorious and to frustrate the efforts of Satan, by snatching from him the prey that he looks upon as already his own'—Some time after, the Blessed Virgin presented herself to my soul. She appeared quite worn out with fatigue. She had in her holy hands some hearts that were covered with wounds. 'See,' she said, 'what I have snatched from the hands of the enemy, who was having his sport with them. But what most afflicts my maternal heart is that some take his part against me. They despise the help that I offer them.'"

It is for us to render fruitful by our prayer, contrition, and penance, united to her sorrow and tears, Mary's reparation to the Sacred Heart for our sins and those of the whole world. Let us confidently present them to Jesus, repeating to Him without wearying: "Remember with all Thy Heart, O Thou best of sons, the agony and the groanings of Thy Mother and, by that remembrance, have pity on us: *In toto*

*Corde tuo gemitus matris tuae ne obliviscaris!*" (1)

### PETITION.

"*Cor Jesu, Filii Virginis Matris, miserere nobis!*" To all the other relations that bind the Heart of Jesus to that of Mary, we must add those of justice; for God Himself has laid it down as a law that whoever has faithfully accomplished here below what was intrusted to him, shall receive in heaven as a recompense jurisdiction over great things: "*Euge, serve bone, quia super pauca fuisti fidelis, super multa te constituam*—Well done, good and faithful servant; because thou hast been faithful over a few things, I will place thee over many things" (2).

Now, Mary wisely, faithfully, and successfully administered all the graces she had received. She valiantly co-operated in the grand work of the Incarnation and the Redemption. She was a Mother as courageous in delivering her Son for the world on Calvary as she was faithful in giving Him to the world at Bethlehem. It is due

---

(1)  Eccli. vii, 29.
(2)  Matt. xxv, 21.

to her that Jesus was able to fulfil the will
of His Father, redeem mankind, and regain for Him the eternal empire which He
now possesses in His glory. These works
were infinite and worthy of infinite reward.

Jesus must, then, recompense His
Mother with glory, power, and royalty.
Having placed her at His right, crowned
Queen of heaven and earth, His Heart
tastes ineffable satisfaction in putting at her
disposal all the treasures of Redemption,
all the created forces of the world of nature,
grace, and glory, so that nothing is done
without her, nothing bestowed but through
her, nothing, whether of expiation, prayer
or praise, accepted but by her mediation.
Jesus has constituted her the universal
mediatrix between mankind and Himself,
the constant co-operatrix in His government, the sovereign dispensatrix of all His
treasures.

"*Deus totius boni plenitudinem posuit in
Maria: ut proinde si quid spei in nobis est,
si quid gratiæ, si quid salutis, ab ea no-
verimus redundare quæ ascendit deliciis af-
fluens, innixa super Dilectum suum.*—God
has placed in Mary's hands the fulness of
all good, so that we can have no hope of

grace and salvation, but through her who, taken up into heaven and there inundated with the delights of the blessed, rests on the Heart of her well-beloved Son "(1).

It is, then, our duty as well as our interest to pray by the name of Mary, to trust in the merits of Mary, to cover ourselves with the sanctity of Mary, to bear as far as in us lies a resemblance to Mary, if we would touch the Heart of Jesus and become pleasing to Him. She is the Queen and the Sovereign of His Heart, because she is His unique love, He having loved her, as He still loves her, more than all other creatures together of whom He loves not one but on account of His Mother. This is what the glorious title, " Our Lady of the Sacred Heart," proclaims. With this title the Church has crowned her. She, like a mistress, disposes of that Sacred Heart as is pleasing to her. She inclines It to what she desires, gives It to whom she wills. Jesus finds exquisite and infinite delight in being thus delivered into the hands of His Mother! All that she asks of Him, her Son owes her, since she it was who fur-

---

(1) St. Bernard, *Sermo in Nativitate B. M. V*

nished Him with the means of acquiring it by giving Him her blood. God Himself is her debtor: *" Euge, euge, quæ debitorem habes Filium tuum, qui omnibus mutuatur; Deo enim universi debemus, tibi autem etiam ille debitor est!"* (1)

Mary one day said to Blessed Margaret Mary: " I wish to enrich all men with the precious gold which has become under the blows of the Passion inappreciable currency, marked with the coin of the Divinity, in order that they may be able to pay their debts and negotiate the great affair of their eternal salvation." This salvation is what she operates in her children. They, also, form her glorious and immortal crown, as the confidante of the Sacred Heart, that most privileged child of the Blessed Virgin, tells us: " I received," she says, " great marks of the protection of the Blessed Virgin on the day of her triumphal Assumption. She showed me a crown which she had made of all the daughters in her suite, and she gave me to understand that she wished to appear with that ornament before the Most Holy Trinity."

---

(1)   St. Methodius Const., *Sermo de B. Virg.*

" *Cor Jesu, Filii Virginis Matris, miserere nobis!* "

Make frequent ejaculations during the day to Our Lord in the Tabernacle.

Jesus, my God, I love Thee above all things.

(50 *days' Indulgence.*)

# Seventh Day.

## THE SACRED HEART IN THE GIFT OF THE EUCHARIST.

THE Sovereign Pontiffs who instituted the Feast of the Sacred Heart declare that the motive for this worship is to recognize and honor under the symbol of the human Heart of Jesus Christ, His love for mankind, shown above all in His Passion and in the institution of the Eucharist. It is to this second manifestation of His love that we render homage in the following adoration.

Nowhere has the Sacred Heart stamped an impression more profound, more visible than in this institution, since the Eucharist is the most magnificent gift, the highest effort of Its power, the masterpiece that exhibits His love as never before. His twofold nature, divine and human, appears therein in the marvels and the goodness that He scatters abroad without measure. The double phase of His existence, the mortal here below, the glorified in heaven, are revealed therein in the throes of sorrow and in the sovereign mediation which He began by the oblation of the Eternal Sacrifice upon the altar of the Cenacle.

It is, then, the Heart of the God made man, revealing Itself at the Last Supper as the Institutor of the Eucharist, that we are going to acknowledge and adore: *"Cum dilexisset suos qui erant in mundo, in finem dilexit eos*—Having loved His own who were in the world, He loved them to the end."

### ADORATION.

The Heart of the Son of God, carrying in It the eternal love which is the very nature of God, possessing almighty power to show forth that infinite love in works worthy of Him—the Sacred Heart, which labored for thirty-three years to prove Its love for the world by innumerable benefits of prayer, devotedness, teaching, goodness, and mercy, *having loved His own*, wishes, at the end of Its mortal life, to sum up all Its gifts in one which surpasses them all, in a masterpiece which crowns all others, and so instituted the Eucharist: *"In finem dilexit*—He loved them to the end."

The Gospel tells us: "*Sciens quia omnia dedit ei Pater in manus et quia a Deo exivit et ad Deum vadit*—Knowing that the Father had given all things into His hands, and that He came from God and goeth to God," that is to say, that He is as truly God as His Father, Jesus recalls this truth to His disciples. Under the influence of this remembrance, wishing to love in God, He loves even to the end, that is to say, infinitely, without other measure than that of these two terms which have no measure: the divinity of His origin and the divinity of His end. *In finem dilexit.* And as the works and gifts of love must be proportioned to its power and extent, the gift, the work springing from this appeal to His Divinity, is a marvel of infinite beauty, of infinite goodness, of infinite extent: *In finem dilexit!*

It is a marvel of the two natures, the divine and the human, integral and living, which constitute the Man-God, glorified, confined in the narrow limits of what appears to be a morsel of bread! It is the most marvellous of all the great love, of all the great benefits of God and of His Christ, creation, the Incarnation, Redemption, grace, and glory, all concentrated, summed up in this one proof, this still greater proof of love, the gift of the Eucharist! It is the marvel of the actual abiding on earth of the Son of God made man, after He had re-ascended to heaven, the sojourn due His dignity! It is the marvel of an unbloody immolation, wrought upon Himself and by Himself, although through the agency of a visible minister, and renewing in all its efficacy the sacrifice of His death, giving to God the same satisfaction and obtaining for man the same redemption! It is the marvel of a little bread that has lost its natural substance by changing it, at the breathing of a sacerdotal word, into that of Jesus Christ! Under its frail envelope it contains Jesus Christ in His whole being. It feeds the human soul with Him, pouring into it the perfections of His Divinity, the virtues of His Soul, the living properties of His Flesh and Blood, the merits of His sacred life, His heroic death, and the victorious spoils of His Resurrection. It is the marvel of time conquered by this fragile Host, which sways all ages, giving strength and duration to all that lean upon It, like the Church which, persecuted by enemies without, weakened by the corruption of her children within, still exists while the most solid empires crumble! It is the marvel of distance cleared, oceans filled up, mountains crossed by this bond of the Host, wholly present everywhere, forming the connecting link between souls and creeds and morals, among nations the most diverse, in one same adoration, in one same eating of the Bread of Life! And the wonder of this Bread, so precious that a single one of its atoms is of more value than the whole world, that it multiplies with superb magnificence, is renewed with inexhaustible fecundity, is offered daily to all: *Quantum isti, tantum ille, nec sumptus consumitur!*

All these marvels of love—for being gratuitous, they can come only from Him —proclaim that the Heart that inspires them, that operates them, is the Heart of a God, who brings His almighty power into play.

What do all these marvels call for from us? That in admiration, astonishment, amazement. but also in firm faith, we adore from the depths of our soul the Gift, the Marvel of the Divine Heart, the Most Blessed Sacrament! It was this Gift that the Divine Saviour had in view when, casting aside the Sacramental veils in order to reveal His Heart, which had given It at the Last Supper, and which gives It still upon our altars, He said to Blessed Margaret Mary: "Behold the Heart that has so loved men that It has spared nothing even to exhausting and consuming Itself in order to testify to them **Its love!**"

### THANKSGIVING.

Truly the Heart of a man, formed to express in a human manner the love, the goodness, and the mercy of God, thus to gain the human heart, which responds only to sympathy and yields only to kindness, the Sacred Heart reveals Itself in the institution of the Eucharist by the tenderness, the intimacy, the familiarity of the most sincere friendship that can be imagined between equals and brethren.

"Knowing," says the Gospel, "that His hour was come to go from this world to the Father," and that He must, consequently, be separated from His "own whom He loved so much," the Saviour felt His Heart oppressed with sadness and compassion for them. So, He resolved to "love them to the end," that is, to remain with them under the form of the Sacrament while ascending to heaven in His human form. It is the sincerity of His human Heart which expresses itself by this attachment " for His own," from whom He cannot depart without feeling It torn and breaking. His " own! " Who were they? They were those bound to Him by the ties of blood, by the affection that He had shown them, by that which He had received from them, by the call followed, by the common labors undertaken, the hatred braved, the sufferings endured. His " own " are they who, abandoning father and mother, house and business, have given themselves to Him, and who depend wholly on Him.

While suffering in His Heart at being obliged to leave those loved ones, the sight of their grief and the tears that filled their eyes roused His tender compassion and the desire to console them. " Because I have told ye that I am going away, sorrow hath filled your heart. No! I am going away, but I will return to you! " Lastly, the thought of what they would have to suffer from the world and its prince, made Him resolve to sustain and defend them: " No!

I will not leave you orphans. I will remain with you all days even to the end of the world ! "

Under the pressure of all these sentiments, He made Himself the kind, the affectionate, the familiar Sacrament, in which appear all the tenderness, all the condescension of the most human of all hearts. It is a Sacrament which is taken at a banquet of friends; which gives Itself under the well-known form of bread broken, of a cup drunk at a hospitable table; which, concealing the human form of Him whom It contains, renders access to Him more easy, His frequent reception more unconstrained. It is a Sacrament which, descending into the breast of man to mingle with his substance, proves to him to what intimate union Jesus aspires, and that He aims at being associated with his labors, his trials, his joys, his whole life in this valley of tears. Ah, how truly human is the Heart of the Son of God, who came into this world to live with men and to gain them by the charms of His Humanity! He longs to abide forever " with His own, who must still remain in this world."

Jesus betrayed His inmost Heart when He ended the bestowal of Himself with these words: "*In memoriam facite.*—Do this in remembrance of Me!" Remember Me! What an appeal, what a request, what a command to love Him are contained in these two words! In them we have the proof that He loves us with a truly human love based on reciprocity, that He cannot bear to be forgotten, He cannot bear not to be loved by us: *In mei memoriam!*

Ah, let us, then, remember Him with faithful and loving friendship, for which He is hungering and thirsting! "One day, Good Friday," says Blessed Margaret Mary, "having a great desire to receive Our Lord, I said to Him with many tears: 'Sweet Jesus, I would wish to be consumed by desire for Thee! Not being able to possess Thee today, I shall not cease to desire Thee.' He came to console me with His dear Presence, and said to me: 'My daughter, thy desire has so touched My Heart that, if I had not already instituted this Sacrament of Love, I would do so now in order to give Myself to thee as nourishment. I take so much pleasure in being desired that, as often as a heart forms that desire, so often do I look upon it lovingly to draw it to Myself!'"

## REPARATION.

The Saviour had prophesied that the lot of His Heart on earth would be " reproach and misery: " *Improperium exspectavit Cor meum et miseriam* (1). And, in fact, from the first moment of Its being, when It accepted the responsibility of the sins of men, even to Its last pulsation on the Cross, It was never without the weight of all the sorrows, all the humiliations that they had merited.

His sorrowful life here below was reproduced in the institution of the Eucharist, and that the more notably as He intended this Sacrament to be the memorial of all His sufferings and of His death. The anguish, the opposition endured, the repugnance surmounted, the heroic resignation to support everything, were very clearly foreseen at the Last Supper. By them we can trace the cruel martyrdom confronted by the Sacred Heart in order to bestow upon us the best of His gifts.

The instrument of that martyrdom is personified in Judas whose heart, possessed by Satan, filled by him with implacable hatred

(1)  Ps. lxviii, 21.

for Jesus, resolved to betray Him in the Cenacle by a sacrilegious Communion, and in the Garden by the kiss which was to point Him out to the executioners: *"Cum diabolus jam misisset in cor ut traderet eum Judas*—The devil having now put it into the heart of Judas to betray Him "(1). The struggle of Jesus' Heart full of love against that of Judas full of hate, constituted the Eucharistic Agony of the Sacred Heart. Jesus still loved the disciple chosen by Him like the others, whom He had associated to His mission, to whom He had confided His secrets, and upon whom He had conferred the power of working miracles, and He longed to rescue him from his murderous design. To soften his heart, He lovingly washed and kissed his feet. But all in vain, and He signifies it to him in the ambiguous words: " Ye are pure, but not all." Alas!

While Judas was taking his portion of the Paschal lamb from the hands of Jesus, the Saviour, in order to relieve His own Heart and to remind the traitor, exclaimed in a loud voice: " Amen, I say to you, that one of you is about to betray Me. He that

---

(1) John xiii, 2.

dippeth his hand with Me in the dish, he shall betray Me!"

He had consecrated the Eucharist, saying: "Take ye and eat. Take ye, and drink," and Judas had extended his hand to receive his share of the Divine Bread, and his lips are immersed in the Chalice whence the lips of Jesus had drunk. Then Jesus says in a voice grave and full of emotion: "He that dippeth his hand with Me in the dish, he shall betray Me. It were better for him if that man had never been born!" While the Apostles, agitated and frightened, eagerly declared their fidelity, Judas affected to do the same; and the Saviour, indignant at his hypocrisy, uttered this cry of sorrow: "The Scripture sayeth: and it must be fulfilled: He that eateth bread with Me shall raise up his heel against Me!"

Jesus felt that odious and persistent treason so keenly that, by the allusion which He made to it, He opened a vent for the agony He endured in His Heart. Not being able to contain it, He showed Himself troubled, and He protested against its violence and against him who caused it: *Cum haec dixisset Jesus, turbatus est spiritu et protestatus est* (1). The grief at being thus profaned and betrayed, indignation against the blackness of the crime, persistent pity for the traitor rushing blindly to his own destruction, stirred His very soul, made His Heart shudder: *Turbatus est spiritu*—He was troubled in spirit, and brought to His lips the burning and bitter words of protest: *" Et protestatus est."*

Then Jesus became resigned, for His love would not allow the crime of Judas to be an obstacle to His giving the Eucharist to the world: *" Quod facis, fac citius!*—That which thou dost, do quickly! "  And yet He saw behind Judas all the traitors that would, under the guise of hypocritical piety, approach to receive Him at the Banquet of Holy Communion, to profane Him, and to deliver Him to the demon.

To be betrayed at the very moment in which one loves most, is sorrow supreme, mortal agony for the human heart!  And as, at the Last Supper, Jesus called upon the co-disciples of Judas to repair by their fidelity and compassion, so does He now demand reparation and consolation from faithful souls.

---

(1) John xiii, 21.

He said to Blessed Margaret Mary: "And in return I receive for the most part only ingratitude, expressed by the contempt, irreverence, sacrilege, and coldness that they have for Me in this Sacrament of Love! But what is more hurtful to Me is that there are hearts consecrated to Me who treat Me thus. I feel that more keenly than all I endured in My Passion! Do thou, at least, give Me the consolation of seeing thee supplying as much as thou canst for their ingratitude!"

### PETITION.

If the first phase of the existence of the Sacred Heart is consumed in suffering, the second, a just recompense of the former, is passed in immortality, power, and glory. The Heart of the Eternal Priest, who has ascended even to the throne of God to plead uninterruptedly in our behalf, and who at the Last Supper inaugurated His priesthood, His love, and ever watchful solicitude for us, must exhibit itself in a powerful, ardent, and devoted prayer. That prayer, begun in the august sanctuary of the Cenacle, is continued and it will be continued on all the altars of the world until the end of time.

It is for this reason that the institution of the Sacrament is also the institution of the Sacrifice, the prayer *par excellence,* in which Christ prays not only by His desires and His words, but by His Flesh delivered up and His Blood poured out. Yes, He pays for what He demands by the price of His innocent life.

Asking for us from the Father the destruction of sin, pardon, reconciliation, restitution of former rights, He said, raising to heaven His Flesh and His Blood under the species of bread and wine: " Behold My Body broken for you! Behold My Blood shed for the remission of your sins! "

The Adorable High-Priest, in order to give them efficacy, supported all the prayers that would be made by men throughout the ages upon this fundamental prayer of His Eucharistic Sacrifice. It anticipated at the Last Supper and it was to reproduce at the altar that which on the next day He was to offer on the Cross. Jesus solicited our prayer and roused our confidence by saying: " Amen, Amen, I say to you: if you ask the Father anything in My name, He will give it to you. Hitherto you have not asked anything in My name. Ask, and you shall receive, that your joy may be full." Again, He said: "Whatsoever you shall ask the Father in My name, that will I do: that the Father may be glorified in the Son. If you shall ask Me anything in My name, that I will do that your joy may be full. If you abide in Me, and My words abide in you, you shall ask whatsoever you will and it shall be done unto you " (1).

Behold the Heart of the all-powerful, the all-merciful Priest! He is all-powerful by His sacrifice in which He has spared nothing to satisfy His Father. He is all-powerful by His purity, His love, His perseverance. He is all-merciful, because being laden with our debts, He learned by experience the excess of our evils and the extent of our needs.

Jesus asks us to pray with Him, by Him, in Him, with confidence, humility, perseverance, since every prayer that issues from a sincere heart is secure of finding in His infinitely good Heart *access* and *success*. " My Heart is so passionately in love with men," He said to Blessed Margaret Mary, " that It can no longer contain within Itself

_____

(1) John xv.

the flames of Its ardent charity. It must pour them out by means of thee, and manifest Itself to them to enrich them with Its treasures, which contain all the graces of which they have need to be saved from perdition." And at another time, He said: " I constitute thee the heiress of My Heart and of all Its treasures. I promise that assistance shall never be wanting to thee till power is wanting to Me!"

Pray for greater reverence toward the Holy Eucharist.

O Sacrament most holy! O Sacrament divine!
All praise and all thanksgiving be every moment Thine!

(100 *days' Indulgence.*)

# Eighth Day.

## THE SACRED HEART IN THE PASSION.

When Our Lord allowed the centurion's lance to pierce His Heart, and to end by that solemn and unexpected blow the innumerable outrages of His Passion, He desired to prove what an immense rôle that Heart had played in it. That Wound was never effaced from His Sacred Person. It remains open even in His glorified flesh, like a master's seal on his work. It proclaims that it was the Sacred Heart which conceived, willed, and suffered the Passion. Revealing It to Blessed Margaret Mary, with Its most striking wounds, encircled by a crown of thorns, pierced through and through by a cross, the Saviour said to her: " These instruments of My Passion signify that the immense love of My Heart for mankind has been the source of all its sufferings." The Church, when approving the worship of the Sacred Heart, declared that its object is to honor His love, above all, in His Passion and in the Eucharist. There is

118

no question of the pains directly endured by the Sacred Heart, but only of the part It took in the drama of the Passion from the Cenacle to Calvary.

## ADORATION.

The rôle played by the Sacred Heart in the Passion is of primary importance. It was the responsible inspirer of that Passion. It endured the greater part of the pains that make it up. It was fitting that it should be so, for this double rôle belonged to It of necessity.

Nothing could oblige the Word to become incarnate and to die for guilty man. It was love alone that led Him to do so, spontaneous love, a love full of divine generosity and infinite power. This was the love that burned in the Heart of Jesus from Its first formation.

Yielding to the ardor of that love, pressed on by its irresistible impulse, the Saviour delivered Himself as a sacrifice for us: " *Christus dilexit nos et tradidit semetipsum pro nobis oblationem et hostiam Deo in odorem suavitatis*—Christ hath loved us, and hath delivered Himself for us, an oblation and a sacrifice to God for an odor of sweetness " (1).

No work nor prayer nor suffering of guilty man being capable of giving satisfaction to Divine Justice and restoring the kingdom of God in creation, Jesus, so loving His Father that He feared not to confront death for His honor, said on leaving the Cenacle: " That the world may know that I love the Father, let us go to Calvary: *Ut cognoscat mundus quia diligo Patrem, eamus hinc* " (2). To love, then, and consequently to the Heart all loving, belongs the sublime, the heroic design of the Passion.

Upon that strong and magnanimous Heart fell the greater part of the sufferings and humiliations of the Passion. Yes, we may say that directly or indirectly the Heart of Jesus supported the whole weight of that dolorous Passion.

Directly, It endured all the anguish that has the heart, the affections for its seat: treason, denial, the abandonment of His own. In the Garden, It endured the terror,

---

(1)   Ephes. iv, 2.
(2)   John xiv, 31.

the agony, the bitterness and disgust, the weariness and mortal sadness of the Agony, all those pains with which Jesus said His Heart was filled: *" Repleta est malis anima mea*—For My soul is filled with evils "* (1). Ah! it was those evils overflowing that produced the exhaustion, the tears, the groans, the bloody sweat under which He succumbed and fell prostrate on the earth. Again, upon the Cross, it was the Sacred Heart that directly agonized at the sight of Mary and her grief, and at the abandonment of His so-loved Father who, though long invoked, responded only by a disheartening and grievous silence.

Indirectly, the Heart of Jesus suffered all the torments of the Passion both moral and physical. There was not a single one of the outrages, humiliations, denials of justice, buffets, pricks of the thorns, blows of the whip, wounds of all His members, effusions of blood, so abundant, so painful, so ignominious, which had not its rebound upon that Heart, the furnace of life, the source of life-blood, and the organ of sensibility. And it had to be so. The root of sin and its es-

---

(1) Ps. lxxxvii, 4.

sential malice being in the perversion of the ungrateful heart, which turns away from God to attach itself by disorderly affection to the creature,—if Christ wished to satisfy God by expiating our sins, it was right and just that His Heart should suffer most and bear the heaviest load of chastisement.

Let us, then, adore the Sacred Heart, through the great wound which, upon the Cross, opened It to us forever. In this Book of Life, whose characters are deeply engraven in blood, let us read, let us contemplate, in amazed and compassionate adoration, all the suffering, the love, and the virtues, all the redeeming power of the Passion: " *Et aspicient ad me quem confixerunt; et plangent eum planctu quasi super unigentium*—And they shall look upon Me whom they have pierced; and they shall mourn for Him as one mourneth for an only son "(1).

### THANKSGIVING.

The Sacred Heart is revealed in the Passion by the goodness, meekness, and mercy, which we can trace in it from the beginning

---

(1) Zach. xii, 10.

to the end of that terrible drama. Throughout its whole enactment, Jesus never ceased to love, to show Himself kind to those who, in any manner whatever, contributed to His sufferings. His providential love was, at the same time, preparing for the redeemed of all future ages treasures of merit and example.

As we can trace the course of a gentle stream over the sharp rocks and down the rugged sides of a mountain to the narrow valleys below where, after spreading its fertilizing influence, it rushes on to wider plains, so in the tumult and horror of the Passion, we see the benevolence, the condescension, the forgiveness, the tenderness of this most sweet and loving Heart. Neither man's excess of hatred and fury, nor Its own excess of sufferings can cause that Heart to cease from loving: " *Aquæ multæ non potuerunt extinguere charitatem* —Many waters cannot quench charity "(1).

Its indulgent goodness received the traitor Judas, and hastened to cast on Peter, who denied Him, a glance that smote his heart. Its considerate goodness protected

---

(1) Cant. viii, 7.

the liberty of His Apostles that they might not share His captivity. Its sweet goodness in the spirit of obedience bore with the ignoble treatment and the iniquitous judgment of the prætorium. Its generous and magnanimous goodness prayed for the salvation of those that decreed and executed His death-warrant. Its merciful goodness granted pardon and salvation to the prayer of the good thief. The provident tenderness of Its filial piety strengthened Him to tear Himself away from His Mother by giving her John to hold to her the place of a son when He Himself should be no more. Its loving confidence committed His soul into the hands of His Father at the very moment that He appeared to be the most abandoned by Him. All these exhalations from the Heart of supreme goodness created around the terrifying summit of Calvary an atmosphere of sweetness, benevolence, and peace.

Forgetful, at the same time, of Its pains, and rising above all the torments that later caused His death, the Sacred Heart urged Jesus to occupy Himself only with us, our welfare, our salvation. With every one of the sufferings that oppressed Him, with every humiliation that covered him with ignominy, with every drop of the blood which He shed with so much agony, He mingled the love and resignation, the humility and meekness, the sweetness and perseverance with which He bore them, thus forming the necessary and efficacious remedies for our soul. From them He accumulated the treasure of merits from which we can draw to enrich ourselves and purchase heaven, and He wrote that book of beautiful and magnificent examples, which the generations of all ages will read for their encouragement in trial and suffering. Jesus took care to make Himself " the redemption and the justification of all—*Factus est nobis a Deo justitia et sanctificatio et redemptio* " (1). Ah, what devoted goodness, what disinterested benevolence were necessary for that! But His Heart, which had willed the Passion, never ceased to act, transforming it entirely into a work of love for our immense benefit.

Shall we ever be sufficiently grateful to the Sacred Heart for Its goodness, for the benefits that we derive from the Passion that It endured for us? Do we understand that

---

(1) I. Cor. i, 30.

the best way to show our gratitude is to take as a proof of love the trials that It sends us?

"What shall I render to Thee for all the favors Thou hast done me?" exclaimed Blessed Margaret Mary. "O my God, how excessive is Thy goodness to me in wishing that I should eat at the table of the saints the same food with which Thou dost nourish them! Ah! dost Thou not well know that without the Cross and the Blessed Sacrament, I could not live, I could not support the weariness of my exile in this vale of tears, in which I do not desire any diminution of my sufferings?"

### REPARATION.

By Its resolution to confront death, by the immense share that It took in the sorrows and humiliations of the Passion, the Sacred Heart wished, and with good reason, to expiate the leading part that the human heart takes in sin. It desires at the same time to give sinners the grace and model of true contrition and conversion.

It is the heart that is the guilty instrument of sin, for the radical malice of sin consists in the ungrateful abandonment and injurious contempt of the Infinite Good, which the heart commits by turning away from God, and in the perverse and disorderly attachment by which it gives itself to the created, passing, and finite good by its insulting preference. " Be astonished, O ye heavens, at this, saith the Lord. My people have done two evils. They have forsaken me, the fountain of living water, and have digged to themselves cisterns, broken cisterns, that can hold no water!"(1). Every sin springs from this outrageous ingratitude of the heart as from its source.

From the heart, as from their principle, says the Divine Master, "come forth all sins," even those of which the other members are the direct instruments. " For from the heart come forth evil thoughts, murders, adulteries, fornications, thefts, false testimonies, blasphemies. These are the things that defile a man "(2). Sin is so much the more grievous as the heart is the more attached to it, the more resolved upon it. It is the more grievous as it is the more

---

(1) Jer. ii, 12.
(2) Matt. xv. 19.

loved, desired, and concealed in the heart, which will not renounce it, which dissimulates it under the cloak of deceit and hypocrisy, and which tries even to justify it. Sins of surprise, impulse, or weakness are small in comparison with those to which the heart is attached, glued, as it were, in which it takes its delights and appears to make its final end and aim. Ah, this is why the Saviour's Heart, which had taken them upon Itself, had to expiate them by torments so cruel!

Holy Scripture, in terms expressive of every form of excessive sorrow and humiliation, depicts this most pure Heart struggling with the sins of the human heart. It is a Heart "troubled and shaken even to its very depths by mortal terror; a Heart devoured by pitiless fire; a Heart which melts like wax in the fire, and is liquefied like water; a Heart reduced to nothingness; a Heart abandoned, struck, bruised, broken, humbled, rejected, plunged in darkness, afflicted with innumerable tribulations, filled with anguish, sighing and groaning with sorrow, incapable of one sentiment of self-defence or justification. And the Gospel recounts the agony of this poor

Heart in these short words, wide and deep like oceans of interior sorrow: " Jesus began to fear and to be heavy, and He fell flat on the ground, and He said: ' My soul is sorrowful even unto death!'"

Ah, this is the true sorrow of the Just One endured for sinners, the perfect contrition, the satisfaction that pays every debt, the sincere return to God by contempt of every created joy, the sacrifice of every attachment to creatures! With this contrition of infinite efficacy, conceived and offered to God by the Heart of Him who, having no sin, was burdened with the malediction incurred by our trangressions, we must penetrate our heart in order to return it to God by a true conversion, torn and bruised by repentance: *" Convertimini ad me in toto corde vestro; et scindite corda vestra et non vestimenta vestra!*—Be converted to me with all your heart, in fasting, and in weeping, and in mourning, and rend your hearts, and not your garments " (1).

Unless we hearken to these words of the inspired prophet, terrible will be the chastisement that will strike our heart both in

---

(1)  Joel ii, 12.

this life and in the next, for if the pure and
living Heart was thus afflicted, what will it
be with a dry and withered one? *"Si in
viridi ligno hæc faciunt, in arido quid fiet?*
—For if in the green wood they do these
things, what shall be done in the dry?"(1).
All the heartaches that cast a gloom over
life and fill it with bitterness; that long and
sad privation in purgatory of the possession
of God, more cruel than the flames of the
fiery prison itself; the absolute abandonment
of the soul by God, with no hope of any
possible communication with Him under the
weight of His wrath and malediction in hell
—such are the chastisements of the guilty
heart that refuses to cast itself into the
wounded Heart of Jesus, thence to draw
contrition, repentance, and love, which wash
away every fault, deliver from every punishment, and reconcile with God in eternal
peace!

Ah! rather let us imitate Blessed Margaret Mary who, after Communion, having
seen Jesus under the figure of the *Ecce
Homo* laden with His Cross, covered with
wounds and bruises, heard Him say to her

---

(1) Luke xxiii, 31.

in a voice full of sadness: "Will no one have pity on Me?" The Blessed Sister fell at His feet with tears and sighs. "The Saviour," she tells us, "laid upon my shoulders His heavy Cross, which was bristling with iron points. While sinking under its weight, I began to understand as never before, the malice and grievousness of sin. I detested it so heartily that I should have preferred a thousand times to cast myself headlong into hell than ever commit a single one. 'O abominable sin!' I exclaimed, 'how detestable thou art, on account of the injury thou didst inflict on my Sovereign Good!'"

PETITION.

The grace that comes from the contemplation of Jesus in the Passion is chiefly the love of suffering such as He Himself had, the love of it for His sake, because He loved it for ours.

Although He fully understood all its extent and horror, Jesus voluntarily chose suffering. He took upon Himself far more than was necessary to satisfy the Father and to redeem the world from sin, and this He did only because to embrace greater suffering is a proof of greater love.  Will not this example of His, this proof of His immense goodness toward us, convert us to the love of suffering, or, at least, to love God in that which He sends us even if we have not the courage to ask for more and still more?

To love God in suffering is to submit without undue sadness or murmuring to His will in time of trial.  It is to offer Him our pain as a sacrifice of prayer and expiation. It is to continue to hope in Him, to believe in His goodness, in spite of the appearance of severity that accompanies the trial, to think well of Him:  *" Sentite de Domino in bonitate*—Think of the Lord in goodness "* (1).  To love God in suffering is to cultivate the virtues that it requires and that it so quickly perfects, namely, humility, meekness, patience, fortitude, and love: *" Patientia opus perfectum habet*—Patience hath a perfect work "* (2).

To love God in suffering is to transform suffering into apostolic charity by offering all that it holds in the way of sorrow and

---

(1)   Wisd. i, 1.

(2)   James i, 4.

humiliation for the neighbor, his salvation and sanctification, for the conversion of sinners, for the dying, and for the deliverance of the souls in purgatory.

How easy this Christian love of suffering, though so horrible to the senses, so inexplicable and repugnant to reason, would become if we beheld and understood it in the light of the Sacred Heart! The love of suffering is, in fact, only the love of Jesus Himself. It is true that all imaginable sufferings were heaped upon Him, and that He willed, endured, and embraced all. It is also true that every suffering sent by Him is an effusion of His Heart. As it is from the plenitude of His grace that we receive every grace, it is from the plenitude of His sufferings comes every trial that we have to bear. It was once endured by Him. It comes steeped in His Blood, adorned with His virtues, transformed by His loving patience into love and merit for us. Oh, what intensified misfortune, what manifold trials, is suffering without love, is suffering deprived of the light and support of the Sacred Heart! Suffering must be borne even if there be no supernatural strength, no hope, and no fruit. How much more severe, more bitter, and more crushing it then is! Oh, how much easier it is to endure for love, to pay a debt of love, to share the pain of one beloved, to relieve him, to be inseparably united with him, to press the heart wounded by trial against the Heart crushed by the Passion! The Apostle experienced this, and gave us the example of it when, enumerating the torments and death that threatened him, he exclaimed: "*Sed in his omnibus superamus propter eum qui dilexit nos!*—But in all these things we overcome because of Him that hath loved us "(1).

And Margaret Mary, the confidante of the Heart that was broken on the Cross, that is annihilated in the Sacrament for love of us, says: " I know not how a spouse of Jesus Crucified can fail to love the Cross, can flee from it, since in doing so she despises Him who bore it for our love and made of it the object of His delights. We can love Him only inasmuch as we love crosses. He has Himself told me that, as often as I shall encounter the Cross and lovingly place it in my heart, I shall with it receive and taste

(1) Rom. viii, 37.

the sweets of His Presence, for He accompanies it everywhere as being the true character of His love. I had this assurance after Holy Communion."

May it be for us, also, the fruit of each of our Communions and the practical conclusion of this adoration!

Beg Our Lord to give you sincere sorrow for your sins.

Eternal Father, I offer Thee the Precious Blood of Jesus in satisfaction for my sins and for the wants of Holy Church.

(100 *days' Indulgence.*)

# Ninth Day.

### THE SACRED HEART IN GETHSEMANI.

### ADORATION.

THAT part of the drama of the Passion which was played in Gethsemani may properly be called the Passion of the Sacred Heart. Although the Heart of the Saviour, in all the torments that He underwent for us, ceased not for one instant to suffer, even till the last pulsation with which He breathed forth His soul upon the Cross, yet it was in Gethsemani that every pang sprang from the depths of His Heart, fell back upon His Heart, flowed in torture over His Heart. It was from the Heart alone that His agony then came, for no external violence from the hands of the myrmidons who seized Him, the iniquitous judges who condemned Him, the executioners who scourged, buffeted and crucified Him, then struck the Divine Victim.

From this almost limitless domain of the Passion of the Sacred Heart, we shall choose as our subject of adoration the

136

prayer of Our Divine Master during this night of agony. We shall reflect upon it as the motive and example of prayer by night, which in our own day receives the name of Nocturnal Adoration, and which was demanded by the Sacred Heart from Blessed Margaret Mary as one of the chief means of Its worship.

"Every night, between Thursday and Friday, you shall rise to share in the sadness that I willed to endure in the Garden of Olives, and to bear Me company in the humble prayer I then presented to My Father."

The Gospel tells us very plainly that the Saviour desired with a formal desire several times expressed, that His Apostles should watch and pray with Him on the night preceding His Passion.

It was by night that Christ went to Gethsemani to pray. He consecrated three hours to that earnest prayer, which His grief changed for Him into an "agony."

The Pasch was celebrated after sundown. Jesus entered the Cenacle at nightfall and, after the three repasts, that of the Paschal lamb, that of the ordinary supper, and that of the Last Supper, it was night, as says the Sacred Text. Then Judas, the double traitor toward his Master, went out, to deliver Him to His enemies: *" Erat autem nox*—And it was night "* (1). It is probable that Jesus entered the Garden about the ninth hour, and we are led to believe that He prolonged His prayer for the space of three hours. We know for certain that He spent one full hour in prayer before going to the Apostles, and saying to them: *" Sic non potuistis una hora vigilare mecum?*— What! Could you not watch one hour with Me? "* (2) As the Evangelists describe in the same terms the other two stations that Jesus made afar from His Apostles: " He went again the second and third time, and prayed, saying the self-same words: *Et iterum secundo abiit et oravit, eundem sermonem dicens* "(3), it is very probable that each one of those prayers lasted an hour. What makes this the more likely is the fact, that St. Luke says: *" Et factus in agonia, prolixius orabat*—And being in an agony, He prayed the longer "(4).

---

(1) John xiii, 30.
(2) Matt. xxvi, 40.
(3) John xiii, 30.
(4) Luke xxii, 43.

Commentators tell us, also, that in resuming His prayers, despite the violent struggle that He experienced, the Saviour wished to give His Apostles an example of perseverance in prayer. He desired to teach them that it must be prolonged until the soul feels itself drawn nearer to God, its hope enlivened, its needs supplied, or its will more perfectly submissive to that of God. They say, also, that it was only at the third period of His prayer that an angel " was sent to console and to strengthen Him."

The foregoing reasons render it very credible that the Saviour prolonged His prayer in the Garden three hours. He passed, in consequence, a great part of the night in adoration before His Divine Father. By His own example, He consecrated in advance the nocturnal prayer which the Church was to practise at all periods of her existence. He Himself set the example before demanding it formally of His Apostles, His first disciples, priests, and religious.

### THANKSGIVING.

Yes, it is first of all for Himself, for the support and consolation of His Heart, so truly human, that He desires His Apostles to share in His sorrowful prayer. He has need of sympathy, companionship, and fidelity. In all His strength as the Son of God, He willed to be feeble as the Son of Man! He is plunged in death-like sadness, and His Heart is about to begin a mortal combat. Nothing is more necessary to a sufferer than the constant and faithful presence of a sympathizing friend, who understands, enters into, and compassionates his pain. And so does Jesus " look for some one who will console Him by sharing His sadness." He is about to descend into the arena, to begin, in accordance with the will of His Father, a combat of tears and supplications, to mitigate His rigor and obtain that He will be pleased " to allow that chalice to pass! " His Heart revolts at the thought of all the treason, abandonment, and denials in store for Him, and He has to combat against that repugnance. He has to struggle with His own soul to make it yield voluntarily to a flood of opprobrium and ignominy, and even against His flesh itself when imposing upon it the most horrible sufferings. He feels all the horror of one that has to combat alone, for " if he falls, who will raise him up? "

Oppressed by the necessities of the human nature which He so freely assumed, Jesus implores the presence and assistance of those whom He has a right to think His friends, since He had so loved them. He makes known to them the need that He has of them: "Ah! watch ye and pray with me, for my soul is sad unto death!"

And when yielding to the inexorable decision of His Father, who will pardon the guilty only at the price of the death voluntarily embraced by the Innocent One; when overcome by grief and shame at the thought of the cruelty, the excess of humiliation, which are about to make of Him "the last of men and the outcast of the people," He fled the field of His defeat to find in the vigilant solicitude of His own a little respite and relief, how did He appear? Ah, behold Him; His face wan, His eyes sunken, His head bowed down, His shoulders stooped, covered with the bloody sweat that has been forced from His pores by the weight of His mental sufferings! Listen to Him begging His Apostles to have pity on Him, not to refuse "to watch and pray at least one hour with Him."

### REPARATION.

Although the prayer of the Saviour in the Garden of Olives is in itself a deep mine for meditation, we shall very briefly indicate according to the Gospel, its exterior character and interior composition, since it should serve as a model for " all the servants of the Lord," who, leaving their couches, pass the night in the temple, their hands raised toward the tabernacle, and blessing the Lord: " *Ecce nunc benedicite Dominum, omnes servi Domini  .      In noctibus extollite manus vestras in sancta, et benedicite Dominum*—Behold now, bless ye the Lord, all the servants of the Lord
In the nights lift up your hands to the holy places, and bless ye the Lord " (1).

Let us contemplate the Saviour's prayer in its religious exterior in the sombre sanctuary of Gethsemani. He withdraws some paces from even His most intimate disciples, in order to separate Himself from every creature, buries Himself in solitude favorable to prayer, and presents Himself alone before His Divine Father: " *Et progressus*

----

(1)   Ps. cxxxiii.

*pusillum, avulsus est ab eis quantum jactus est lapidis*—And when He had gone forward a little, about a stone's throw," He fell upon His knees in prayer, acknowledging before the Divine Majesty the inferiority and weakness of His human nature: "*Et positis genibus orabat*—And falling on His knees, He prayed." But that posture is not sufficiently humiliating. He falls face downward on the earth, overwhelmed by the weight of Divine Justice. He hides His face because, covered with our sins as with a filthy leprosy and struck on that account by the wrath of God, He cannot endure the brightness of His sanctity: "*Procidit super terram in faciem suam, orans*—He fell on His face to the earth, praying." Struck, humbled, rejected by His Father, for whose honor, however, He was suffering, He fell into an agony, "*Factus in agonia.*"

The struggle between His spiritual will which wishes at any price to satisfy the demands of God and His sensible will which He permits to feel and express insurmountable repugnance, is such that from His whole person, crushed under the weight of agony, a bloody sweat breaks out. Soon He is covered with it from head to foot. It flows down on the earthen floor of the grotto: *"Et factus est sudor ejus sicut guttae sanguinis decurrentis in terram* —And His sweat became as drops of blood, trickling down upon the ground."

In this abasement, in this agony, Jesus prays for three hours!—Ah, how humble, respectful, submissive, and at the same time loving and confident toward His Father! "Father, if Thou wilt, remove this chalice from Me! Yet not My will, but Thine be done!"—And again: "Abba, Father, all things are possible to Thee! Remove this chalice from Me, but not what I will, but what Thou wilt!"—And again: "My Father, if this chalice may not pass away but I must drink it, Thy will be done!"

In the Saviour's soul, His agony was still more cruel. It was from the exhaustion of His Heart that His knees had given way and that He had fallen to the earth. It was from the extreme sadness of His Heart, tortured by the most cruel agonies, that had sprung the bloody sweat which inundated Him.

### PETITION.

The "Master of Prayer" gave in the Garden the ideal model of every prayer.

Though under different conditions, He continues this example in the Eucharist.

Instituted to be the perfect and perpetual memorial of the Passion of the Saviour, the Eucharist carries down through the centuries the remembrance of the prayer and the agony of Gethsemani. It recalls the fact itself together with the sorrow and the love. It applies its virtues, and confers its fruits.

It continues it in reality, but under conditions compatible with the glorified and impassible state which the immortal Christ retains even under the sacramental veil of death. Of the mental and physical sufferings, of the bloody sweat, of the abandonment of His Father which marked His agony, the Eucharistic Christ retains only the remembrance, a remembrance blessed and recompensed. But desirous to perpetuate as much of His Passion as is possible, He continues His prayer in the lowliness of a state of inertia, which abases Him before His Father even below that of Gethsemani. There, the pallor of His divine countenance, the agony and the blood, without doubt, disfigured Him; but here, He is no longer human, He is but a little dust. He dwells alone, abandoned by indifferent, ungrateful, or hostile men, an abandonment far more displeasing to Him than was the sleep of the Apostles; and there He will remain night and day until the consummation of ages. Every morning at the Consecration, He descends, perseveringly overcoming all repugnance, into the Gethsemani of the Sacrament, there to resume His prayer, in the humility of His attitude and the ardor of His desires for the redemption of the world and the coming of His kingdom.

But remaining truly man in His Heart and affections, seeking a return of love from us, still feeling the need of our presence and fidelity, of our sympathy and compassion, in which He finds consolation for His past sufferings and present humiliations, He calls upon us, He supplicates us to keep Him company, to stay with Him, to unite with Him in prayer as much for His sake as for our own. It was this desire that He earnestly expressed at the moment He instituted the Eucharist, when He said: "*Manete in me, manete in dilectione mea*—Remain in me, remain in my love." He did this in a manner still more precise when He deigned to throw off the sacramental veils and reveal the mystery of His existence, the love and the needs of His Heart in the Eucharist.

To His blessed confidante, Margaret Mary, He said: " Every night between Thursday and Friday, thou shalt rise between eleven and twelve o'clock and bear Me company in the humble prayer which I offered to My Father in the Garden of Olives. During this hour thou shalt do what I shall teach thee.

" Thou shalt prostrate, face downward on the ground, as much to appease the Divine anger while imploring mercy for sinners, as to sweeten in some degree the abandonment of My Apostles, which forced Me to reproach them for not having watched one hour with Me.

" I shall make thee share in the mortal sadness which I then willed to endure, and it shall reduce thee, without thy being able to understand it, to a species of agony more insupportable than death itself."

Beg Our Eucharistic Lord to increase the devotion of the Holy Hour among the Faithful.

Jesus, meek and humble of Heart, make my heart like unto Thine.

(300 *days' Indulgence.*)

# Tenth Day.

## THE SACRED HEART IN AGONY.

### ADORATION.

THE Saviour called the whole Apostolic College to accompany Him in His prayer: "*Sedete hic donec vadam illuc et orem*—Sit you here, till I go yonder and pray." To three chosen friends among them, whom He took with Him to the vicinity of the grotto into which He descended to pray, He said: "*Tristis est anima mea usque ad mortem: sustinete hic et vigilate mecum!*—My soul is sorrowful even unto death: stay here and watch with Me." Is this only a simple recommendation? Is it an order? Is it a task that He assigns? a prayer that He addresses to them? We cannot read these words without being impressed by their earnestness and their sorrowful accent, without beholding the august countenance of the Saviour already clouded by mortal sadness, without comprehending that His Heart, terror-stricken, agonized, filled with bitter-

148

ness and disgust, is already in the throes of anguish.

If Jesus commands the Apostles to watch, it is that they may pray with Him; for when, after an hour of struggle, He returned to seek relief and comfort in their fidelity and found them sleeping heavily, He roused them with these energetic words: "Why sleep ye? Arise, pray!—*Quid dormitis? Surgite, orate!*" He reproached them with their sloth: "*Sic non potuistis una hora vigilare mecum!*—Could you not watch one hour with me?"

Twice did He return with the same entreaties, which He supported on the motive of their own interest and the threat of seeing it compromised: "*Vigilate et orate, ut non intretis in tentationem*—Watch and pray that ye enter not into temptation." "*Spiritus quidem promptus, caro autem infirma*—The spirit indeed is willing" (to resolve and to promise), "but the flesh is weak" (to execute). Being able neither by prayer nor recommendation nor reproofs nor threats, to overcome their pitiful torpor, He said to them at last in a tone of gentle irony: "Sleep ye now, and take your rest: —*Dormite jam et requiescite.*" The hour for prayer is past. But no: "*Sufficit*—It is enough. The hour is come. Behold the Son of Man shall be betrayed into the hands of sinners. Rise, let us go. Behold, he that will betray Me is at hand.—*Surgite, camus: ecce qui me tradet, prope est.*"

There can be no wish more clearly defined, no demand more pressing. The Saviour surely wills that His followers should unite with Him in His watching and praying.

He even deigned to give the reasons for it, and they are both urgent and touching. He sums them up in these two words: the pressing need of His Heart, and the chief interest of their soul.

### THANKSGIVING.

But, alas! This consolation, so legitimate and so humbly sought after, He does not find: "*Consolantem me quaesivi et non inveni!*—And I looked for one that would comfort me, and I found none!" This disappointment was for Jesus' Heart what the draught of biting vinegar and the bitter gall were to His parched lips and mouth: "*Dederunt in escam meam fel, et in siti mea potaverunt me aveto!*—They gave me gall for my food, and in my thirst they gave me vinegar to drink!" (1)

The Heart of the Saviour is too generous, too disinterested to desire the Apostles to watch and pray only on His account. He was seeking their own most sacred interests, their victory over the most formidable temptations, their perseverance in faith. The capture of their Divine Master, the chaining of His power, which has suddenly become inert, the insolent triumph of His enemies were to be for them a terrible occasion of scandal and ruin. Satan, who had asked to sift them, is now about to rain blows upon them. When Jesus, His hands bound, will have been led away to malicious and perfidious tribunals, they will be alone, the "dispersed sheep of the Shepherd that has been struck."

Humble, prolonged, persevering prayer, united to that of their Master, vivified and perfected by it, can alone strengthen them against the furious assaults of those temptations. Ah! "Watch and pray that ye enter not into temptation! Reckon not on the impulse of the spirit, ready to promise,

---

(1) Ps. lxviii, 22.

but inflated by presumption. Fear the flesh subject to weakness and drawing the spirit downward in its fall!" And how He insisted when care for their safety, which He knew depended on the prolonging of their watching and the earnestness of their prayer, snatched Him from His own agony, and led Him back to them: "What, sleeping still? Arise! Pray, lest ye yield to temptation!"

Thus, for His own sake and for theirs, the Saviour called upon His followers to pass with Him a part of that frightful night of His Passion in prolonged watching and prayer.

### REPARATION.

Four elements unchained in the tempest against the Saviour, had penetrated His Heart, breaking and crushing It in their fury. The Gospel names them, and it is sufficient to recall them to have some idea of the frightful agony of the Sacred Heart during this prayer, which they transformed into a bloody sacrifice, into a consuming holocaust. As His sadness was, as He says Himself, "even unto death," the paroxysms of fear, weariness, and disgust that seized

Him were capable of causing death. Their attacks were mortal, and would really have cut short His life had not the superhuman effort of His will and the special assistance of the Divinity preserved it: "*Tristis est anima mea usque ad mortem*—My soul is sorrowful unto death."

He was attacked by fear: "*Coepit pavere*—He began to be afraid." Anxiety, disquietude, fright, terror seized upon His soul, agitating and crushing Him before His Father's angry countenance. He found that beloved Father implacably exacting all the horrors of His Passion and death, before restoring Him to His friendship and granting Him the salvation of the world.

He was seized by sadness: "*Coepit contristari*—He began to be sad*" when He saw the inevitable necessity of suffering those evils. Black, deep, frozen, like a bottomless abyss whose waters madly rose to overwhelm, to engulf Him without chance of escape,—such was the sadness that filled the Sacred Heart at that dread moment.

He was attacked by weariness: "*Coepit taedere*—He began to be heavy." Blinding Him as with a thick veil, weariness of soul weighed heavily upon His will, stifling hope, nullifying effort, and annihilating courage.

Lastly, disgust filled the soul of our agonizing Saviour: "*Coepit moestus esse*—He began to feel disgust." The humiliating bitterness arising from the deception, the perfidy, the betrayal, the indifference, and abandonment of His own made His Heart sick. It heaved within His Sacred Breast and melted like water.

Now, these terrors, this sadness, weariness, and disgust sprang from the necessity to drink the chalice presented Him, and which His Father refused to remove from His lips. And what did this chalice of the divine wrath contain? All the sins of the world, even the most horrible, the most filthy—all were placed upon Him that He might expiate them. He had to endure all the chastisements that they merited and all the evils by which God's wrath is poured out upon the sinner. The ignominy, the violence, the iniquity, and the sufferings of the Passion—death upon the accursed Cross in total abandonment of God and men—all are before him. And still more, the immeasurable sorrow of His innocent and much loved Mother fell upon His Heart along with the knowledge of the utter uselessness of His sufferings for so large a number of ungrateful creatures, who obstinately refused the salvation they were to purchase for them.

It was in this struggle, this prayer so sorrowful and crucifying, that the Saviour persevered for long hours, and which He prolonged in proportion as it became more painful: *" Factus in agonia, prolixius orabat*—Being in agony, He prayed the longer."  He prayed the longer, because persevering prayer alone is heard. And, in effect, He did obtain, with strength to overcome all torments by His patience, God's pardon for sinners, the salvation of the world, the resurrection of His Body, and the glory of His eternal reign.

### PETITION.

It cannot be doubted that though nocturnal prayer as practised in all ages of the Church by her canons and religious, draws one of its greatest powers of praise, reparation, and intercession from the prayer of Christ in Gethsemani, yet the prayer here demanded by the Sacramental Christ notably differs from it as to form and spirit.

It is a new fruit of this garden of prayer, fertilized by the Blood of the Agony, vivified forever by the breath of the prolonged supplication of the Saviour floating through the olive trees. Instead of vocal prayer, what the Master of every form of prayer here demands, is mental prayer, interior prayer, silent contemplation. Instead of the various liturgical attitudes observed in public prayer, it is the imitation of His humiliated posture, the kneeling, the prolonged prostration with the face against the earth. It is not praise of the perfections and benefits of God, but the spiritual participation in the sadness, in the abandonment of the Son of God made Man and the Victim of men. It is communion by compassionate love with Christ agonizing. It is the apostolate of charity for sinners by prayer and reparation, offered for them in union with the Divine Priest, who continues on the altar to present to His Father the supplications, tears, and blood which He shed for them as well in Gethsemani as on Calvary. It is, in fine, every prayer made at the foot of the altar in presence of the Sacred Victim, in order to honor that Presence and to render our own prayer effectual, to console the Heart of Him, " whose delights are to be with the children of men," and to petition for those that have the most need of His mercy.

Is not all this the Nocturnal Adoration, the prayer of the night, to which, interrupting their repose, religious in their cloisters, priests and men and women of the world in their parish churches, give themselves up prostrate or kneeling? They unite by meditation, by silent contemplation, by loving colloquies, with the prayer which the Agonizing One of the Garden, the annihilated Christ of the Eucharist, still continues before their eyes.

O all ye who believe in Him, hearken to the call which the Sacred Heart makes to you for Nocturnal Adoration! Arise! Leave your couch unhesitatingly, and sacrifice to Him your repose! Watch with Him! Combat courageously the attacks of sleep, torpor of the mental faculties, and comfortable positions that favor it. Let us prostrate before Him! Let us kneel as long as possible at His side, uniting our adoration to His, for He is both the God whom we adore, and the only perfect Adorer by whom we can adore Him as we should!

Let us obey His teachings, let us detest sin, first, in ourselves by rousing in our soul something of the horror that He feels on account of the injury it does to God His Father and to the souls of His brethren. Then let us appease the divine anger by our tears and supplications, our sentiments of reparation and penitence while begging pardon for sinners.

Let us by an attentive, earnest, and compassionate consideration, try to comprehend in some degree the terror, sadness, weariness, disgust, which filled the Sacred Heart in Gethsemani, and which are still so fresh in His memory, since men are constantly renewing them by their manifold offences.

Then let us earnestly pray for ourselves that we may not fall into temptation, into the temptation of infidelity to the duties of our state, into the temptation of the pleasures of the world and of the flesh, into the temptation of discouragement in our pains and trials, into the temptation of apostasy from our faith when confronted with persecution. Like Jesus, let us pray for strength to desire the will of God, whatever it may be. Let us ask this for ourselves and our loved ones in sickness, misfortune, abandonment, and death. If while making this prayer, while in the actual Presence of God in the Eucharist, and at the moment in which He is listening to it, our soul should fall into the agony of disquietude, weariness, disgust or sadness, let us press close to the Agonizing One, who was weighed down by all these afflictions even unto death. Let us persevere, let us go on with our prayer, satisfied to repeat after Him and with Him in our heart or with our lips: "*Verumtamen, non mea, sed tua voluntas fiat!*—Nevertheless, not my will, but Thine be done!"

Ah, yes! Jesus' prayer in the Garden on the night of His Passion is the reason for the invitation, the example, and the grace, the justification and the pledge of success of Nocturnal Adoration.

May its remembrance always accompany and sustain us there: "*Sustinete hic et vigilate mecum!*—Stay ye here and watch with me!"

Let your visits to the Blessed Sacrament be more frequent and fervent.

Eucharistic Heart of Jesus, solace in our exile, give peace to the Church.

(50 *days' Indulgence.*)

# Eleventh Day.

## THE WOUND OF THE SACRED HEART.

IF there is in the history of the Sacred Heart one fact of supreme prominence, it is that of the thrust of the soldier's lance that was buried in the Side of the dead Redeemer. In the worship of the Sacred Heart, consequently, what most rouses the ardent faith of him who contemplates It, what most excites the compassion of the tender soul, is this Wound. When revealing His Heart, the Divine Master always shows It open like the hospitable door of an asylum or sanctuary, like the orifice of a gushing stream, like the hearth of a burning furnace. "One day," says Blessed Margaret Mary, " the Divine Heart was shown me on a throne of fire and flames, emitting rays on all sides, more brilliant than the sun and transparent as crystal. The Wound that It had received on the Cross was strikingly visible."

The subject of this *adoration* will be the reality of this Sacred Wound; the *thanks-*

*giving,* the love that **It** shows to us; the *reparation,* the sin that caused **It**; the *petition,* the fruits that we ought to derive from **It**.

### ADORATION.

The following passage from the Gospel of St. John insures to us the right to recognize and adore the Wound of the Sacred Heart:

" Jesus, therefore, when He had taken the vinegar, said: It is consummated. And bowing His head, He gave up the ghost. Then the Jews (because it was the parasceve) that the bodies might not remain upon the cross on the Sabbath-day (for that was a great Sabbath-day) besought Pilate that their legs might be broken, and that they might be taken away. The soldiers therefore came: and they broke the legs of the first, and of the other that was crucified with Him. But after they were come to Jesus, when they saw that He was already dead, they did not break His legs. But one of the soldiers with a spear opened His side, and immediately there came out blood and water " (1).

---

(1) John xix, 30-34.

From the foregoing words we may positively believe that the Side of Jesus was pierced by the thrust of a lance. It appears, moreover, indubitable that that same blow transpierced the Heart, also, of the Divine Crucified. The Evangelist does not say so in precise terms, but reason and authority combine to make this assertion absolutely incontestable.

First, reason tells us so. It is very probable that the soldier, either to assure himself that the Christ was really dead, or to give Him the final death-stroke, designedly drove his lance into the very Heart of Jesus. The Wound of the Side, moreover, was so large, so deep, that one might easily thrust his hand into It, as St. Thomas did on the invitation of the risen Redeemer. Such a wound could not have been dug in the breast without transpiercing the Heart. Again, the abundant flow of blood and water which spouted out under that blow, proves that the Heart had been struck; for the Heart is the source of the blood. It alone could still retain some after the other members of the body had shed theirs by the wounds of the scourging and the Crucifixion. Again, Christ willed that His Heart should be wounded that it might be apparent with what love He regarded His Church, to whom He says with so much tenderness: " Thou hast wounded My Heart, O My well-beloved Spouse! " Lastly, it is evident that this Wound of His Side had a mystical relation with His Heart. Christ willed that It should be the open gate which, revealing to us His Heart, should afford us an assured entrance into It.

Secondly, the weight of authority is added to reason. In the Decree of Beatification of Blessed Margaret Mary, Pius IX thus expressed himself: " Who, then, will be so hard, so insensible, as not to be forced to return love for love to this most sweet Heart, which was wounded, transpierced by a lance, in order that our soul might find in It a refuge, a secure asylum from the pursuit, from the deceits of its enemies: *Cor illud suavissimum idcirco transfixum et vulneratum lancea?* " This Decree repeats the tender, the burning words of St. Augustine, of St. Bernard, of St. Bonaventure on the mysterious opening of the Side of the Saviour, which calls to us to enter into His Heart, to abide therein, to live and to die therein.

To unfold to the eyes of faith the full reality of the Wound of the Sacred Heart, we add that the Blood and water, though issuing from It at the same moment, did so without mixing with each other. The Blood was substantially blood; the water, pure and natural, with no foreign tinge whatever. That Blood was miraculously preserved and that water miraculously formed in the Sacred Heart Itself. It was by a miracle, also, that they streamed forth instantaneously and abundantly under the stroke of the lance, and yet without mingling.

The Saviour willed, likewise, that this Wound should remain open in His resuscitated Body, not like the scar of a wound badly closed, not painful to look upon as it was in the Side of the Christ dead upon the Cross, but wonderfully harmonizing with the beauty of His glorified Humanity. It was shining with light, or, as St. Bernard says, It was " the most beautiful of the five roses that expanded upon the fruitful stem of our most sweet Saviour, by the heat of His ardent love: *Intuere et respice rosam Passionis sanguineae, quomodo rubet in indicium ardentissimae charitatis"* (1).

Let us, then, approach with respect the Saviour who, in the Most Blessed Sacrament, presents to our adoration this Sacred Wound, so authentic, so profound, so lasting. A living memorial of the past, It is in the present a powerful centre of action, and the sure guarantee of the eternal future. It repeats to us with open lips not only all the sufferings, but all the love of Our Saviour's death. It continues, It untiringly perfects in our behalf the work of Its Redemption. It proclaims that heaven is open to all who raise a sincere and suppliant glance to " Him whom they have transpierced: *Et adspicient ad quem confixerunt"* (2).

"One day," says Blessed Margaret Mary, " the Blessed Sacrament being exposed, Jesus Christ, my Divine Master, presented Himself to me, radiant with glory, His five Wounds brilliant as so many suns. From all parts of His Sacred Humanity, there issued flames, above all, from His sacred breast, which resembled a furnace. Opening it, He showed me His Divine Heart, the burning centre of those flames."

(1) *Ex. Off., Quinque Vulnerum, Lect. IV.*
(2) Zach. xii, 10.

### THANKSGIVING.

Love, supreme love, which the Wound of the Sacred Heart so plainly manifests, calls for our gratitude. One of the principal reasons that led the Son of God to allow His Heart to be wounded was, that it might serve as an unmistakable sign, as an authentic seal of His love for men.

The Sacred Wound, chaining the attention to the Heart of the Saviour, proclaims that it is from that Heart, that is, from His love, proceeds all the self-sacrifice of His life, whether in sentiments of tenderness, pity, and mercy, in words of instruction and consolation, or in works of healing and conversion. From It, also, came forth all the sufferings embraced and supported even to the end of His Passion. From It, in fine, originated that death undergone upon the accursed Cross for the expiation of sin and the liquidation of its insolvent obligations, for the satisfaction of Divine Justice, and for the reconciliation of Divine Mercy with mankind repentant and forgiven. " Behold," says St. Bernard, " the secret of the Sacred Heart revealed by the wounds opened in the Saviour's flesh! Behold the grand mystery of Divine Goodness laid bare! Behold the bowels of mercy disclosed to view! *Patet arcanum Cordis per foramina corporis; patet magnum pietatis sacramentum; patent viscera misericordiae!* (1)

" By allowing His Heart to be pierced after His death, the Divine Master disclosed both the supreme gift of His Heart and the supreme proof of His love. While still alive, He had delivered His head to thorns, His shoulders to the scourges, His hands and feet to the nails. His Heart alone, although It had cruelly suffered from all Its effusions of blood, had escaped without a direct bruise, without a wound dug in Its very substance. That He might not appear reluctant to deliver for our salvation the most noble organ of His Sacred Body, Christ offered His Heart to be transpierced by the thrust of the soldier's lance " (2). He testified thereby that He truly loved us to the end: *In finem*—to the end of His life, even unto death, yes, and beyond death.

---

(1)   Serm. lxi, 4.
(2)   Fr. Lucas Brug, in Joan. xix.

It is the excess, the superabundance, of the evidences of His love!

That Wound is, also, the authentic seal of God's reconciliation with us, the proof that having banished us from His Heart as well as from Paradise, He has now restored to us both the one and the other. The lance of the soldier opened and holds open the gate that the archangel's flaming sword kept closed. " Behold ! " exclaims St. Bernard, " the gate of Paradise reopened and the fiery sword thrust aside by the bloody lance ! Behold the Tree of Life pierced not only in Its branches, but in Its very core ! Behold the treasure of eternal love opened ! Enter, then, those large openings of the Sacred Wounds: *Ecce aperta est janua Paradisi et per lanceam militis gladius versatilis est amotus! Ecce Lignum vitae tam in ramis quam in stipite perforatum! Ecce apertus est thesaurus charitatis æternæ! Intra per vulnerum aperturam!*"(1)

Will not such love open our heart with its fiery flame, as did the lance the Heart of Jesus, that tears of tender love, of grateful love, may gush from it, which, mingling

---

(1) Stim. div. Am. Pl. c.1.

with His Blood and with His love, may perfect in us the Saviour's Passion? It is this return that Jesus expects from us: *"Adspicient ad quem confixerunt et dolebunt super eum ut doleri solet in morte primogenti!*—They shall look upon Me whom they have pierced: and they shall mourn for Him as one mourneth for an only son, and they shall grieve over Him, as the manner is to grieve for the death of the first-born "(1).

One day, when Blessed Margaret Mary, to overcome her natural repugnance, had performed an heroic act toward a sick person seized with vomiting, Our Lord testified the pleasure that she had afforded Him. " The following night," she tells us, " for about two or three hours, He kept my lips pressed upon the Wound of His Sacred Heart. It would be very hard to express what I then experienced, or the effects that favor produced in my soul and in my heart."

### REPARATION.

Sin, alas! is at the root of the great fact of the transfixion of the Sacred Heart,

---

(1) Zach. xii, 10.

which fact, however, Its love transforms for us into benefit.

It was, indeed, a real crime on the part of the soldier, who exhibited as much contempt as ferocity toward the Divine Condemned. Even while executing the orders of the civilized rules of pagan Rome, it was his own innate cruelty that urged the barbarous soldier to deal as heavy a blow on the limbs of the Saviour as upon those of the two thieves. But finding Christ dead, he vented his disappointment and rage by driving the iron of his lance into His Heart. He was fully aware of the uselessness of that proof of the Saviour's death. He meant it as a supreme insult to the Condemned upon whom, from the very beginning of His Passion, gratuitous outrages had been heaped, to the exclusion of those guarantees by which the law protects both the accused and the condemned. He wished, moreover, to please the High Priests who had hired him, and whose imperious eyes were upon him.

It was, however, the infinite malice of our own sins that nerved the arm of the soldier and urged him to commit the crime. It exacted this expiation of the Holy Victim, who willingly took upon Himself its responsiblity. The seat of sin is, then, in the heart of man, in the disorderly preference that he gives to the creature above the Creator, in the outrageous abandonment in which he leaves his God in order to give Himself up to the depraved pleasures in which he seeks his delight and happiness instead of placing them in the Infinite Good. Now, the Lord, who looks at the heart in order to recompense the intention which prompts the good action, pursues sin even to its primitive source by striking that heart: *"Dominus intuetur cor*—The Lord beholdeth the heart"* (1). Let, then, the Heart of this Man, this Substitute for all mankind, His brethren, to pay their debt of sin and to expiate its malice by submitting to its chastisement, be struck and broken! The divine wrath will be appeased only when it can fall upon this Heart truly broken by the most humiliating blows: *"Ad quem respiciam nisi ad pauperculum et contritum spiritu?*—To whom shall I have respect but to him that is poor and little and of a contrite spirit?"* (2) See, now, why the

----

(1)   Reg. xvi, 7.
(2)   Is. lxvi, 2.

Heart of Jesus which, during His whole life, and still more during His agony in the Garden, had been troubled and wounded by a thousand spiritual swords of terror, sadness, disgust, deep humiliation, the treason of the cold indifference of His own, and lastly, by the pitiless abandonment of His Father,—behold why It should be transpierced by the point of the lance. It was the ransom of sin rated upon the human heart.

The sword of grief, prolonging even to ourselves the sharp point of the lance that transpierced the Heart of Jesus,—will it not cleave our hearts of granite and draw from us tears of sorrow over the Innocent One whom we have literally covered with wounds? *" Adspicient ad quem confixerunt et plangent planctu quasi super unigenitum*—They shall look upon him whom they have pierced, and they shall grieve over him as the manner is to grieve for the death of the first-born "(1). But if, indifferent to the chastisements that He once underwent for us, we continue to strike Him daily new blows, what will be our attitude when this

(1) Zach. xii, 10.

Crucified Redeemer, coming in His majesty in the clouds of heaven, shall display His Wounds before the eyes of them that pierced Him, without their being able to flee from the terrible sight? *" Ecce venit cum nubibus et videbit eum omnis oculus et qui eum pupugerunt*—Behold He cometh with the clouds, and every eye shall see Him, and they also that piereced Him "(1). Then will this open Wound, transformed into a mouth of fury, cry for vengeance against us, and will command the infernal flames, penetrating and devouring, to torture us for all eternity!

" One day," says Blessed Margaret Mary, " it seemed to me that I heard the voice of my Saviour, saying: ' My chosen people persecute Me in secret, and they have irritated My justice. But I shall manifest these secret sins by visible chastisements, for I shall sift them in the sieve of My sanctity, in order to separate them from My well-beloved. Having separated them, I shall surround them with that same sanctity, which comes between the sinner and My mercy. And when My holiness has

(1) Apoc. i, 7.

once environed the sinner, it is impossible for him to know himself. His conscience continues without remorse, his understanding without light, his heart without contrition, and at last he dies in his blindness!' Discovering to me afterward His loving Heart, all torn and transpierced with blows, He said: ' Behold the wounds that I received from My chosen people! Others were satisfied with striking My person, but they have attacked My Heart, which has never ceased to love them!' "

### PETITION.

The fruits of the transfixion St. Bonaventure shows in Christ transpierced by the lance upon the Cross, " the Tree of Life gashed in Its branches and in Its Trunk: *Ecce lignum vitae tam in ramis quam in stipite perforatum."* As they pierce aromatic trees in order to gather their precious liquor, so shall we gather in our heart near the Divine Crucified by attentive, confident, and humble prayer, the odoriferous oils of grace which flow from the Wound of the Sacred Heart.

At first, it is the salutary bruising of the heart, holy contrition, the frequenting of the piscina of Penance, filled with the waves of lustral water that jet from the transpierced Heart; then it is the holy habit of assiduously drinking from the Eucharistic Chalice the virginal Blood, the repairing Blood, whose last drops reddened as they fell to the earth of Calvary, and reanimated for the resurrection the bones, long dried up, of the first sinners.

Later on, it is the knowledge of Jesus Christ, of His mysteries, His love, His spirit, gained by contact with His Heart. On the morrow of the Resurrection, Thomas, having lost faith and hope, had fallen into discouragement, which led to denial and apostasy. But he recognized Jesus, " his Lord and his God," as soon as he had plunged his hand through the Breast of the Saviour into His open Heart, burning with love and palpitating with tender pity. Let us do the same. In our doubts, our coldness, our sadness and weakness, let us touch the Heart of Jesus by a look of faith, a cry of hope, a dart of love, an act of humility, and we shall soon find our Saviour and our God: *" Dominus meus et Deus meus!"*

Another fruit, in fine, is supernatural consolation in our trials. This consolation applies the true remedy, which is composed of the sufferings of Jesus, the most cruel and the most numerous that can attack any heart here below. In it He has mingled His purity, His love, His strength, His humility, His obedience, and His patience, with His indefectible hope. Wounds against Wound! Let our torn and broken hearts adapt themselves by their very wounds to the Heart of Jesus Christ so deeply transpierced. He there pours out His virtues with the price of His victories. There, above all, He pours forth His love, and " love is strong as death itself! " Ah! let us, then, cast our bruised hearts into the Wound of the transpierced Heart! It is blindness or cruelty which induces them to come forth from It.

" There," says St. Bonaventure, " are found and dispensed all the balms that calm and cure: *Ecce aperta est apotheca omnibus aromatibus plena!* "—" O blessed lance," continues the holy Doctor, " had I been in thy place, I should never have come forth from the Bosom of Jesus! I should have exclaimed: Behold the place of my rest for endless ages! Here will I remain, for it is the abode that I have chosen forever. *O quam beata lancea! O si fuissem loco illius lanceae, exire de Christi latere noluissem, sed dixissem: Haec requies mea in saeculum saeculi; hic habitabo quoniam elegi eam!"* (1)

Once, when Blessed Margaret Mary was experiencing great interior disquietude, it seemed to her that she heard a voice constantly warning her that she was on the edge of a precipice. With great confidence she thus addressed Our Lord: " Thou only Love of my soul, disclose to me the cause of this disquietude!" Our Lord, all covered with wounds, immediately presented Himself to her soul, and bade her look upon the opening of His Sacred Side, which was a fathomless abyss, dug by an immeasurable arrow, namely, the dart of love. He told her that, if she desired to escape the unknown abyss which she dreaded, she must lose herself in that by which all others are shunned; that it was the abode of those that loved; that in it they found two lives, the one for the soul, the other for the heart. The soul finds therein the source of living water for its purification; the heart finds a furnace of love which allows it to live no longer but by the

---

(1)   Stim. Div. Am. P. I. c. 1.

life of love.   The one sanctifies, the other consumes." On another occasion, she tells us, " My Divine Spouse gave me His Heart for my asylum, my help, and my heavenly resting-place in the tempests of this stormy sea. It is my repose, my retreat, my strength in my weakness.   When I feel myself laden with sufferings and sorrows caused by the sanctity of His justice, which reduces me to the point of death, He says to me: 'Come, take some rest, that thou mayest suffer more courageously!' I then feel myself abyssed in this furnace of love wherein I can think of nothing save loving Him!"

Make frequent spiritual Communions during the day.

O Sweetest Heart of Jesus, I implore
That I may ever love Thee more and more.
                    (100 *days' Indulgence.*)

# Twelfth Day.

SUBJECT.—The sufferings of the Heart of Jesus during the Passion were innumerable. They were not only those that sprang from mental anguish and physical pain, but those that He endured directly in His affections. He suffered from the friends who betrayed Him, forsook and denied Him, and, above all, was He afflicted by the abandonment of His Divine Father. But there was one other pain not less acute, and that was the presence of His most dear and beloved Mother, Mary most holy! If her presence was an heroic act of fidelity and, viewing it from this point, brought Him comfort and consolation, the Saviour suffered infinitely from the sight of the immense grief of the most innocent of mothers, and from the knowledge that He Himself was the cause of it. The compassion of Mary, in which was summed up all His own sufferings, came only from the Passion of Jesus. If

179

we can affirm that the deepest wound in the Heart of Jesus is that which was dug into It by the abandonment of His Father, we need not hesitate to declare that next to it was the sorrow experienced at the sight of His holy Mother at the foot of the Cross. This subject, which so closely binds the Heart of Jesus with the Heart of Mary, both transpierced by the sword of the same sorrows, can not be too frequently meditated upon by souls truly devoted to the Sacred Heart, if they desire to delve into Its profound secrets.

### ADORATION.

" *Stabat juxta crucem Jesu Mater ejus*— There stood by the Cross of Jesus His Mother," sometimes a little nearer, sometimes more removed, according as the surging of the crowd around the Cross or the caprice of the guards permitted. In either position, she was so placed as to be seen by Jesus: " *Cum vidisset ergo Jesus Matrem* —When Jesus, therefore, had seen His Mother "(1). He saw her with His bodily eyes, and still more did He behold her with the interior gaze of His filial Heart. In

_____

(1) John xix.

this double view, which enveloped Mary and penetrated to the depths of her soul, He saw the personification of sorrow the most profound after His own. The Church, our other Mother, so capable of comprehending Mary's grief, depicts it in strophes of deep compassion in the *Stabat Mater,* which we can not read without emotion. She is " the sorrowful Mother, plunged in tears at the foot of the gibbet of her Son: *" Dolorosa, lacrymosa"*(1); the soul weighed down with sadness, wounded, groaning, transpierced with a sword: *" Animam gementem, contristatem, dolentem "*(2). Ah, how afflicted, how agonized was the Blessed Mother of that only Son, that unique Son: *" O quam tristis et afflicta! "*(3) Turning to us, the Church exclaims:

*" Quis est homo qui non fleret,*
*Matrem Christi si videret*
*In tanto supplicio!—*

---

(1) *Stabat Mater dolorosa,*
 *Juxta crucem lacrymosa,*
  *Dum pendebat Filius.*
(2) *Cujus animam gementem,*
 *Constristatem et dolentem*
  *Pertransivit gladius.*
(3) *O quam tristis et afflicta*
 *Fuit illa benedicta*
  *Mater Unigeniti!*

Who is the man who would not weep at sight of the Mother of Jesus enduring punishment so terrible?" If the most degraded of men, the coarsest, the most hard-hearted, are challenged to gaze unmoved on the untold sorrows of Mary, what impression must they have produced upon her Son, the most loving, the most sensitive, the most delicate of all that have ever appreciated a mother? It is His own Blood that thrills and dries up in His Mother's heart, His own tears that course hot or chill from her eyes. He experiences all Mary's sorrow, deep, wide, bitter as the sea, as if it were His own. Mary's compassion is joined to His own Passion to redouble its sharpness and bitterness.

He saw her at the foot of the Cross as the prophecy of Jeremias had described her in terms that burst like sobs from a broken heart: " Weeping she hath wept in the night, and her tears are on her cheeks " (the whcle night of that terrible agony which began in Gethsemani, and ended in the horrible darkness of Calvary) ; " there is none to comfort her among all them that were dear to her; all her friends have despised her, and have become her enemies!"(1) John's fidelity cannot make her forget the abandonment of all the others. And it was prohibited Jesus by the avenging anger of God to afford His Mother the least relief, to say to her one word of pity or consolation!

Still more, Jesus had to listen to these sorrowful lamentations uttered by His Mother: "O all ye that pass by the way, attend and see if there be any sorrow like my sorrow: for He hath made a vintage of me, as the Lord spoke in the day of His fierce anger. From above He hath sent fire into my bones, and hath chastised me. He hath spread a net for my feet, He hath turned me back: He hath made me desolate, wasted with sorrow all the day long. .
My strength is weakened: the Lord hath delivered me into a hand out of which I am not able to rise. Therefore do I weep, and my eyes run down with tears, because my children are desolate, because the enemy hath prevailed. Hear, I pray you, all ye people, and see my sorrow: my virgins and my young men have gone into captivity!"(2) And his Mother

---

(1) Lam. i, 1-2.
(2) Ibid., 12-18.

who saw her Eldest-Born dying of sorrow before her eyes, mourned all her other children buried in the more lamentable death of sin.

In the excess of her anguish, Mary sent forth to her Jesus a cry of agony: " Behold, O Lord, for I am distressed, my bowels are troubled. My heart is turned within me, for I am full of bitterness: abroad the sword (Thy Cross) destroyeth and at home, it is death alike " by the share that I take in the sufferings of Thy Heart: " *Foris interficit gladius, et domi mors similis est!* "(1)

Behold what Jesus saw, what He heard! Behold into what an abyss of pain, agony, and darkness He was plunged by the anxious tenderness, the devoted affection, the compassion of His Heart for the best of Mothers! Oh, what an increase of suffering for this best of Sons! Let it cease, O Son, Thou who dost remain even in the weakness of death, the All-Powerful! Put an end to the sufferings of Thy Mother! Or, at least, console her by a word, a look, an impression of relief in the depths of her

---

(1) Ibid. xx, 20.

soul from Thy sovereign power, which holds souls in its hand and acts in them as it wills!

But no! It had been decided in the council of inexorable justice that, in order to drain the chalice of filial suffering to the very dregs, Jesus should not say one word of comfort, should not cast on her one look of pity, one smile of encouragement. He will see her weighed down without the power of relieving her. He will be condemned to the punishment of being able to do nothing in time of affliction for the loved one. And if, at last, He looks upon her from the height of the Cross, if He speaks to her, it is to pierce her soul with a word sharper than the sword, the cruel nails, and the lance that tore Him from her maternal embrace. By robbing her of her own Son, they gave her John in His place, who, after all, was only a stranger, a sinner,—a man instead of a God! *" Dicit matri suae; Ecce filius tuus!"* Very far from lessening the pain of His Mother, who was watching Him die, that word of Jesus thrust the last sword into her heart and, according to St. Bernard, *" Plus quam Martyrem non immerito praedicemus,* made Mary a martyr and the Queen of Martyrs."

But to this sorrow of seeing His Mother suffer without His permitting Himself to do anything for her relief, there is for the Heart of Jesus a pain still more cruel, still more harrowing, and that is, to know without doubt that He is the cause, the only cause of her suffering. It is most true to say that Mary suffered only on account of Jesus and His pains, which she shared with Him without reserve. The Passion of Jesus gave rise to all the compassion of Mary. The Passion was the cause, the instrument, and the measure of her compassion. It is not on record, indeed, that, during the Passion, Mary had to endure any insult or brutal treatment on the part of the judges, the executioners, or the crowd. Her grave and humble modesty, the extreme dejection of her sorrow enveloped her with a kind of sacred protection, even in the sight of those monsters of hatred and that furious multitude athirst for blood. All her sorrow came to her, then, from the suffering of her Son. This strange law, that Jesus would be her mortal torment was revealed to Mary as soon as she presented Him in the Temple, in the joy of her glorious maternity, " Behold, this Child is set for the fall, and for the resurrection of many in Israel, and for a sign which shall be contradicted. And thy own soul a sword shall pierce." Mary had lived so closely, so constantly united to her Son, that her soul never ceased to envelop Him, so that the sword, insults, condemnation, blows, nails, death itself could attack Jesus only by passing through the soul of His Mother. It was not only by the sentiment of compassion that she participated in the Passion of Jesus. She was present corporally, for she had the courage to follow Him everywhere, from Gethsemani to Calvary, passing through the prætorium, keeping as close as possible to Him, walking in the tracks of His Blood and literally following His footsteps. Her presence at the foot of the Cross authenticates by the Gospel her meeting with Him on the dolorous way, and gives us an assurance of this fact consecrated by tradition. And is it not the same fact that is still recalled by the touching and graphic lamentation of the *Stabat?*

In the Garden, Mary was witness to the Agony of her Son. She shared the terror, the sadness, the languor, the bitterness that inundated His Soul and dragged Him down

to the gates of death.   She heard Him
vainly entreating His Father to remove
from Him the chalice filled with the wine
of His wrath.   She saw Him covered with
the sweat of His own Blood, going to seek
from His Apostles a little drop of comfort,
but which was denied Him by their torpid
indifference.   Her intimate union in those
pains, which she would have been so happy
to sweeten by her maternal tenderness,
caused her inexpressible "torment and
agony:"

> " *Quae mœrebat et dolebat*
> *Pia mater dum videbat*
> *Nati pœnas inclyti!*"

She followed Him from tribunal to
tribunal, heard Him accused of crimes by
false witnesses, and condemned as an
avowed criminal by the hatred or cowardice
of the iniquitous judges; then she assists at
the horrible torments of the flagellation and
the crowning with thorns.   She revealed to
St. Bridget that her veil had been stained
with the drops of blood which spouted from
the flesh of her Well-Beloved under the
violent blows of the scourge:

> *" Pro peccatis suae gentis*
> *Vidit Jesus in tormentis,*
> *Et flagellis subditum!"*

Lastly, she was at the foot of the Cross, where Jesus endured for three hours the cruel throes of His last agony. She assisted at His desolate death, amid the curses and mockery of men and the inexorable abandonment of His Divine Father, and she heard Him draw His last sigh while uttering a loud cry of pain. That death, which freed the Son from His agony, redoubled that of the Mother; and when she received Him into her arms dead, lacerated, disfigured, covered with clotted blood, her martyrdom was at its height:

> *" Vidit suum dulcem natum*
> *Moriendo desolatum,*
> *Dum emisit spiritum!"*

Jesus, Jesus, then, is the cause, the whole cause of Mary's suffering. No sword pierced Jesus without turning its point upon Mary, also. " The dolors of Mary," writes Father Faber, " all come from the presence of Jesus; they were the point of contact between the Heart of Jesus and the Heart of Mary. He Himself was the cause of her woe.  He poured at every instant from His own Soul into hers, every insult, every pain, every outrage, every indignity.  It was He who extended His Mother's members upon the instrument of torture; it was He who spread around her the dreariest darkness. It was He alone who caused her to endure all these woes. Without Jesus, Mary would not have had any sorrows to endure; but for her heart, the best loved of all by Him, He was a fiery cross.  And then, all the immense bitterness that He poured from His own Heart into Mary's, He received again into His, but without relieving Mary.  It entered into the Heart of Jesus like another Passion.  Thus the compassion of Mary flowed from the Passion and returned to it. Between the two there was identity rather than union."

O ye who comprehend in some degree the dolors of Mary, see, understand and adore the truth. the depth, and the extent of the wound that they dug in the Heart of her Son, who saw them without having permission to relieve them, and who had received from the dread justice of His Father the command to inflict them.  Adore in amazement and compassion.  When you shall have comprehended the reasons for this strange punishment, caused to the Mother by the Son, and falling back with double force from the Mother upon the Son, you will bless the love which for you has not hesitated to impose it on both the one and the other!

### THANKSGIVING.

God the Father demanded this terrible suffering, and Jesus embraced it " in order to suffer more," says a profound commentator of the Holy Scriptures: *" Voluit hoc Christus ut magis pateretur!"* To suffer in His filial tenderness, to assume the odious appearance of a heartless Son, to suffer from her faithful and constant presence as He did from the absence of the friends that had abandoned Him, to endure, in reality, two Passions—His own and that of His Mother—this was the aim of Jesus in Mary's dolors. " In olden times," says an ancient author, " it was not lawful to immolate a sheep on the day they had taken away its lamb, but Thou, O God, O Father, didst sacrifice on the same day the Son with the Mother! The love they have for each other is the executioner that carries out Thy sentence; and that nothing may be wanting to their sorrow, they are tormented at the sight of each other. Blessed forever be the excess of Thy mercy toward sinners!" The sufferings so generously embraced by the Son of God prove the measure of His love for us; the excess of His Passion reveals to us the excess of His love!

### REPARATION.

Jesus willed to endure the pain of making His mother suffer the most genuine sorrows and weep the holiest tears, in order to expiate the sins committed by children against the duties of filial devotedness, by children who cause their poor mothers scalding tears. Without having been a bad child, who is he who, at certain times, has not saddened his mother by his caprices, his pride, or his idleness? But how numerous the children who, by their ingratitude and disobedience, their precocious impiety and immorality, by the danger of eternal death which they incur and in which they remain, bow down the aged head of their mother under the weight of dishonor, torture her tender heart with mortal anguish and inconsolable desolation. Insensible to the grief, the tears, the sighs of those gentle and loving mothers, treading under foot the law of nature and the precept of the Lord: " *Gemitus matris suae ne obliviscaris*—Forget not the groanings of thy mother "(1), they bring upon them premature old age and hurry them to the tomb.

O Christ, the best, the most obedient, and the most loving of sons, expiate the crime of these parricides, and endure in Thy filial love the sufferings Thou dost impose on Thy virginal Mother!

Hear, again, the lamentation of that other Mother, the Holy Church, who weeps over the ingratitude and disobedience of so many of her children who pitilessly persecute her. To repair this new crime, O Jesus, sacrifice, immolate Thy Heart under the wine-press of the dolors of Thy own Mother, which flow back upon Thee!

### PETITION.

Jesus confronted this heartfelt sorrow to sustain by His example the courage of those children upon whom God imposes duties and from whom He demands sacrifices which

---

(1)  Eccles. vii, 29.

cannot be made without causing great
anguish to their mothers.

It is not ingratitude that in such cases
makes tears course down the cheeks of those
mothers so loved and venerated; it is the
superior right of divine love to which, when
it pleases God, every other love, however
legitimate, must be sacrificed. Jesus, when
a Child, did not hesitate to leave His Mother
in tears and disquietude when His Divine
Father, in order to affirm His sovereign
rights, commanded Him to do so without
saying adieu. Nor did He hesitate to expose her to the horrible tempest of His Passion, although He might so easily have
closed her eyes as He did St. Joseph's, before casting Himself into that ocean of suffering. Jesus acted thus in order to give to
children who are, by duty to their country,
a religious vocation, or the call to the apostolate, obliged to leave their mother. If
their heart shrinks, if the tears of one so
venerated weaken their resolution and
tempt them to recoil, let them look upon this
admirable Son who immolated His Mother
to the glory of God and the salvation of the
world. That glance will strengthen them to

accomplish their sacrifice, will fortify them against after-thoughts of tender regret.

To gain precious fruits from this mystery, let us take the following resolutions, while earnestly begging the Son by the Mother of Sorrows for the grace to know how to accept and suffer pain, whatsoever it may be, without distinction or reserve: patiently to behold our loved ones suffer, although we would be rejoiced to suffer in their stead; to accept cheerfully what those we most love make us suffer; willingly (and this is the most painful of all to a loving heart) to be a cause of suffering, should it so please God, to our loved ones when we would wish most to be a consolation to them. Yes, we must even be willing, voluntarily and unshrinkingly, to inflict pain on them when some supernatural good or the welfare of their souls calls for it.

O Christ Jesus, perfect Son of Mary, and Model of all good children, Thou who didst love us even to sacrificing Thy own Mother, be Thou forever blessed! Be Thou loved and served by the total sacrifice of all that we hold most dear, if it should please Thee to demand it of us! I press my lips to the Wound opened in Thy

Heart by Thy love for Mary, desiring to find therein with the strength never to refuse Thee anything, the balm necessary to dress the wounds that the sacrifice of its dearest loves may open in my heart!

We read in Blessed Margaret Mary's Revelations of the Sacred Heart: " One Friday, during Holy Mass, I felt a great desire to honor the sufferings of my Crucified Spouse. He told me lovingly that He wanted me to come every Friday to adore Him thirty-three times on the tree of the Cross, which is the throne of His mercy. I was to prostrate at His feet and endeavor to enter into the same dispositions in which was the Blessed Virgin at the time of the Passion, offering it all to the Eternal Father with the sufferings of His Divine Son for the conversion of hardened hearts. To those who had been faithful to this practice, Jesus promised to be favorable at the hour of death."

Pray for vocations to the priesthood.

O Mary most sorrowful, Mother of all Christians, pray for us.

(300 *days' Indulgence.*)

# Thirteenth Day

## ADORATION.

SUBJECT.—The Divine Master pointed out His Heart to men in the different states of His mortal life as the source of the love that He testifies toward them in every one of those states, and as the centre in which they should seek Him if they would everywhere find and taste Him. " Come to Me and learn of Me that I am meek and humble of Heart," did He say to those sheep without a shepherd, to the heavily burdened. " Abide in Me, abide in My love," did He say when He made Himself a Sacrament, when He drew St. John to His Heart. He willed that a soldier should with a thrust of his lance open His side on the Cross, to show to the world in His open Heart the love that had led Him to embrace death for its redemption. To inaugurate the immortal life that He was henceforth to lead to the end of time in our tabernacles and for all eternity in heaven, He called upon Thomas

197

to plunge his hand into His side: *" After
manum tuam, et mitte in latus meum—*
Bring hither thy hand, and put it into My
side," that we might know by contact with
His Heart in Its new life that He is always
our Lord and our God. In His resuscitated
life as in His death, He was consecrating to
our welfare the treasures of His glorified
Heart, as He had poured out for our benefit all the devotedness of His mortal Heart.

The various manifestations of the Sacred
Heart during the days that our risen Saviour passed upon earth after the Resurrection, will form the subject of this Adoration.

While the Body of Jesus, wrapped in the
winding-sheet, lay motionless in the tomb,
His Divinity, which was never separated
from the Humanity even in death, com-
missioned the most glorious of the angels
to gather up in golden cups the drops of
sacred Blood scattered over the wide battle-
field on which the intrepid Christ had combated. Those angelic messengers bore it
with the deepest respect to the source
whence it had issued, to the Sacred Heart,
pierced, broken, lifeless. For three days it
rested before resuming new life, the just

recompense of Its holy and magnanimous death. At the moment of the Resurrection, the Soul of the Saviour, ending Its beneficent visit to the patriarchs of limbo, touched with Its radiant wing the pale countenance of the Christ in His sleep of death and, ardent and joyous, united Itself forever to that Body, so pure and so worthy of It, and from which It should never have been separated. At that touch of intense power, the Heart of Christ awoke and, with an impetuous rush, propelled into the arteries the Blood that filled It. Then began the joyous and rhythmic pulsation of the glorious life by which the First-Born of the Resurrection was to live eternally.

Nothing henceforth could trouble the unalterable joy of this Heart, no power whatever could dim Its glory, no more painful and ignominious effusion of Its Blood. Peace, light, beatitude unending were to be Its portion. The life that it poured into the members of the Saviour was safe from every attack, secure against the ravages of decrepitude, raised above the laws of matter, independent of every created cause, and endued with all the prerogatives of the spiritual life. The Heart of the First-Born among the victors over death, It became the centre of every resurrection for souls purchased to the life of grace, for all that enter into the life of glory, as well as for the body snatched from the dust of the tomb and established in incorruptible life. It is the living and luminous source, from which all souls thirsting for unruffled peace, pure joy, and eternal happiness, shall come to draw, to slake their thirst, and to be inebriated without ever exhausting It: *Haurietis aquas in gaudio de fontibus Salvatoris* (1).

### THANKSGIVING.

Goodness is the principal motive for gratitude. In no other phase of His life did the Saviour more tenderly manifest His goodness than in His Resurrection. The spirit that this mystery inspires is, also, one of joy, happiness, and thanksgiving.

Christ shows that glory has not changed His Heart, as it too often happens among men. His goodness shines forth in His eagerness to show Himself to His own, to multiply His apparitions to them, and to allow Himself to be touched by them: *" Videte et palpate!*—Handle and see! "

---

(1)   Is, xii, 3.

His goodness speaks in His words of peace, repeated insistently: *"Pax vobis! Iterum dico, Pax vobis!*—Peace to you! Again I say, Peace to you!"* It was His condescending goodness that made Him return to the Cenacle, urged by the challenge of incredulous Thomas, in order to impart to him the Holy Spirit, which he had not received with his fellow-disciples.

What familiarity, what goodness on the shore of the sea of Tiberias! *"Pueri numquid pulmentarium habetis?* — Children, have you any meat? Cast the net on the right!"* And He had Himself lighted the coals upon which was broiling a fine fish, which He blessed, distributed, and ate with them: *"Accepit panem et piscem similiter."*—It is His goodness that consoles the weeping Magdalen: "Woman, why weepest thou?" "They have taken away my Lord!" "Mary!" *"Rabboni,* O my Master!"

It was the compassionate goodness of Jesus that encouraged, enlightened, and strengthened the disciples of Emmaus. He explained to them the Scriptures that announced and justified His death. He revived their fainting hearts with the breath of His convincing proofs. He deigned to accept their hospitality and, reversing the rôles, became their host. He fed them with " Bread blessed and broken," with that marvellous Eucharist which they had tasted three days before, and He sent them away full of faith and zeal on their mission of witnesses and Apostles.

### REPARATION.

The very mysteries which glory illumines most with its splendors and replenishes with holy joy, are mingled with sadness, become overcast when in contact with sinful man. They have to amend and purify, hence, the necessity for reparation. In the effusions of Its Paschal joys, therefore, the Sacred Heart feels Itself obliged to inspire the Saviour with remonstrances and reproaches. It inveighs, above all, against the weak and wavering faith of Its own followers, and against the discouragement resulting from it, and which may easily lead to infidelity and apostasy.

On account of their ignorance, which had not comprehended the Saviour's teachings, and their groundless distrust of His goodness, the Apostles were, more or less, a prey to the terrible evil of incredulity. In vain had Jesus announced to them on several occasions His Passion, Death, and Resurrection, and proved that they had been foretold by the prophets. On the very day after the event, they remembered not that the Scriptures declared His Resurrection certain. The holy women, sent to them first by the angel, then by the Saviour Himself, talked foolishly, as they thought, when announcing His Resurrection, and they refused to believe. Even in the presence of their risen Lord, they hesitated and feared being deceived. Still more, after the repeated apparitions in the Cenacle, they failed to recognize Him when He appeared on the shores of Tiberias. It was only the more refined perceptions of John that made Him known to Peter and the other disciples: "*Dominus est*—It is the Lord!"

Such incredulity outraged the Saviour's veracity, and wounded still more His Heart. Indignation, as well as sorrow, may be traced in the reproaches that Jesus made to them. "O foolish and slow of heart to believe in all things which the prophets have spoken," did He say to the disciples when, in doubt and despondency, they were making their way to Emmaus. " Know ye not that Christ had to suffer these things, and so to enter into His glory? " When He appeared to the Eleven as they were at table, He " upbraided them with their incredulity and hardness of heart, because they did not believe them who had seen Him after He has risen—*Ex probravit incredulitatem et duritiam cordis.*"

Oh, how difficult it is to obtain and to preserve faith, though so necessary! When recommending to Thomas to be no longer faithless, but believing, the Saviour, to exalt the merit of faith, made use of these words: " *Beati qui non viderunt et crediderunt!* —Blessed are they that have not seen, and have believed! "

### PETITION.

The Resurrection, in retaining the open Wound of the Sacred Side, reveals the Heart of the Priest who prays, of the Apostle who evangelizes, of the Father who remains ever in the midst of His children to protect them.

" Behold, I go to My Father, to My God," said the Saviour. In these words, He made known the ministry of all-powerful mediation that He was to exercise as the eternal High-Priest in behalf of the world. He is ever standing before the Father, showing Him His Wounds, which tell of His Passion and His victory, and appealing to Him without intermission to grant us all the fruits of His Resurrection.

His Heart is overflowing with pity and inflamed with ardent, apostolic zeal for souls. He must shed light upon the whole earth, and carry salvation to mankind, held by Satan in the chains of death. To His Apostles on the little hill in Galilee, which He had assigned to them as a rendezvous, He said: "All power is given me in heaven and on earth. Going, therefore, teach ye all nations, baptizing them in the name of the Father, and of the Son, and of the Holy Ghost, teaching them to observe all things whatsoever I have commanded you."

But His Heart is that of a father toward the family which He Himself has gathered together, and which He wishes to multiply indefinitely. He knows that the father's presence is indispensable to the children, that he it is who must provide them with food and protection. At no cost will He leave them orphans, so giving to heaven His human Presence, He gives us His Eucharistic Presence by the solemn words of an inviolable testament: "Wheresoever you go to preach My Gospel, I am with you all days, even to the consummation of the world."

Pray that the pious custom of frequent and daily Communion may increase among children.

St. Joseph, model and patron of those who love the Sacred Heart of Jesus, pray for us.

(100 *days' Indulgence.*)

# Fourteenth Day.

## ADORATION.

" *Haurietis aquas in gaudio de fontibus
Salvatoris*—You shall draw waters with joy
out of the Saviour's fountains " (1).

Now, this life, this joy and glory with
which It was replenished in the Resurrection, the Sacred Heart is burning to shed
around, by revealing Itself to the world
and communicating to it unreservedly. It
impelled the Saviour to go to the Cenacle
where, uncertain and fearful, were gathered
the disciples whose faith had received so
rude a shock from the grievous defeat inflicted on Him by His enemies. In spite
of the closed doors, He entered, and His apparition, like a phantom before their
troubled eyes, only increased the terror of
their souls. But He, in that sweet and commanding voice which calmed tempests
and gained hearts, uttered the words:

---

(1)  Is. xii, 3

207

" Peace be to you! " At the sound, their faces brightened, and their hearts grew light. But wishing to strengthen their peace against vicissitudes and establish it on unshaken faith and confidence, He turned to Thomas, still incredulous concerning the Resurrection. Earnestly and tenderly He said to him: " Put in thy finger hither, and see My hands, and put it into My side; and be not faithless, but believing:—*Affer manum tuam et mitte in latus meum!*" Come, draw near, do not fear! Touch, handle, thrust thy finger into these Wounds of My hands and see whether they are not the hands of a living man. Place thy hand into the wide Wound of My Heart, plunge it in, draw it out, put it in again, and feel around in it! Go deep into My Heart, wounded from side to side. Feel Its pulsations. It is living and glowing. Feel the warmth of the Blood that dilates It, the strength of the movement that makes It rise and fall, the ardor of the love that consumes It. Ah! say, is it not the Heart of the Messiah who has called you, of the Friend who has loved you, of the Brother with whom you have lived, of the Priest who has fed you with His own consecrated Flesh, of the God whom miracles have proved to you, of the Sovereign Master to whom you have given yourself? Can you not henceforth believe firmly that it is I, I whom you have seen die, I whom you behold risen again? "*Noli esse incredulus, sed fidelis*—Be not faithless, but believing."

And Thomas, his hand in the Heart which is beating with immortal life, with the joy of meeting those whom It loves so much, with tender condescension toward the rashness of Its incredulous disciple,—Thomas enlightened, won, subdued,—Thomas in a rapture of gratitude, confessed his faith, adored, and rendered homage to Christ risen: "*Dominus meus et Deus meus!* My Lord and my God!" The touch of the Sacred Heart revealed to him the truth of Jesus' Humanity, the truth of His new life, of His personal identity, His victory over death, His glory, His Divinity, and His love for men. All this in the splendors of His Resurrection remains what it was in the humility of His mortal life: "*Dominus meus et Deus meus!*"

It is this resuscitated Heart, glorious and immortal, which beats in the breast of the Eucharistic Christ under the veils of ma-

terial signs, which conceal His splendor. If
you desire that your faith should taste the
joy of certitude and be enlightened with the
clear light of vision so far as to confess your
Lord and your God, enter, penetrate, plunge
your hand into His Heart, which is still
open, and which has been calling you for
twenty centuries! It is His Heart that reveals the Presence, the life, and the love of
the Christ of the Sacrament: *"Dominus
meus et Deus meus!"*

"One day," said Blessed Margaret Mary,
"when the Blessed Sacrament was exposed,
Jesus Christ, my good Master, presented
Himself to me brilliant with glory, His five
Wounds shining like so many suns. Flames
shot forth on all sides from His Sacred
Humanity, above all, from His adorable
Breast, which looked like a furnace. Opening It, He showed me His Divine Heart,
the living source of those flames. It was
then that He discovered to me the inexplicable marvels of His pure love and to what an
excess it had led Him in His love for man."

### THANKSGIVING.

It was Jesus' merciful and delicate goodness that, without making any painful al-

lusion to it, raised up Peter after his triple denial. He simply demanded of him in the presence of those that he had scandalized, three acts of love, after which He confirmed him in his charge of universal pastor: "*Petre, diligis me plus his? Pasce agnos, pasce oves*—Peter, lovest thou Me? Feed My sheep, feed My lambs."

It is the generous goodness of Jesus which is satisfied only when making others happy, shedding joy into hearts, and causing them to forget all sadness: "*Gavisi sunt discipuli, viso Domino*—The disciples were glad when they saw the Lord." He goes to meet the faithful, but disquieted, women with the words: "*Avete, nolite timere*—All hail! Fear not." And He allowed them in their joyful emotion to cast themselves at His glorified feet, and cover them with their pious kisses. The Church forever resounds with the echoes of the pure joy with which He replenished the heart of His Mother when, like a loving son, He pressed her to His Heart, making her taste as much happiness as she had experienced bitterness: "*Regina coeli, laetare, quia quem meruisti portare, resurrexit sicut dixit, alleluia!*—O Queen of heaven, rejoice, because He whom thou didst deserve to bear, has risen as He said, Alleluia!"

"Once," says Blessed Margaret Mary, "when I had retired into a little corner to be nearer the Blessed Sacrament, the adorable Heart of my Jesus was presented to me more brilliant than a sun. It was in the midst of the flames of Its pure love, and surrounded by seraphim, who sang in wonderful harmony:

Love triumphs, love possesses,
The love of the Heart of Jesus rejoices!

These blessed spirits invited me to unite with them in magnifying this amiable Heart, and to render It an unending homage of love and praise."

### REPARATION.

But if His most merciful Heart dictated to the unrecognized Saviour the necessary reprimands, It did not fail to incline Him to pardon the guilty and apply a remedy to their faults. It was in one of those consoling visits of the Resurrection that He instituted the Sacrament of mercy, through whose all-powerful action every sin will be remitted to them who humbly accuse themselves. The breath of pardon which will pass with the Holy Spirit over guilty souls to purify them from sin and lead them back to the divine life, will first have issued from the Sacred Heart, victorious by the Resurrection over sin and its principal causes, Satan and the world. " He breathed upon them, and He said to them: Receive ye the Holy Ghost. Whose sins ye shall forgive, they are forgiven them; and whose sins ye shall retain, they are retained."

Let us, then, make reparation for all our incredulity of mind, of heart and deed toward Christ risen from the tomb, and who appears to us constantly under the accidents of the Sacrament. Appearances are deceitful; but he who accepts in all their fulness the Eucharistic words, shall never feel his faith and confidence grow weak. " This is My Body, this is My Blood!" If it is the human Body of Jesus, it must be animated by a human Soul, for life necessarily results from the union of soul and body. Now, as the Humanity of the Saviour existed only to be borne and deified by the Person of the Word, this Body, this Soul, this Blood are those of a God. The Eucharist is, therefore, the Word Incarnate, Christ resuscitated and living under the appearance of bread. As no obligation retains Him under the abject bonds of the Sacrament excepting His own Heart, that is, His love, it follows that the Eucharist is Christ loving as well as Christ living. Lord, guard, increase, strengthen ever my faith in Thy Heart, give me light indefectible which enlightens the abysses of the mystery of Thy Eucharist!

Our incredulity, our forgetfulness, our diffidence and discouragement, are felt very keenly by the Saviour in this Sacrament of life and love. Like thorns constantly driven into His Heart they wound Him. Like a new Cross laid on His shoulders, they crush Him.

"One day," says Blessed Margaret Mary, "this Divine Heart was shown me on a throne of fire and flames, shooting out rays on all sides more brilliant than the sun and transparent as crystal. The Wound that It had received on the Cross appeared in It. A crown of thorns surrounded the Divine Heart, and It was surmounted by a Cross. My Divine Master gave me to understand that these instruments of His Passion signified all the outrages to which His love for men would expose Him in the Holy Eucharist to the end of time."

### PETITION.

The glorified Heart of the risen Christ, without abandoning us, consecrates to us in the Sacrament, which preserves Him for us present and living, His immortal life, His devoted love, His most pure joys, His untiring solicitude, His uninterrupted prayers and Sacrifice, the daily Bread, and His invincible protection. All this is secured to those that believe in Him and invoke Him with firm confidence. Let us pray, then, through the Heart of the risen Christ. Let us obtain resurrection for all who are dear to us, but whom sin holds in the thraldom of death. Let us, above all, obtain the resurrection of Christian France. To it was revealed the victorious Heart for the cure of its mortal evils and to restore to it, with the plenitude of Christian life, the power of a world-wide apostolate.

" What happiness for us," wrote Blessed Margaret Mary, " and for those that help to make the Sacred Heart known, loved, and glorified! They will draw down upon themselves the friendship and eternal benediction of the loving Heart of Jesus, and obtain a powerful Protector for our country. No less a power is necessary to appease the bitterness and severity of the just wrath of God for so many crimes. I hope that this Divine Heart will become an abundant and inexhaustible source of mercy and grace, as It has promised me."

Pray for the intentions of our Holy Father, Pope Pius X.

Sacred Heart of Jesus, let thy Kingdom come!

(300 *days' Indulgence.*)

# Fifteenth Day.

THE PRECIOUS BLOOD OF THE SACRED HEART.

*" Unus militum lancea latus ejus aperuit, et continuo exivit Sanguis et aqua."*

LET us fix our eyes on the Heart of the Saviour, opened by the lance of the soldier on Calvary, whence flowed the last streams of the redeeming Blood. Let us gaze upon this Heart always open in the Eucharist, laving and cleansing souls, and fertilizing the field of the Church with its inexhaustible fountains. Let us render to It our service of adoration, gratitude, compassion, and prayer for the sublime destiny which God has given It, for the powerful, beneficent, and loving office that It exercises for the glory of the Father and for our salvation by containing and pouring forth the most Precious Blood of Our Lord Jesus Christ.

" Behold the Heart that has so loved men, that has spared Itself in nothing, that has exhausted Itself, in order to prove to them Its love!" (Words of Our Lord to Blessed Margaret Mary.)

### ADORATION.

"*Hic est calix Sanguinis Mei:* This is the chalice of My Blood."

Such were Jesus' words when presenting to His own the golden cup of His Precious Blood, which He had substituted for the substance of the wine, though retaining the ruddy appearance of the grape, in order not to shock our fastidiousness. Ah! I know a chalice made of material more precious than gold, enriched with the rarest stones, shining with a far purer brilliancy, a chalice not formed by the hand of man, a chalice living and loving, holy and sanctifying, a chalice which contains the adorable Blood of Jesus in its reality, in its life, in its constant and indefatigable action—that chalice is the thrice-holy Heart!

I adore that Heart as the furnace in which the Blood of the Son of God was elaborated during the time of His human life, as the reservoir in which it is preserved, as the unfailing source from which it is shed abroad, as the centre to which it incessantly returns only to pour itself out again! I adore that Heart of the First-Born of mankind condemned to death, as the immaculate vase, fragile and passible, whence flowed all the Blood that was shed through the wounded members of the Saviour, and which was Itself broken by a last blow, that Its remaining drops might be shed for the salvation of the world! I adore that Heart of the First-Born of the Resurrection, impassible and immortal, overflowing with the unalloyed joys of beatitude, and offering to the ravished adoration of the elect the victorious Blood that had purchased them from death! Lastly, I adore It, still the incorruptlble vase, but concealed under the material appearance of the Sacrament, blending the semblance of death and humiliation with the realities of life and glory, in order to send up to God from the depths of this earth of sin and indigence the atonement that He expects from it, to pour out unceasingly upon mankind during the hardships of their earthly pilgrimage the elixir of eternal life, and to have always in readiness for them the bath which cleanses from every stain.

I adore in the Eucharistic Heart of My Saviour His true and real Blood in its perfect and incorruptible purity. I adore it in its life independent of every exterior cause, rising above time, its vicissitndes and its decay. I believe in its inestimable price, which renders it worthy of the adoration that angels and men give to God Himself. Why do I believe in its worth? I believe, because it was formed of the purest drops of the Virgin-Mother's blood, carefully selected by the Holy Spirit Himself. I believe, because it has become the Blood the most exquisite, the purest, the most quickening, and the most worthy of existing among all the children of men. I believe, because it was taken by the Word as His own Blood, penetrated by the Divinity even to its least globules and substantially deified. I believe, because it has been enriched by all the virtues of the Holy One of God, by actions to which it has lent its faithful and generous concurrence, by sufferings that consummated its perfection, and by all the merits of the triumphant Resurrection which recompensed them.

O Heart of infinite love, Thou didst appear environed with flames when Thou didst shake off the dust of the sacramental state in order to reveal Thyself in our day! I adore Thee as the inextinguishable furnace in which the Blood of My Saviour boils up with glowing fervor, and whence it flows in burning wave to enkindle in all hearts the fire of its love! I adore Thy Blood consumed by Uncreated Love which eternally desired it, and which takes in it infinite complacency. I adore Thy Blood consumed by all the sacred loves that the Holy Spirit enkindled therein at the moment of its formation, which were increased by the wind of contradiction, and which reached their height in the sufferings of the Passion! I adore Thy Blood, devoured with the hot breath of longing, of hunger, and thirst to be loved in its Sacrament which allows it no repose!

Lastly, O Jesus, in absolute dependence and obedience, I adore the sovereign rights of Thy Blood over me, for it is the Blood of my Creator, of my Redeemer, of my Sanctifier. It is the Blood that will judge me for eternity! I acknowledge the absolute necessity that I have of it for I know that without it, there is no salvation for me. I know that it is the indispensable condition of my life, and that, if I do not nourish myself assiduously with it, eternal death will be my portion. I accept the infallible word coming forth from Thy lips, which it empurples: "*Nisi   .    .      biberitis   ejus Sanguinem, non habebitis vitam in vobis!* Except   .     .   you drink His Blood, you shall not have life in you" (1).

### THANKSGIVING.

"*Hic est Sanguis meus qui pro multis effundetur:*—This is My Blood which shall be shed for many" (2).

The term shedding, pouring out, by which the Divine Master designates the gift that He makes to us of His Precious Blood, does, indeed, well express the powerful streams, the perpetual diffusion, the universal inundation of His Blood. The showers of spring and autumn do not fall more abundantly from the skies, the rivulets do not gush more quickly from their source, the torrents do not rush more impetuously down the mountain side, the seas do not extend further their broad expanse of waters, than flows the Precious Blood from the Heart of Jesus under the impulse of Its love.

The Heart of Jesus is the only source whence originate those streams of purity, of life, and of consolation, carried forth by

(1)   John vi, 54.
(2)   Matt. xxvi, 28.

the Precious Blood: *" Haurietis aquas in gaudio de fontibus Salvatoris:*—You shall draw waters with joy out of the Saviour's fountains."  He who has received under what form soever, one of those gifts of grace, which are all tiny portions of the Infinite Good, has drawn from the Sacred Heart a drop of the Precious Blood; for every grace, every help from On High, every celestial gift, is a fruit, a transformed drop of the Precious Blood.

The characteristics that mark the vivifying effusions of the Heart of Jesus, their spontaneity and readiness, their abundance and liberality, their prodigality and magnificence, their fidelity and constancy, are all characteristics of love.  Love alone has willed to turn itself into Blood, in order to save us, since salvation could be procured only through the Blood of the Man-God. It was love alone that urged Him to pour it forth.  In fine, it is only love that gives gratuitously, that gives without counting the cost, that gives without regret: *" Christus dilexit nos et lavit nos in Sanguine suo:* —Christ hath loved us, and washed us in His own Blood "(1).

---

(1)  Apoc. i, 5.

Let us apply our soul to the source of the Precious Blood that we may taste abundantly of its effusions and bless it in them. The liberal, the prodigal Heart of Jesus shed it by the wound of the Circumcision made in the tender flesh of the Infant of eight days, by the ruddy sweat that bathed the whole person of the Man-God in His agony, by the furrows opened on His shoulders and His breast, by the biting blows of the flagellation, and by the punctures in His forehead and head made by the sharp thorns of the mock crown. Again, did that Heart shed Its life-blood through the cruel wounds dug by the weight of the Cross on His sacred shoulder, and those of His knees from the triple fall on the way to Calvary; through the gaping wounds of His hands and feet; and lastly, through the opening in His side made by the lance after death.

All the Blood of the Sacred Heart flowed even to the last drop in those successive effusions.

But not yet satisfied, and desiring to give all at one stroke, He took the Eucharistic chalice and, presenting it to all men of all times, He gave to each the whole plenitude of His Blood! And when all have satiated their thirst, it still remains in all its fulness, always offered, always fresh, always sweet, always inebriating: "*Calix cui benedicimus, nonne communicatio Sanguinis Christi est?*—The chalice which we bless, is it not the communion of the Blood of Christ?"(1)

Flowing over the Eucharistic cup, the Precious Blood, propelled by the Sacred Heart, runs through the channels of the Sacraments and Sacramentals, finds an outlet in Indulgences, in the institutions of the Church, in the Supreme Pontificate, in the episcopacy and the priesthood, in that admirable economy of actual graces, which stretches like a net-work over souls, and whose salutary action is everywhere felt!

Not only in the Church Suffering does the Sacred Heart pour out with Its redeeming Blood floods of relief, light and peace, it shoots its luminous jets up to heaven, where they fill the saints with new joys and the Most Holy Trinity with satisfaction and glory.

How is it possible not to taste even to inebriation the invigorating joys of grati-

---

(1) I Cor. x, 16.

tude when we drink at the source of the Sacred Heart, accessible to all, the living waters of the Precious Blood, which love sends forth with eagerness so spontaneous, with abundance so liberal, with perseverance so magnificent: *"Et calix meus inebrians, quam praeclarus est!*—And my chalice which inebriateth me, how goodly is it!"    What can prevent us from intoning with gladness the canticle of thanksgiving: *"Calicem salutaris accipiam et nomen Domini invocabo.*—I will take the chalice of salvation, and I will call upon the name of the Lord "(1).

### REPARATION.

*"In remissionem peccatorum*—This is My Blood of the new testament which shall be shed for many unto remission of sins "(2).

It was for the remission of the sins with which Christ charged Himself that He shed His Blood.   This determinative reason for the effusion of the Precious Blood necessarily impressed upon it the character of humiliation and suffering, because it was an

---

(1) Ps. cxv.
(2) Matt. xxvi, 28.

expiatory punishment imposed and accepted. And the Sacred Heart, the luminous source of every joy, became the dark and sorrowful piscina, in which sinners ought to wash away their stains in the humiliaticn and sorrow of penitence: *"In die illa erit fons patens in ablutionem peccatoris*—In that day there shall be a fountain open for the washing of the sinner "(1).

Approaching with fear and contrition to the Sacred Heart in the Sacrament which is a memorial of His Passion, we shall see how cruel and ignominious were the effusions of the Precious Blood when the Sacred Victim was capable of suffering; and we shall discern, also, that even now, when endowed with impassibility, It embraces a state of humiliation which forcibly recalls the abasement of His Passion and death. The sight ought to fill us with as much compassion for the sweet and patient Victim of our crimes as contempt for ourselves and hatred for sin.

Certainly, there are some glorious occasions to shed one's blood; for instance, it covers the soldier with a glorious and

---

(1) Zach. xiii, 1.

coveted purple when it gushes from wounds received in defence of " his altars and his fires." But to shed it under the blows of the public executioner, is the very depth of ignominy. Now, Jesus, the Holy One, poured out His in the Garden, prostrate, His face to the earth, weighed down by fear and sadness, and upon the Cross, despised and abandoned by His Father, as a culprit condemned by the divine wrath. He poured it out under blows, rods, and nails, like a criminal executed by public justice. His Heart thrilled with indignation under the undeserved chastisement, the cruel outrage done Him; but at the same time, He abased Himself in humble resignation, since we had merited them, we whose place He had taken! Ah, with what excess of love He pours out every drop, He who was so delicate and sensitive, although its effusion was provoked by the barbarous whips, clubs, and nails, by the cruel flagellation, the crowning with thorns, and the Crucifixion!

The mysterious effusion of the Consecration or of the Eucharistic Communion is not less humiliating, even when celebrated by saints for the good of saints, since it reduces the immortal Christ to the state of a mere potion. But how often, alas! is It accompanied by indifference, if not by contempt, treason, and profanation! How often It wins but ingratitude or even hatred! It is the Blood of the Immaculate Lamb sullied by contact with impurity: *" Sanguinem Testamenti pollutum "*(1). It is the Blood of the Resurrection condemned to bring forth death. It is the supreme outrage which for all eternity renders a man guilty of the " Blood of the Lord: *Reus erit Sanguinis Domini "*(2).

And how many other abuses and profanations, how much contempt and squandering of the Precious Blood by mortal, by venial sin, in the bad or imperfect use of the Sacraments and infidelity to grace!

What injuries, what humiliations for the Precious Blood, a single drop of which is worth more than innumerable worlds, and would suffice to redeem them all were they created! But what bitter deception for the Heart that poured it out at the price of so many sacrifices so generously embraced!

---

(1) Heb. x, 29.
(2) I Cor. xi, 27.

Reparation! Consolation! Compassion for the Sacred Heart which vainly sheds Its Precious Blood " for the remission of innumerable sins! " Contrition, humility, sorrow for our sins!

### PETITION.

" This is My Blood which was shed for you!—*Qui pro vobis effundetur.*"

These words tell us that the effusion of the adorable Blood at the Last Supper and on the altar, as well as on Calvary, was offered to God as a pacific Host, or an impetratory Sacrifice, to obtain for men all the divine benefits of which they have need in time in order to obtain the Eternal Good.

The Sacred Heart here disclosing Itself behind the double veil of the sacramental Species and the Breast of Jesus, like a living sanctuary in which the Precious Blood, pure and august priest, enveloped in its splendid purple, exercises its eternal Priesthood. It offers to God its prayers in the name of all men whom it has redeemed. It sends up its voice even to the Father's throne interceding for earth and pleading the cause of sinners. At length, it appears before the face of the Father in the lustre of its brilliant charms, in the omnipotence of its love, with the infinite merits of its sufferings, and the rights conferred on it by its victories. How could God remain deaf to the voice of the Blood of Jesus, more eloquent than that of Abel's blood, which cried for vengeance, while that of Jesus asks only for mercy? Why should the Father not thrill with joy at the voice of His own Blood, for it is the Blood of His Well-Beloved Son that sounds in His ear. Again, God is the debtor of the Precious Blood. He promised His Son, if He would consent to sacrifice Himself to His justice, to give Him sovereign dominion in heaven and on earth. Now, this means the disposal of all the treasures of grace and glory.

If the Divine Majesty sees Jesus in His glory in heaven, retaining of His past combats only the marks of the Five Wounds, which shine in His hands and feet like brilliant rubies, He beholds Him at the same time humbly poured out in the poor form of some drops of ordinary wine. He sees Him annihilated in dust and ashes, hiding His beauty and glory under the dense veil of the Sacrament, constantly pouring forth His prayer of self-abasement while multiplying His Divine Presence on altars all over this vale of misery and tears.

What an omnipotent prayer is that of the Precious Blood, issuing from the Sacred Heart with such love and innocence, enriched with so many merits, accompanied by self-oblation so perfect, manifested by immolation so entire upon so many altars, and continued both in heaven and on earth with perseverance so unwearied!

Let us, then, always pray in union with the Precious Blood and through the Precious Blood. Let us plunge our petitions into the Precious Blood. Tinted with its hues, so pleasing in the sight of God, purified by its purity, penetrated by its virtues, enriched with its merits, our prayers will surely be acceptable to God and will gain what they ask. "*Te ergo quaesumus, Domine, tuis famulis subveni, quos pretioso Sanguine redemisti!*—We beseech Thee, O Lord, help Thy servants whom Thou hast redeemed with Thy Precious Blood!"

Let us sprinkle ourselves spiritually with the Precious Blood when we pray, and let us pour it over all for whom we intercede, for every oblation sprinkled with blood is agreeable to God. We cannot better enter into the designs of the Sacred Heart than by incessantly drawing from It the redeeming Blood to pour it over the souls of sinners, over those of the just who are still combating, and over those that are suffering in the purifying flames.

" The Precious Blood conquers, and it is for God that it makes its conquests. It invades the kingdom of darkness and illumines whole countries with the rays of its brilliant light. It puts down rebels, brings back exiles to their country, and re-claims wanderers. It re-establishes peace, grants amnesties, and wonderfully adminis-ters the kingdom which it has marvellously conquered. It is the crown, the sceptre, and the throne of the invisible royalty of God ! " (1)

Let us not end this hour of adoration without asking for the grace and taking the resolution ever to make good use of the Precious Blood, by fidelity to grace and the accomplishment of every duty, by patience in suffering and zeal to receive the Sacra-ments eagerly and fervently. May one of

---

(1) Father Faber.

our most habitual aspirations be that which the priest recites at the moment of receiving the Adorable Blood: " May the Blood of Jesus Christ guard my soul to eternal life !— *Sanguis Jesu Christi custodiat animam meam in vitam aeternam!* "

Pray for an increase of religious vocations.

Eternal Father, I offer Thee the most precious Blood of Jesus Christ, in expiation of my sins and for the wants of Holy Church.

(100 *days' Indulgence.*)

# Sixteenth Day

*Cor Jesu, virtutum omnium exemplar, miserere nobis!*

### ADORATION.

ONE of the most clearly marked ends of the different Revelations of the Sacred Heart, both of the evangelical and the Eucharistic life of the Saviour, is to offer Himself to our imitation as the model of all virtues, an example to follow, an example at one and the same time the most perfect and the best suited to our weakness.

At Naim, the Saviour, calling to the crowds, thus addressed them: "Come to My school, become My disciples. You will never find a master so good, so devoted, so disinterested, so patient, for I am meek and humble of Heart: *Discite a me, quia mitis sum et humilis Corde.*" And again, which amounts to almost the same: "Learn of Me, by coming to Me, by stay-

235

ing with Me, by living with Me, how meek
and humble of Heart I am—*Discite a me,
quia mitis sum et humilis Corde."*

At Paray, " My Well-Beloved presented
Himself to me," says Blessed Margaret
Mary, " and said: ' I intend to make thee
read in the Book of Life wherein is contained the science of love.' Then disclosing to me His Heart, He let me read these
words: ' My love reigns in suffering, it
triumphs in humility, and it enjoys in
unity.' " Love, patience in suffering,
humility, meekness toward the neighbor,
union with God by prayer and conformity
with His will, resemblance carried so far
as even moral unity—behold what is shown
forth in Him, what He teaches. and
what He desires all to imitate in
His Sacred Heart. He is, at once,
the Master and the Model of holiness.
What He has Himself practised, He communicates to souls and impresses upon them.
Again, says Blessed Margaret Mary: " As
soon as I began to pray, my Sovereign
Master showed me that my soul was a piece
of canvas upon which He desired to paint
the features of His own suffering life, which
had been spent in love and privation, in

silence and labor, and which ended in sacrifice. He gave me to understand that He was going to impress it on my soul after purifying it from every stain that might remain in it, as well from affection to earthly things as from love for creatures for whom I felt some natural inclination. But He despoiled me at this moment of everything and, after having emptied my heart and stripped my soul, He enkindled therein so great a desire to love Him and to suffer that I had no repose, so occupied was I with the thought of what I could do to love Him and to crucify myself."

We cannot doubt that the Sacred Heart reveals Itself as the living and magnetic model of all the virtues that are comprised in perfection and holiness. The heart is the symbol of the soul, the source of virtuous acts, which are such only on account of their conformity with reason. It is the symbol of the will, whose free adhesion to the moral beauty of those acts and its effort to produce them, in spite of contrary passions, bestow upon them their value and merit. It is, in fine, the symbol of love, the life of every virtue, as being the power that tends to the possession of good by its resemblance to God, the Infinite Good, the substantial Perfection.

This increated Perfection, our eyes wounded by sin can no longer view in supernatural light. To punish man for his rash curiosity and foolish pretention to gain by his own efforts the knowledge of God, of good, and of evil, that blessed light was hidden from him. By merely natural light, dimmed as it is by heavy shadows, he can but very imperfectly understand the divine and adequate Image of the Word come in immense pity to bring to the world, by making Himself man, a created, finite image proportioned to the weakness of our sight, and to manifest the transcendent perfection of God in human virtues. He teaches their nature, proclaims their necessity, promises their magnificent recompense, and thus makes them known to the world.

But as in the matter of morality, example is more efficacious than precept, He Himself practised perfectly every virtue demanded by the various states through which He successively passed. He was a child growing in wisdom and grace; a youth laborious and submissive to His parents; an apostle, prepared by penance and devotedly consuming Himself in the service of the people; a mediator passing whole nights prostrate in prayer. He was the inexhaustible benefactor of the needy; the compassionate physician of all maladies; the welcome consoler, patient and gentle under all trials; the faithful and disinterested friend; the intrepid champion of truth; the courageous defender of justice; the invincible vindicator of the rights and honor of His Father; in fine, the heroic victim freely offered to Divine Justice for the salvation of the world. He endured every sorrow, every unmerited ignominy in sublime silence, with strength that overcame death itself, and in abandonment to the will of God, which was for Him the triumph of love. All these virtues He practised in exact measure, with no excess, with perfect balance. The one did not injure the other, and He presented them in a manner imitable by all men of good will. Without demanding anything impossible, He could say: "*Exemplum enim dedit vobis, ut quemadmodum ego feci vobis, ita et vos faciatis*—For I have given you an example that, as I have done to you, so you do also" (1).

---

(1) John xiii, 15.

By inviting us to study the examples of
His virtues in His Heart, the Master wished
to make them more lovable, consequently,
He encourages us with the words: *"Venite ad me omnes!*—Come ye all to Me."* He
wished to sweeten, to lighten the practice of
virtue, which restrains and mortifies the
passions: *"Jugum meum dulce et onus
meum leve*—My yoke is sweet and My
burden light."* By proclaiming His Heart
meek and humble, He wished to show us
His great condescension in making Himself all to all, demanding of everyone only
what he can give. He shows, also, His
patience in supporting our sluggishness and
delays, His compassion in raising us up
when we fall and receiving us after infidelity more or less prolonged: *Discite a
me, quia mitis sum et humilis Corde.* He
wished, in fine, that the works and struggles
of virtue, however painful, however sorrowful they may be at certain times, should
be performed without too great trouble of
soul, that they should leave it in the possession of a peace too exquisite to be any
other than celestial and a foretaste of the
eternal repose promised to such as shall
have fought to the end: *" Requiem inve-*

*nietis animabus vestris*—You shall find peace to your souls."

## THANKSGIVING.

We shall go, then, to the school of Thy Heart, O infinitely good Master! We shall enter therein and try to see all Its virtues. We shall make profession of dwelling therein, and we shall comprehend their beauty, taste their charm, accept their law and sacrifices. We shall draw from Its inexhaustible treasures the grace, the strength, and the helps we need. Confiding in Its guidance, our own heart closely united to It, we shall apply courageously and perseveringly to the practice of Its virtues in order to please and glorify Thee!

We have heard Thee say to Thy faithful confidante: "Enter, My daughter, into this delicious garden that thou mayst revive thy languishing soul." She understood that He meant the garden of His Sacred Heart, the diversity of whose flowers is as delightful as their beauty is admirable. "After I had looked at them, but without daring to touch them, He said to me: 'Cull what thou pleasest!'" O beauty! O liberality! O magnificence of the Heart of a God become Man in order to enrich man with all the treasures of Its perfection and holiness!

When example is directly under our eyes, the more powerfully does it excite us to imitation. Certainly those from the mortal life of the Saviour, preserved with their circumstantial and vigorous details in the holy Gospels, may be said to be present under the eyes of all generations. The Spirit of Life which animates every one of their syllables gives to their assertions a supernatural vigor capable of penetrating the coldest hearts and leading them to imitation. The generous Restorer of the moral world was not satisfied with leaving to us the book of His Gospels, in which His virtues are engraven in characters deeper and more lasting than the precepts of the Law upon the tables of Sinai. He wished to be here below and until the end of time the living Exemplar of all sanctity. That is one of His reasons for instituting the Holy Eucharist. He desires to be able to show Himself present at all times and in all parts of the world, to be able to say to every one of its inhabitants: " Look and do according to the example that I give you!" When, at the Last Supper, He was explaining the effects that His Flesh ought to produce in the soul of those that would receive It, He said: " He that eateth My Flesh abideth in Me, and I in him. He that keeps My commandments loves Me and abides in Me; and I will love him and manifest Myself to him—*Et ego diligam eum et manifestabo ei meipsum*" (1). This intimate manifestation, this interior revelation is, without doubt, that of the grandeur and the mysteries of the Divinity and the Humanity of Jesus. But what more admirably grand, what more harmoniously mysterious than His virtues at once divine and human, in which are allied so much sovereign power, so much humility, and so much human weakness? Jesus will reveal the secrets of all this to him who, having received sacramentally, will abide in communion of spirit with Him by doing His will.

Again, He said: " I am the way, the truth, and the life—*Ego sum via, veritas, et vita.*" He is the true way, the living

---

(1) John xiv, 21.

way, the way that leads to life by the illumined paths on which, walking after Him, we cannot wander in the darkness of error. Way and example are here synonymous, for if the example invites to action, the way leads us on. Jesus has, then, instituted the Eucharist in order to lead us to perfect life, namely, His own life and that of His Father, and He assures us that all who eat His Flesh live that life. To allow one's self to be guided by Him, to follow Him, to tread in His footsteps, is to imitate His virtues and reproduce His life. That this way may be always open before us, it is found all over the earth, like a royal road leading from all points of our exile to our eternal home.

The Saviour again tells us: "He that eateth My Flesh abideth in Me, and he that abideth in Me beareth much fruit—*Qui manet in Me, hic fert fructum multum.*" This fruit which, without Him, we cannot bear, which ripens only upon the branch vitally united to the trunk of the vine, is evidently the fruit of the supernatural virtues which, borne first by Jesus, ought to extend to us and ripen in us, who are shoots ingrafted on the divine stock. As every branch is nourished by sap from the trunk, which it passes on into the fruits produced among its foliage, so the Christian virtues are produced, developed, and nourished by the sap of Jesus Christ poured into the soul by the sacramental manducation of His Flesh. The Saviour here lays down His Eucharist as a fundamental condition for the production of the virtues. It is in It that we must receive them, by It that we must nourish them, with It that we must practise them. But as the virtues are things essentially spiritual and, consequently, rational, things of intelligence which comprehends them, and things of the will which turns to them freely, we can know them only when Jesus shows them to us, and we are borne to them only when He attracts us and gives us the strength to follow His attraction. Hence, the institution of His Eucharistic Presence, to reveal to us His virtues by sowing in us the seed, by cultivating and nourishing it, by sheltering it from the storms of the passions and of the world, and from the destructive tempests of sin.

In His Sacramental Presence, which will last as long as the world, just as during

His mortal life of thirty-three years under the skies of Galilee and Judea, He calls men to His Heart that they may learn there to understand and imitate His virtues. " Abide in Me, abide in My love—*Mancte in me, manete in dilectione mea!*" And He drew John down upon His Heart in order to reveal to Him all Its secrets, to communicate to him all Its virtues, and to transform him into His other Self.

What passed in the Cenacle was reproduced at Paray. " Showing me one day His loving Heart," says Blessed Margaret Mary, " He said to me: ' Behold the Teacher whom I give to thee, from whom thou wilt learn all that thou shouldst do for My love. Thou shalt be Its well-beloved disciple.' " Let us now see how this great Master of love acted in her regard: " Being one day before the Blessed Sacrament, I felt myself encompassed by the Divine Presence. He made me rest a long time on His breast, discovering to me the marvels of His love and the inexplicable secrets of His Sacred Heart. He disclosed It to me in a manner effective and sensible, saying: ' My Divine Heart is so passionately in love with men that, not being able to contain the flames of Its burning love, It must of necessity pour them forth, manifest them, in order to enrich them with Its precious treasures, which contain the sanctifying graces and all that is necessary to withdraw them from the abyss of perdition.' "

" Sanctifying graces," the graces of sanctification for the soul, are, indeed, the graces of the Christian virtues, whose sustained and progressive culture constitute the perfection of the Christian in every state. They are poured into the soul by the Sacraments, above all by the Eucharist, first, like so many seeds, and then as the forces that germinate those seeds and develop them more and more perfectly. But they also act morally on the soul, enlightening it, stirring it up, and encouraging it to imitate its Model.

### REPARATION.

But, O good Master, in the bread, in that state of material inertia in which Thou hast chosen to remain amongst us, can we truly say that Thou dost practise the virtues, and that they are sufficiently apparent to serve us for models of imitation? That such is true of Thy life spent among men during Thy mortal existence, which flowed on in a human manner under the eyes of all, we well know. The Gospel preserves, living and ineffable, Thy touching and admirable examples of all virtues. But in this sacramental existence, speechless, . motionless, hidden, with no external relations with men —how admit, how see Thy virtues?

I hear Thee answering me through Catholic doctrine that Thou hast freely chosen the exterior signs of the Sacraments to express sensibly what their spiritual reality operates spiritually, and that this is true of the Eucharist as of all the other Sacraments. Still more, that while in them Thou dost act only by a power distinct from Thyself and limited to the moment in which they are applied to the soul, under the Eucharistic Sign, so long as It retains Its integrity, Thou dost remain personally present and living. In fine, that it is Thyself, although invisible, who, freely and by a personal action, in which Thou art visibly seconded by the priest, dost constantly renew in the Holy Sacrifice Thy Sacramental Presence.

From these certain principles there evidently flow these consequences, namely, that if the sensible sign of the bread tells of the spiritual nutriment of the soul operated by the Eucharist, the materiality of this same bread, its inertia and dependence, its mean appearance, speak just as clearly of the humility of Him who, in order to remain therein, annihilates Himself to this state of matter, although He is Man, of glorified condition, and already in possession of His eternal kingdom. The outward signs of the Eucharist tell of Christ's submission and obedience to the laws of nature from which His glorified state has freed Him, and to the will of man over whom He has acquired the indisputable right to reign. They tell of His love of poverty, mortification, and silence, which He displays in this state which binds His lips, closes His eyes to every external sight, chains His members, and gives Him for abode a perishable Host, a crumb of bread, poorer than the poorest coverings of the most destitute beggar. The multiplication of the Host, which places Him unceasingly at the service of all; His manner of giving Himself by manducation, which delivers Him unreservedly to all for their good; His abiding Presence daily renewed—do not all these tell us of the most perfect love for all those of whom, only Son of God as He is, He has willed to become the neighbor, in order to contract the obligation of loving them as brethren, of dying, of rising from the tomb, and of incessantly renewing the double miracle of His life and His death for their advantage alone?   And lastly, that sweetness, that longanimity, that absence of retaliation, and even of resistance in supporting ingratitude, contempt, abandonment, outrage, sacrilegious attempts and the most horrible profanations—are not these the sign of that sublime and heroic patience which, sustained by the victorious strength of love, is the queen of virtues, their perfection and their crown?

Yes, assuredly, the virtues which Thou dost practise in the Blessed Sacrament are real and true, O Eucharistic Christ! They are visible to all eyes, since it is sufficient to look upon the Host, and there behold the material sign of the bread which sensibly expresses them! They recall all the virtues of Thy life and continue them under a new form. Shall I dare affirm that this Eucharistic form, which is the inspiration of Thy supreme love, by which Thou hast willed to touch the limit of the possible in point of generosity and gift, communicates to Thy virtues the same character of perfection, of completion, of having reached the highest possible degree: *In finem dilexit?* And as it is Thy love in its consummation which has reduced Thee to this state, and led Thee to carry Thy virtues to a point that cannot be excelled, it is to Thy Heart that we owe those inestimable examples that incite us to holiness, sustain us in its attainment, and lead us to perfect resemblance with Thee, O Jesus, and with Thy Father, the eternal Unity of beatitude! It is, also, Thy Heart in the Sacrament that we should study in our adoration. There we shall learn the secret of Thy virtues, and to It we should recur for grace and help!

Doing this, we shall follow the lessons of her whom Thou hast crowned with the glorious title of " Well-beloved disciple of Thy Heart," and whom we shall desire to follow as a consummate mistress in the art of making It known. Behold the very lucid instruction that she gave her novices to impel them to the imitation of the Eucharistic virtues of Thy Sacred Heart:

### PETITION.

### COVENANT OF LOVE TO HONOR THE DIVINE HEART OF JESUS.

" Live Jesus in the heart of His faithful servants who desire to consecrate all their actions as homage to His Sacred Heart in the Blessed Sacrament!

" First, in the morning, after having placed ourselves under the protection of the Blessed Virgin, let us beg her to offer us to Jesus in the Most Blessed Sacrament, in order to render homage to the offering which He there makes of Himself to the Eternal Father.   Let us unite our soul to His that He may preserve it from sin, our heart to His Heart that He may consume in it all that is displeasing to Him.   Thus must we unite all that we are to all that He is, and beg Him to supply for what is wanting in us.

" Let us unite our prayer to that which Jesus makes in the Blessed Sacrament for us.   At the end of it let us offer to God that of His Divine Son to repair our defects and loss of time.

" At the Office, let us unite our praises with those of Jesus, endeavoring to enter into His holy dispositions and ardent purity, that He may in everything supply for us before His Divine Father.

" He is obedient to priests good or bad, He places Himself in their hands to die therein mystically, assuming the character of victim in order to allow Himself to be sacrificed and immolated according to their designs, without testifying the least resistance. To conform myself to Him I shall be prompt to obedience. Like a victim of immolation, I shall place myself in the hands of my superioresses, of whatever kind they may be, in order that, dying to my own will, passions, inclinations, and aversions, they may dispose of me in any way they wish without my manifesting the least repugnance. The violence that I shall do myself shall be to honor that which Jesus does Himself to enter into souls stained by sin. He has so much horror of them that, every time He enters such a one, He renews in it the mortal agony that He suffered in the Garden of Olives.

" His life is entirely hidden from the eyes of creatures, who perceive naught but the poor, vile species of bread and wine. In the same way, I shall endeavor to keep myself so hidden that I shall have no greater joy than to allow whatever is meanest and most abject in me to appear, in order to keep myself concealed under the dust of humility, by the rebuffs and contempt of creatures. Thus shall I console my Jesus in the contempt, injuries, sacrileges, profanations, and other indignities He receives in this hidden life, and of which He never complains. For the same reason, I shall neither pity nor excuse myself, always remembering that every one has a right to accuse me, humble me, and make me suffer, since the love of the Sacred Heart obliges me to endure everything without lamenting or saying it is enough.

"Jesus is always solitary in the Most Blessed Sacrament, conversing therein with God alone. To conform to Him, I shall try to be everywhere alone, conversing interiorly only with my Jesus. My understanding shall seek to know Him alone, that my mind may be ever attentive to adore Him and my heart ever yearning to love Him.

"With regard to the life of the senses, He is there as in a state of death. I, then, should find my pleasure in having none, in renouncing everything that could procure me any, trying to mortify everything that brings the least satisfaction.

"Jesus made Himself poor in the Most Blessed Sacrament. To imitate and gain His most amiable Heart, I must forsake self, despise self, and be well pleased that others should do the same in my regard.

"Jesus keeps perpetual silence, which I desire to imitate by interior and exterior silence, speaking only by the order of my Rule and charity.

"O Sacred Heart of my Jesus, I choose Thee for my dwelling-place that Thou mayest be my strength in combat, the support of my weakness, my light and my guide in darkness and in fine, the Repairer of all my faults, the Sanctifier of all my intentions and actions, which I unite to Thine and offer to Thee to prove my unceasing disposition to be one with Thee!"

*Cor Jesu, exemplar virtutum omnium, miserere nobis!*—Heart of Jesus, Model of all virtues, have mercy on us!

To honor the silence of Jesus in the Host, endeavor to observe such silence as is compatible with your state of life.

O Sacred Heart of Jesus, I confide in Thee!

(300 *days' Indulgence.*)

# Seventeenth Day.

## JESUS HUMBLE OF HEART.

SUBJECT.—"*Discite a Me, quia mitis sum et humilis Corde*—Learn of me that I am meek and humble of Heart." The subject of this adoration is the study of the meaning of the words: "*Humilis Corde*—Humble of Heart." What sense do they convey? What do they mean? What do they reveal to us of the Sacred Heart? What do they teach us and what do they exact of us? The answer to these questions will furnish us with ample matter for *adoration, thanksgiving, reparation,* and *petition.*

Blessed Margaret Mary writes: "Look upon Our Lord in the Blessed Sacrament as the Good Master who says to you: 'Learn of Me to be meek and humble of heart, otherwise you shall not be recognized nor loved by My Heart, which will not acknowledge you for Its disciples unless you conform to It by the practice of Its holy maxims.'"

256

ADORATION.

I adore Thee, O My Master! I have heard Thy call. I come to Thy school, and I want to know the full meaning, the truth, and the depth of this word by tasting its grace and its sweetness, for it attracts me as much by its sweetness as it impresses me by its solemn gravity.

"Humble of Heart!" What means this declaration, in which Thou dost appear to define Thyself, to discover to us the bottom of Thy soul, to reveal to us the secret of Thy life, to propose Thyself to the admiration as well as to the love of men, in order to gain them, to succor them in their needs, to console them in their pains?

How important for us to understand the "Humility of Thy Heart," since Thou dost attribute to it effects so wonderful as "the restoration from all fatigue and exhaustion, the sweetening of all yokes, the lightening of all burdens, along with rest and peace for all souls."

I come to ask from Thyself the explanation of this great word, because there is no human teacher, no saint, no angel who can give it to me, and because, also, Thou hast said: "Learn of Me—*Discite a Me!*"

"Humble of Heart!"—The heart is love. Love is its spontaneous impulse, its free choice, its reasonable and definitive attachment. Love is the gift of self, prompt, entire, perpetual, without hesitation, without reserve, without regret. Love is diametrically opposed to necessity, interest, or calculation.

"Humble of Heart!"—O my Christ adored, is it not for Thee to be humble by the free choice of Thy eternal love, by the preference of humility to every other virtue, by the yearning of Thy soul toward humility, by the adhesion of Thy whole being to humility?—humble by all the convictions of Thy divinely enlightened mind, all the force of Thy impeccable will, all the ardor of Thy most pure and loving Heart? It is not to be humble by necessity, no law obliging Thee to it, O Thou Son of the Eternal! Nor is it to be humble through interest. Thou hast nothing to expect from it. O Thou Master of all things, Thou hast need of nothing! It is not to be humble merely on some occasion, by accident, or because it is suitable, humble only in appear-

ance, in some one point, in a passing
manner. No! "Of heart," that is, from
the very bottom of one's soul in our liveli-
est and strongest feelings, in that which
shows the hidden springs of life, in that
which endures as long as ourselves, is confounded with self, is in fine our very self!
And Thou dost think it well to add: *"Quia
mitis sum et humilis Corde*—Because I am
meek and humble of Heart."

*"Sum*—I am" humble by My being and
by My nature, by My character and by My
mission, as I am by My determination and
My choice. I am humble by My Divinity,
annihilated in the lowly condition of creature and slave. I am humble by means of
My soul and My mind, which fully comprehend the nothingness of their origin and
their absolute dependence on the Creator.
I am humble by My will which has chosen
humilitation as the best means of giving
satisfaction to the Sovereign Justice, of
snatching man, dead through pride, from
the yoke of the prince of pride, and of gaining him by abasing Myself lower than he.

"Behold why I am humble of Heart."—
It is through love, through passion! I
have yearned for humility, I have espoused

her, I love her! I am hers. She possesses
Me, captivates Me, and I love her sway. I
love her bonds, I love her laws, I love the
abasement that she imposes upon Me. I
love even her excess, and I love the ignominies with which she has drenched Me and
the death to which she conducted Me. I
regret so little the extreme humiliation
which I have endured from her that I still
remain attached to her, lovingly bearing her
yoke, rendered even heavier in the Eucharist!

This may appear incredible, inexplicable,
incomprehensible, since no human heart can
love humility with such love; only divine
love can reach such a height. Being infinite, it finds its reasons above human hori-
zons, manifests itself in ways inaccessible
to human power, and aims even at the infinite. I have loved, I still love humility
with all the strength of My divine love, in a
divine manner, and in divine proportions.
I love it beyond the power, beyond the aspirations, beyond even the conception of any
creature human or angelic. My humility is
My love, My Heart, Myself, God made
Man, the God-Man put to death upon the
accursed gibbet, the God-Man annihilated

under the dust of the Sacrament. Whoever knows My humility knows Me, knows
My Heart, for I am humility personified,
humility in its sum and substance, humility
in infinite and eternal proportions: *"Quia
mitis sum et humilis Corde!"*

### THANKSGIVING.

How explain, excepting by the passion for
humility, the Incarnation of the Son of God,
come only to humble Himself and to be
humbled, descended into those humiliations
of which St. Paul says: "Although He
was God, by nature equal to His Father; although He enjoyed the incommunicable
prerogatives of the Divine nature; although
He was incapable of submitting to a will
superior to His own, or of seeking out of
Himself any good whatsoever, *"Cum in
forma Dei esset,"* "He has so loved the
world" that He annihilated Himself, made
Himself a creature and a slave, clothing
Himself with human nature: *"Exinanivit
semetipsum, formam servi accipiens, et
habitu inventus ut homo."* He made Himself man, a creature of nothingness, that is,
He placed Himself in a state of dependence
and inferiority. Now, to take the state of

sinful man, was to make Himself a slave to the divine wrath, subject to labor, chastisement and death. It is, however, to this state that He descended. Under these laws the only Son of God willed to live, " out of His too great love for us " and for our misery. His whole life here on earth was but the manifestation of that extraordinary annihilation under the pressure of these three derogatory forces: humiliation, obedience, and suffering: *" Humiliavit semetipsum, factus obediens usque ad mortem, mortem autem crucis."*

He humbled Himself in the poverty of His birth, in the persecutions of His early infancy, in the submission of His youth, in the rough labors of His manhood, and in the ignominious temptations of Satan in the desert. He humbled Himself in the contradictions, the calumnies, the attacks that assailed His apostolic life; in the agony of fear, distress, and disgust that inaugurated His Passion; in the infamous accusations made before the tribunals against His doctrine, His conduct, and His influence over the people. He humbled Himself by submitting to the condemnation, to the punish ment of the accursed; to the flight, the treason, the denial of His followers; to the implacable abandonment of His own Father in fine, to a death despised, mocked, blasphemed, which sealed the depth of His degradation!

All this humiliation and ignominy He had foreseen, desired, willed. He had embraced it with all His Heart. He identified Himself with it, appearing " as one struck by God and afflicted, despised and the most abject of men: " *Tanquam percussum a Deo et humiliatum;—Opprobrium hominum et abjectio plebis;—Novissimum virorum,—* the last of men;" no longer a man, but a worm of the earth: " *Humiliavit semetipsum!* "—crushed under the heel of the passer-by!

" He humbled Himself, becoming obedient unto death." He was obedient all His life, in the fulness of mature age as well as in childhood, from the first pulsation of His Heart, which was a profession of perpetual obedience to the will of His Father, until His last sigh when He delivered His soul into His hands by an act of supreme abandonment. He was obedient and submissive to all the powers of nature, to all laws human and divine. He was obedient to

all the masters whom the sovereign authority of God delegated to rule over Him or
to chastise Him, such as Caiaphas, Pilate,
and Herod; or those others monstrously
stupid and sanguinary, such as the servants
of the High Priest at Gethsemani, the
drunken soldiers of the prætorium, and the
executioners of Calvary. He was obedient
to all their orders, caprices, and violence.
He offered without resistance and without
complaint His hands to those that bound
them; His shoulders to those that scourge 1
them, His cheeks to buffets, His face to
spittle, His head to thorns, His hands and
feet to crucifixion, His Mother to the disciple John, His life to death, and all at the
precise moment that His Father demanded
of Him the sacrifice.

And this obedience, which is the accen-
tuated form of humility, He loved as a delicious bread. " He nourished Himself
with it constantly as His only necessary
food," and He experienced ever an insati-
able hunger to obey still more: " *Factus
obediens usque ad mortem!* "

He annihiliated Himself "even unto
death, even to the death of the cross—
*Usque ad mortem, mortem autem crucis.*"

There are some deaths glorious and without suffering. But the Son of God, captivated by humility, delivered Himself to the painful and ignominious death of the Cross, because suffering is the highest form of humiliation. It depresses, it debases, it subjects, it allows no resistance, it destroys happiness, joy, peace. It is the privation, a privation violent, repugnant, horrible to nature, of all the legitimate gifts of soul and body, of society and life, and its end is death itself.

It was for this reason that the Son of God, descending from the sublime heights of His beatitude, bathed in pure light and environed by unalterable peace, plunges into suffering and the most cruel of deaths. He does so to satisfy His thirst for humility and to attain the last degree of humiliation. This is what St. Paul has called the folly, the insane love, excessive and immeasurable, of the Cross.

### REPARATION.

Jesus loved the Cross. He sighed so ardently after it that His inability to obtain it at once was torture to His Heart. He had, indeed, delivered Himself to suffering without reserve. It possessed Him interiorly, since He had celebrated with it His betrothal in the sanctuary of His Mother's womb, under the eye of His Father, and in presence of the Archangel Gabriel. But when the hour came to espouse it before heaven and earth, He delivered Himself to it in a frenzy of passion. His love goaded Him on, and made Him refuse anything like delay. He called it His glory, His triumph, and He begged His Father not to delay it a single moment. He gave Himself to this spouse of His choice in a way that made Him one with her, and He appeared the Man of sorrows, and of all sorrows: "*Virum dolorum,*" clothed with every sorrow, penetrated with sorrow even to the marrow of His bones. He endured it under every form: "*Scientem infirmitatem.*" He was changed into sorrow. He was sorrow become a man. A tempest of all kinds of sorrow in its highest intensity was precipitated upon Him. It swept over Him. It inundated, submerged, engulfed Him. It ravaged His Flesh, His Heart, His Soul, tearing everything from Him, His honor, His friendships, His works, His life. With unexampled joy, He gave Himself up to its devouring attacks: *" Proposito sibi gaudio sustinuit crucem! "* He died of its violence and He was happy to owe to it His death, for even unto death He loved it: *" Dilexit et tradidit semetipsum! "*

This is what is to be understood, partly at least, and in this manner is verified the great word of Jesus: " I am humble of Heart—*Humilis Corde.*" When Jesus had reached the last degree of humiliation, His Father desired to recompense His heroism by " exalting Him above every name " according to the measure of His abasement, giving Him over men and things an empire in extent equal to His own obedience and, in exchange for His sufferings, pouring into His soul and body the plenitude of life and happiness, of which He is to be the inexhaustible source for all the blessed. He called Him to Himself by the triumph of His glorious Ascension. He made Him sit on His throne at His right. He placed in His hand the sceptre of eternal royalty, while the angels and saints adored Him, joyfully hailing and serving Him who had abased Himself below them.

But Christ loved humility too much to renounce humiliation! The latter being impossible in heaven, He descended again to earth to find and embrace it in a love even more rapturous than that of the Incarnation! Having so loved it already, He wished to love it " to the end," to the greatest limit possible, so He shut Himself up with it in the annihilations of the Eucharist: *" In finem dilexit!"*

He made Himself this humble, common food, this miserable particle, this mite of bread, which showing to His own at the Last Supper, He said: *" Hoc est corpus meum*—This, this particle, this nothing,—this is My Body! " Yes, in truth, this is My Body, immortal and glorious. This is My Blood, ruddy and rippling with joy. This is My Heart overflowing with love. This is My Soul and My Divinity. Yes, this is I Myself in person! It is I, the Conqueror,—I, the immortal King of ages,—I, the God of majesty, the Sovereign Master of all that exists! Behold Me without beauty, movement, or life, inferior to the insect or the blade of grass, which live, at least, however low they may be in the order of beings. I—I am below them by the condition of the sacramental state which I now take, and which I shall retain till the last day of the world!

"This, this is My Body! It is I, the Living One, who can no longer die. This is I, delivered for you and for the remission of your sins, a Victim immolated by the acceptance perpetually renewed of the humiliations and sufferings of My death, buried in the winding-sheet, and crushed under the tombstone of the dead and inert species of the Sacrament!"

PETITION.

"Take and eat My Flesh. All ye, take Me and eat Me!—I am only a morsel of bread, destined to disappear in the breast of my creatures for their benefit. I am the bread of sinful man, sinful by nature, today actually a sinner, tomorrow again a sinner. I am ordinary bread, by some disdained,— bread that negligence renders useless,— bread without flavor, causing nausea to some,—bread which, given as a sign of friendship, will be dealt treacherously with by the perfidious. I am bread which the impious will profane, which the sacrilegious will cast to the impure beasts of hell that swarm in their soul!—Take ye all, and eat of It! I have made of My immortal Flesh a simple remedy to cure your infirmities,

an ointment to dress your wounds, an antidote for your sinful desires.   To whatever
degrading usage you may wish to devote
Me, I shall willingly lend Myself, I shall
consume Myself in it, for I am in heaven the
Bread of light and glory for the angels and
the blessed.   Here I wish to be the ob-
scure Bread of the voyager and the humble
Viaticum of the dying!

"All this supposes unheard-of and incredible abasement, an increase of humiliation which would seem to exhaust even the
imaginable and the possible, yes, even that
of My own wisdom and power.   But 'I
have loved humility to the end,' and My
love carries Me away, drives Me to de-
lirium, to excess: 'I am humble of Heart:
*Quia mitis sum et humilis Corde!'*"

"Humble of Heart!"   Oh, yes, I see
very plainly that Thou art all that Thou
sayest, O Christ, annihilated through pure
love, through Thy own free choice, through
inviolable attachment to humility, in the
multiplied annihilations of the Crib, of
Calvary, and of the Altar!   Have I comprehended the whole truth, the whole depth
of this word?   Have I praised its marvellous grandeur, its ineffable harmony?   Have

I tested all its sweetness? Have I seen all its influence over God and the world, all the consequences it ought to have in the direction of my thoughts and works?

Do I comprehend, even to effective conviction, that it rigorously obliges me not merely to esteem humility, not merely to submit to its law, not to attempt to acquire it in some small degree for the sake of the spiritual advantages that it confers, but that I must love it, cherish it, prefer it to everything else? Have I delighted in being humbled, in obeying, in suffering? Have I looked upon such things as the satisfaction of my best desires, as the gaining of a sovereign good? It is only at this price that I shall truly learn of Jesus what it is to be " humble of heart."

I adore, in the meantime, acknowledging my inability to comprehend the greatness, inappreciable to every created intelligence, of this word great as Thy love and, consequently, great as Thyself, O Son of the Infinite! I admire, praise, love, and bless all the wonders hidden in it. I invoke all its vivifying virtues, all its deifying influences. I am lost, annihiliated, with the cherubim and the seraphim so perfectly humble, with

Joseph and Mary, more humble still, in adoration of Thy " humility of Heart." O my God and my Saviour, my Victim and my Bread of Life!    .  .   *" Discite a me, quia mitis sum et humilis Corde!"*

Blessed Margaret Mary possessed a just and lively sentiment of the humility which Jesus embraced with all His Heart in the Most Blessed Sacrament.

" He is there as in a state of death with regard to the life of the senses.  His life is perfectly hidden from the sight of crea-tures, who perceive nothing but the poor and lowly species of bread and wine.  He is always alone, in perpetual silence, convers-ing only with God.  He divests Himself of everything in the Most Blessed Sacrament, giving us all that He has, and reserving nothing for Himself.

" Beholding Him obedient to priests, good and bad; putting Himself in their hands to undergo a mystical death; assum-ing the quality of victim in order to allow Himself to be unresistingly immolated and sacrificed according to their designs, to con-form to Him, I am prompt to obedience. Like a host of immolation, I place myself in the hands of my superiors for whatever they will that, dying to my own will, to my passions, inclinations, and aversions, concealing the repugnance that I may feel, they may dispose of me according to their pleasure. The violence that I shall do myself will be to honor that which Jesus must undergo on entering souls sullied by sin. Of such souls He has so great horror that, every time He enters one, He renews His mortal agony of the Garden of Olives."

Honor the obedience of Jesus-Hostia by faithfully fulfilling all your religious obligations.

Jesus, meek and humble of Heart, make my heart like unto Thine.

(300 days' Indulgence.)

# Eighteenth Day.

## ADORATION.

OBEDIENCE is the concrete form of humility, its proof and its measure. It has its seat in the will, the proper symbol of which is the heart. It is sufficient to say what place and with what perfection this virtue occupies in the Sacred Heart of Jesus. Obedience establishes the glorious empire of God over the reasonable creature, perfects him by conforming him in every particular to the will and, consequently, to the idea of God. The reality of obedience in the Sacred Heart, the great advantages that it brings to us, the immense and universal evil of disobedience, the obligation to obey, and the most opportune means of doing so —will furnish successive motives for adoration, thanksgiving, reparation, and petition. Through their consideration we shall implore an abundant participation in the most obedient Heart of Jesus, the Divine Master, who here, as elsewhere, " began by doing before teaching."

Blessed Margaret Mary once wrote to a novice: " Your challenge (1) will be obedience both interior and exterior. First, you will promptly obey the inspirations of grace urging to acts of the virtues, bearing in mind these words: ' If today you hear the voice of the Lord, harden not your heart,' for grace comes once and returns no more. As for the exterior, you will obey all who have authority over you promptly, simply, lovingly, and without reply, having at heart these words: ' I am not come to do My own will, but the will of Him who has called Me.' At the first sound of the bell, you will run as if at the voice of the Spouse, saying: ' He became obedient unto death. I, too, will obey till the last sigh of my life.' " . . Let your obedience honor that of Jesus Christ in the Blessed Sacrament.

" Lord," said Solomon in the days of his wisdom, when he took possession of the throne of David, his father, " give to Thy servant a docile heart, *Dabis servo tuo cor*

---

(1) A *challenge* is an invitation to the practice of some special virtue.

*docile"* (1).    This was the prayer that was made by the eternal Son of God, the same gift that He received when He annihiliated Himself by taking our created nature, in order to enter the service of His Father and restore to Him the human race, subject to His empire.    " In the head of the book it is written of Me that I should do Thy will. O my God, I have desired it, and Thy law in the midst of My Heart—*Deus meus, volui, et legem tuum in medio Cordis mei"* (2).

These words, which St. Paul places on the lips of the Word at the moment of His Incarnation :  *" Ingrediens mundum,"* proclaim in what light the Son of God made Man considered and embraced obedience. Equal to the Father in glory, with the power of remaining so for all eternity by right of His eternal birth, *" Qui cum in forma Dei esset,"* He voluntarily became inferior by taking human nature. This He did in order to be able to offer the homage and reparation of an obedience truly worthy of the Divine Majesty, *" Semetipsum exinanivit, factus obediens."*    The Word Incarnate,

---

(1)    III Kings iii, 9.
(2)    Ps. xxxix, 9.

therefore, accepted obedience not only as a necessity of His humanity, and as a chastisement of man's sin, with which He had charged Himself, but He chose it freely. He elevated it by a love of predilection that He might espouse it and give Himself to it forever without reserve. He placed it in the centre of His Heart, to love and cherish it above every other affection; to be possessed, ruled, and directed by it in everything; to serve it and satisfy it forever: "*Et legem tuam in medio Cordis meo*— And Thy law in the midst of My Heart."

It measured the first pulsation of His Heart, says St. Paul, by giving It over in Its formation to the accomplishment of the will of God: "*Ingrediens mundum, dicit: Ecce venio ut faciam voluntatem tuam*— Coming into the world, He said: Behold, I come to do Thy will" (1). And it arrested Its last throb in the supreme moment when the obedient Victim clung without reserve to the will of the Father who demanded ·His life: "*In manus Tuas, Domine, commendo spiritum meum!*—Into Thy hands, O Lord, I commend My spirit!"

---

(1) Heb. x, 5-7.

### THANKSGIVING.

We owe eternal gratitude to the obedience of Jesus Christ, for it merited for us justification and salvation. " For as by the disobedience of one man, many were made sinners; so also by the obedience of one many shall be made just—*Ita et per unius obeditionem justi constituentur multi*"(1).

Adam's outburst of proud independence of the Creator, manifested by revolt against His formally expressed will, outraging His majesty, wounding His sovereign rights, despising His love and His benefits, had broken the bond of friendship which, uniting the Heavenly Father to His adopted children, shed upon them the divine life, that is, holiness, immortality, and happiness. Then it was that sin, suffering, and death chastised both in time and eternity the ungrateful, the stupid disobedience of Adam, leaving him no power to efface his fault or expiate its punishment. Obedience alone could re-establish what disobedience had destroyed. But it had to be an obedience altogether worthy of God, an obedience altogether free, without imperfection or

(1) Rom. v, 19.

weakness. It had to be an obedience which would attain supreme perfection, one inspired by love alone, and embellished by holiness, whose merit would far transcend the debts of disobedience; in one word, it should in every way be infinite.

No son of sinful Adam could possibly render such obedience; no, not even the Virgin preserved from original sin, since her qualities, her power for good are limited like those of every other creature. It was necessary that the Son of God, equal to His Father, by becoming man without ceasing to be God, should render Himself capable of communicating to His obedience an infinite value, in order to infuse into it infinite love, infinite holiness, infinite merit. The Word Incarnate rendered such an obedience in the full extent exacted by the Father to satisfy His justice, propitiate His mercy, expiate man's disobedience, and obtain pardon for the guilty. And thus by " the obedience of the new Adam, all His sons have been justified—*Ita et per unius obeditionem justi constituentur multi.*"

While Jesus rendered that obedience in the terrible trials imposed upon Him by the justice of the Father, He seemed Himself to be accursed by God. What were those trials? Poverty, exile, labor, fasting, privations, temptation, contradictions, the abandonment of ingratitude, the persecutions of hatred, calumnious and infamous accusations. They were ignominy and torment, the intolerable struggle of a double agony, and lastly, death itself, in which, cursed by man, He appeared also accursed by God. To nerve Himself to endure to the end, He thought of us, of our deliverence, of our reinstatement in grace.

### REPARATION.

Disobedience is the fundamental, the universal evil. It is the concrete form and the bitter fruit of pride. It is the essence and the substance of every sin. Whatever may be the diverse objects, the specific nature, and the particular circumstances of any sin whatsoever, it is radically and before all a disobedience. It exists only by the violation of some law. St. Thomas has well defined it: " *Factum, dictum, concupitum aut cogitatum contra legem divinam*—a thought, a desire, a word, a deed contrary to the divine law, contrary to the will of God manifested by some law."

What constitutes the malice of disobedience is the injury that it does to the sovereign rights of God and the disorder that it introduces into the relations of the creature with his Creator. In the sight of God, it is the denial of His sovereign right over the most noble work of His hands. But God's right is confounded with His will and with His very Being. Disobedience is, then, the negation of God, an apostasy, and a practical form of atheism: *"Initium superbiae hominis est apostatare a Deo*—The beginning of man's pride is a turning away from God."  In man, it is disregard of his essentially dependent situation with respect to God; and therein lies the fundamental disorder.  Inasmuch as he is a creature, it is absolutely necessary for man to depend upon the Creator. This dependence he should acknowledge by obeying His will in whatever way He may be pleased to exercise it over him. Created, that is, beginning to exist, man tends to the fulfilment of his being, namely, to his end; and He alone who called him into existence can conduct him to his end.

Of necessity, then, man depends on God; but God having created him free, he should recognize the legitimacy of his dependence and accept it without constraint. To accept it, is to obey; to deny it, is to disobey. The consequences of obedience are virtue, merit, and recompense; those of disobedience are sin and chastisement.

Such is the teaching of the Holy Spirit: " God made man from the beginning, and left him in the hand of his own counsel. He added His commandments and precepts: ' If thou wilt keep the commandments and perform acceptable fidelity forever, they shall preserve thee.' . Before man are life and death, good and evil—*Ante hominem, vita et mors, bonum et malum* That which he shall chosse shall be given him: *Quod placurit ei, dabitur illi* "(1).

### PETITION.

We can ask for nothing better or more useful than for our heart to have some resemblance to that of our Saviour. He warns us by the example of David that He finds no heart like unto His own excepting that which " does all His wills," that is, a heart perfectly obedient: " *Inveni David*

---

(1) Eccles. xv, 14.

*secundum Cor meum, qui faciet omnes voluntates meas"* (1).

If we wish to make progress in obedience, let us reanimate in our soul faith, love, and humility, the elements of this capital virtue.

Faith, throwing light upon the end of obedience, shows us in those clothed with authority the majesty of God, Jesus Christ Himself. It is to Him alone, in reality, that we submit our will, our reason, our judgment itself. Are we not assured that "he who hears the Church and all those that have received authority from her, hears Christ: *Qui vos audit, me audit?"* Faith, removing the veil of appearances, shows us in the things we have to do, the orders we have to execute, different forms of the one only substantial thing, the sweet and amiable will of God alone. We shall be, then, according to the teaching of St. Peter, "Children of obedience," like unto the Son of God, who saw in everything only His Father and His will, "not fashioned according to the former desires of your ignorance: *Quasi filii obedientiae, secundum eum qui vocavit vos, sanctum"* (2).

---

(1) Act. xiii, 22.
(2) I. Peter i, 14.

Let us reanimate in our soul the love of the Heavenly Father by accomplishing His will; the love of Jesus Christ, by following and glorifying Him, and by the acknowledgment of His sovereign rights; the love of our neighbor set over us by obeying him; the love of our brethren by serving them in obedience. Divine love animating our obedience, will purify and ennoble our soul, banishing servile fear which would debase it by hypocrisy, and mercenary interest which would render it narrow by egotism: "*Animos vestras castificantes in obedientia charitatis*—Purifying your souls in the obedience of charity"(1). Love alone can give us strength to confront the sacrifices, the forgetfulness of self, the privations, and sometimes the confusion that is met in obeying; for to be perfectly accomplished in every point, the law must be loved, cherished, followed, and fulfilled with a sort of passion far above that which seeks after earthly advantages. To the obedient heart, David says: "*Dilexi mandata tua super aurum et topazion*—I have loved Thy commandments above gold and the topaz"(2).

--------

(1) Ibid. 22.
(2) Ps. cxviii, 127.

Thus taught Jesus, the Great Master, the ideal, and the persuasive model of obedience: "If you keep My commandments, you shall abide in My love; as I have also kept My Father's commandments, and do abide in His love "(1).

Beg Our Lord to increase your faith in the Real Presence.

Eucharistic Heart of Jesus, have pity on us!

(*300 days' Indulgence.*)

---

(1) John xv, 10

# Nineteenth Day.

## OBEDIENCE, THE GLORIOUS HOMAGE OF THE EUCHARISTIC HEART.

### ADORATION.

THE Son of God, obedience personified: "*Factus obediens,*" lived only to love, to cultivate, and to satisfy the demands of obedience. During the thirty years of humble labor at Nazareth: "*Et erat subditus illis* —He was subject to them." During the three years of His apostolate, His "bread," that which He loved above everything else and upon which He lived, was to accomplish the will of God who sent Him: "*Meus cibus est ut faciam voluntatem ejus qui misit me*" (1). During His Passion, on the terrible eve of that most agonizing last day of His life, to which He gave Himself up to testify to the world with what love He would fulfil the Father's commands, He clung to obedience: "*Ut cognoscat mundus quia diligo Patrem et sicut mandatum dedit mihi Pater, sic facio, surgite eamus*

_____

(1) John iv, 34.

286

*hinc!*—That the world may know that I love the Father, and as the Father hath given Me commandment, so do I. Arise, let us go hence!"(1)

Lastly, to perpetuate here below under the humiliating yoke of human masters and in conditions of dependence and abasement which surpass all that He endured during His mortal life, to perpetuate an obedience which in heaven is all glory and felicity, He delivered Himself to His Apostles and gave to every priest full power over His Body and Blood by binding Himself in the fetters of the sacramental state. Every day of the world, even to the very last, shall we see this almighty God, this King of the nations, crowned with glory, " obeying the voice of a man," laboring and suffering for the good of a redeemed people: *" Obediente Domino voci hominis et pugnante pro Israel!"*(2)

Is obedience, then, so great, so noble, so beautiful as to have power to allure, to conquer, to captivate the Son of God to such a degree? Ah! it is to God the most glorious homage that He can receive from His creatures. It is the homage of their in-

(1) Ibid. xiv, 31.
(2) Jos. x, 14.

telligent will, the spiritual sacrifice of their immortal soul, the free gift of their meritorious life, offered by love to His good pleasure: *"Melior est obedientia quam victimae"* (1). It is for man true sanctity and consummate perfection: *"Deum time et mandata ejus observa; hoc est enim omnis homo.*—Fear God and keep His commandments, for this is all man "* (2).

" Beholding Jesus Christ rendering obedience to all priests whether good or bad," says Blessed Margaret Mary, " and placing Himself in their hands to die mystically, concealing Himself in the Host that, without showing any resistance, He may be immolated and sacrificed according to their designs, I am prompt at the call of obedience. Like a host of immolation, I place myself in the hands of my superiors for whatever they may command that, dying to my own will, to my passions, inclinations, and aversions, they may dispose of me as they please without my allowing the repugnance I may feel to appear.

" And the violence I shall have to do myself will be to honor that which Jesus does

---

(1) Matt. ix, 13.
(2) Eccles. xii, 13.

Himself on entering souls sullied by sin. He has such horror for these souls that every time He enters them, He there renews the mortal agony of the Garden of Olives."

### THANKSGIVING.

At the moment in which He offered Himself freely to suffer for the crimes of all and to assume their burden, He recalled the Father's promise: "If He shall lay down His life for sin, He shall see a long-lived seed—*Si posuerit pro peccato animam suam, videbit semen longævum*" (1). Of His sufferings and His obedience, mingled with His Blood, He formed remedies to cure us of the evil of independence and all the disorders it brings with it: "*Cujus livore sanati sumus*—By His bruises we are healed." In His obedience, He multiplied the most perfect acts, examples the most sublime of all the virtues, in order to induce us to imitate them and to teach us obedience sanctified and perfect: "*Passus est pro nobis, vobis relinquens exemplum, ut sequamini vestigia ejus*—Christ also suffered for us, leaving you an example that you should

(1) Is. liii, 10.

follow in His steps "(1). Lastly, in this rude school of obedience, and tried by all kinds of sorrows, He formed for Himself a Heart of infinite compassion to bear with all our difficulties, struggles, and even falls, in the fulfilment of the perpetual and universal duty of obedience, which is the very foundation of man's life here below: " He learned obedience by the things which He suffered—*Didicit ex eis quæ passus est obedientiam* " (2).

And now, become by His sacramental state obedience consummated, mercifully continuing before our eyes the lessons of the humblest, the meekest, the most heroic, and the most persevering obedience, He gives Himself as the food, the strength, the con·solation, and the pledge of infinite reward to all who, in order to reign with Him, bind themselves to Him till death in the bonds of Christian charity: " And being consummated, He became to all that obey Him, the cause of eternal salvation—*Et consummatus, factus est omnibus obtemperantibus sibi, causa salutis æternæ* " (3).

---

(1) I Peter ii, 21.
(2) Heb. v, 8.
(3) Ibid. 9.

Once when Blessed Margaret Mary had some difficulty in submitting to obedience, the Divine Master let her see His sacred Body covered with the wounds that He had received for her love. He reproached her with ingratitude and with tepidity in overcoming herself for love of Him. "What dost Thou will me to do, O My God," she asked, "since my will is stronger than I?" Jesus told her that, if she would place it in the wound of His Sacred Side, she would have no trouble in surmounting self. "O my Saviour," she exclaimed, "do Thou place it therein so deeply and shut it up so securely that it can never come out!" She tells us that from that moment everything appeared to her so easy that she never again had any difficulty in overcoming herself.

### REPARATION.

Man, alas! disdains to receive from the Most High the light to guide him in his way. He pretends to have, like God Himself, the knowledge of good and evil; therefore choosing death by despising the divine commandment, he is condemned to darkness and torture for time and eternity. It is just that, refusing to obey God willingly, he should be chained in spite of himself under the murderous yoke of the leader of all revolts. It is just that, not having wished to accomplish the noble commands of the Lord and of His Church, he should be obliged to submit to the cruel and ignominious caprices of the demons and to the reprobate. The confession they are then obliged to make, can do them no good: " For we have not obeyed Thy commandments, therefore are we delivered to spoil and to captivity and to death, and are made a fable and a reproach to all nations ! "(1).

It is true that every disobedience is not opposed to the absolute will of the Creator, and does not carry with it a total revolt of the human will. A great number of these acts of disobedience regard things not imposed upon us as necessary. Respecting the substance of the precepts, some souls violate only the accidental circumstances: others only half comprehend or half will. These are slight disobediences, partial or venial. God punishes them with temporal pains during life or after, in order to pardon them in the end.

---

(1) Tob. iii, 4.

But whatever they be, they displease His Heart. If He at once casts the gravely disobedient into the abyss of death, He declares His Heart turned away from those tepid souls that disobey in all things. He threatens to "vomit them out of His mouth." Let us seriously examine ourselves upon this capital point of the Christian life. Let us remember that the most deeply rooted inclination of fallen nature, the most impetuous, the most difficult to destroy or even to repress, is the passion of independence, of resistance to authority, and tendency to disobedience. Let us listen to the severe admonitions on this subject given by the Sacred Heart to the most intimate confidante of Its thoughts, Blessed Margaret Mary:

". My Divine Master having ordered me to rise every night between Thursday and Friday, in order to recite five *Pater* and *Ave* prostrate on the ground, I replied to Him: 'My Lord, Thou knowest that I am not my own, and that I shall do what my superioress orders me.' 'I do not intend it otherwise,' replied my Lord; 'for, all-powerful as I am, I desire nothing from thee but in dependence on thy superioress.'"

Hearken to these words from the mouth of Truth: "All religious disunited and sepa rated from their superiors, must be looked upon as vessels of reprobation, in whom all good liquors are changed into corruption, and upon whom the Divine Sun of Justice darting His rays, produces the same effect as the sun shining upon mire. Such souls are so utterly rejected by My Heart that, the more they try to approach Me by the Sacraments, prayer, and other exercises, the more I withdraw from them in horror. They will fall from one hell to another, for it is this disunion that has lost so many, and that will lose so many more. Since every superior holds My place, be he good or bad, the inferior who injures him wounds his own soul in the same measure. It is vain for him after so doing to weep at the door of My mercy. He shall not be heard."

### PETITION.

Lastly, humility, that perfect form of the religious fear of God, will bow our neck under the yoke of obedience, will bend our will to that of superiors, so that we shall even prefer the non-success of obedience to the success of revolt. Like the proud, alas!

we have in our excitement and eagerness. preferred the present and deceitful satisfactions of disobedience. Lacking humility, we have not sought the conscientious and lasting observance of the divine commandments: "*Deum time et mandata ejus observa*—Fear God and keep His commandments." Therefore it is that, wishing to propose the yoke of His law, sweet but inevitable, the Divine Master manifested His meek and humble Heart to all men crushed under the weight of inexorable obligations, that they may seek in It, as in an inexhaustible source, humility, meekness, and sweetness, without which it is impossible for obedience to be sincere or lasting: "*Discite quia mitis sum et humilis Corde: tollite jugum meum super vos: Jugum enim meum suave est et onus meum leve*—Learn that I am meek and humble of Heart: take up My yoke upon you, for My yoke is sweet and My burden light."

After having earnestly implored grace of the most obedient Heart of Jesus, which we adore in the consummation of obedience in the Blessed Sacrament, let us take the resolution to obey, each in his own state, every law to which we are subject, every superior

who has authority over us.   Let us obey all
the general obligations of the Christian contained in the Gospel, in the commandments
of God and of the Church, in the liturgical
laws.   Let us render obedience to all the
Decrees, all the directions of the Sovereign
Pontiff, the universal Pastor, and to the lawful ordinances of diocesan Bishops.   Let us,
each in what concerns him, obey the laws
that regulate particular states; for instance,
the laws of marriage, of trade, of public
functions, of the priesthood, and of the religious state.   Let us render obedience to
those that have a right to exact it; wives to
their husbands, children to parents, servants
to masters, employees and workmen to em-
ployers, subjects to the legitimate laws and
to magistrates, parishioners to their pastors,
penitents to confessors, religious to superiors, vicars to rectors, priests to their
Bishop.   It is at this price that notable victories of the spirit over the flesh are gained,
of humility over pride, and the public ascen-
dency of Christians over the enemies of their
Faith:   *"Vir obediens loquetur victorias—*
The obedient man shall speak of victories!"(1)

_____
(1)   Prov. xxi, 28.

" Lord, give to Thy servant a docile heart: *Dabis servo tuo cor docile!* "

Ask Our Eucharistic Lord to increase your spirit of recollection.

Our Lady of the Most Blessed Sacrament, pray for us.

(300 *days' Indulgence, when said before the Blessed Sacrament exposed.*)

# Twentieth Day.

*Invenisti Cor ejus fidele.*
*Thou didst find His Heart faithful.—II. Es-*
*dras IX, 8.*

SUBJECT.—The fidelity which we are now going to consider is not that which Jesus testified to His Father in His love for Him by the accomplishment of His will even at the cost of His life, but that which urged Him to love us and help us without fail, standing faithfully by all the promises which His gratuitous love made to mankind. It is the Heart of "the faithful Friend," the treasure-house of His tender mercies to us, that we are going to adore, bless, and invoke. It is the Heart which revealed how far Its fidelity extends by these words whose full meaning we shall understand only in heaven: "Behold this Heart which has so loved men that It has spared nothing, even to exhausting and consuming Itself to testify to them Its love!"

298

## ADORATION.

Fidelity of Heart is one of the distinctive moral characteristics of the Incarnate Word. He had announced it by His prophet in order that men might with more confidence await His coming upon earth: From the root of Jesse, shall be born the virginal rod (Mary), which shall be crowned by the magnificent rose (Jesus), and the Holy Spirit shall fiil Him with the Spirit of wisdom and of understanding, the spirit of counsel and of fortitude, the spirit of knowledge and of godliness, of piety, and the fear of the Lord. "And fidelity shall be the girdle of His reins—*Et erit fides cinctorium renum ejus*"(1). As the girdle closely clasps the body and forms for it a support, so does fidelity envelop the Heart of Jesus and prevent Its ever swerving from Its promises to help us. The girdle, which gathers the clothing in graceful folds around the person, is, likewise, the symbol of love. The Heavenly Spouse appeared in His glory, "His breast, that is His Heart, supported by a cincture of gold: *Praecinctum ad ma-*

---

(1) Is. xi., 5.

*millas zona aurea"* (1).   It was certainly
of the Heart of Jesus that Isaias prophesied
when he depicted It gloriously encircled by
the bands of invincible fidelity.

It is meet that the most perfect of all
hearts should possess this perfection, which
is "the most sacred treasure of the human
heart, the honor of Divinity as well as of
humanity: *Sacratissimum humani pectoris
bonum"* (2).   According to Eternal Wisdom it is the most precious of all treasures
and the most assured of all protection.
*"Amicus fidelis protectio fortis; qui autem
invenit illum, invenit thesaurum*—A faithful friend is a strong defence, and
he that hath found him hath found
a treasure "(3).   It is not upon honor,
honesty, fidelity—these three are one and
the same—that rest all relations between
mankind and God Himself?   Do they not
form the bonds of friendship, the peace and
joy of the domestic circle, the security of

---

(1)  *Cur ad mamillas cingitur Christus? Quia
Cor Christi. quod est inter mamillas, plenum est
charitate.*   Corn. a Lap. *in Apoc. I,* 13.

(2)  *Seneca, Ep.* 89.—*Decus divumque hom-
inumque.   (Cicero, Lib. I. offic.)*

(3)  Ecclus. vi, 14.

business transactions, our confidence in prayer and every religious exercise? He that is faithful, no matter what his condition, perhaps that of a lowly servant, merits esteem and affection: " *Si est tibi servus fidelis, sit tibi quasi anima tua: quasi fratrem tuum sic cum tracta*—If thou have a faithful servant, let him be to thee as thy own soul: treat him as a brother, because in the blood of thy soul thou hast gotten him "(1).

Alas, it is too true! Fidelity is very rare on this earth. We do, indeed, often find hearts capable of pity, ready to perform an act of devotedness at their own time and convenience; but fidelity implies disinterestedness, devotedness and constancy under every form, and that is very difficult to the heart wounded by original sin. At the bottom of that heart lie egoism, weakness, and inconstancy: " *Multi homines misericordes vocantur: virum autem fidelem, quis inveniet?*—Many men are called merciful, but who shall find a faithful man? "(2)

How good, then, it is for our poor heart, always deceived both by itself and others,

---

(1) Ibid. xxxiii, 31.
(2) Prov. xx, 6.

to contemplate and adore in all security the fidelity without fail or weakness of that only One who can in truth be called " the faithful Friend: *Amicus fidelis!* " He is our efficacious and ever present help: *Protectio fortis,* whose heart is a treasury of every kind of fidelity: " *Et qui invenit illum, invenit thesaurum!* "

The Heart of Jesus bears in Itself the eternal fidelity of God, along with His munificent liberality, His infallible truth, and His very Being: " *Fidelis Dominus in omnibus verbis suis*—The Lord is faithful in all His words "(1). The Heart of Jesus possesses human fidelity under all the forms in which it can be exhibited: the fidelity of a father remaining with his children that they may not be left orphans; the fidelity of the shepherd going before his sheep to lead them to good pasture, and to give his life in their defence against the wolf; the fidelity of the priest praying indefatigably for the needs of his people; the fidelity of the Spouse toward the Church, which He daily washes in His Blood and feeds with His Flesh; lastly, the fidelity of the Friend who said to His

---

(1) Ps. cxliv, 13.

Apostles invited to His table, and in them to all men who communicate: " I will not now call you servants, but I call you My friends, because all things whatsoever I have received from My Father, I have made known to you, and I shall be with you all days even to the end of the world."

Let us adore the Heart of the faithful Friend, Its truth, sincerity, and the generosity and abundance of Its fidelity. Let us abandon ourselves unreservedly to Its fidelity!

" I constitute thee heiress of My Heart and all Its treasures for time and for eternity, and I permit thee to use them according to thy desires. I promise thee help shall fail thee only when My Heart shall fail in power." (Words of Our Lord to Blessed Margaret Mary.)

### THANKSGIVING.

Nothing is so beautiful as fidelity. The Holy Spirit does not hesitate to say: " *Amico fideli nulla est comparatio, et non est digna ponderatio auri vel argenti contra bonitatem fidei illius*—Nothing can be compared to a faithful friend, and no weight of gold and silver is able to countervail the goodness of his fidelity"(1). A friend is a gift of God above all gifts, and he who has it possesses a benefit above all benefits. Considered even in the natural light, fidelity is peace of heart, security in the present, certitude for the future, assurance in daily relations with the neighbor, confidence in the communication of secrets and sorrows the most delicate. It means sincere and de-voted concurrence in time of need, assured help, the sharing of difficulties, and, in cases of misfortune, the continuation of esteem and affection along with the presence of the trusted one. We may say that, among all the goods of the heart, it is the treasure.

What will not be the fidelity of the Divine Friend, whose Heart is full of infinite love, of all the noble affections that dispose Him to be the unique Saviour of men?

The friendship of Jesus is entirely gratuitous, entirely disinterested, for He is always the first to love, and that without any other end in view than to do good. It accommodates itself to the needs, to the character, the situation of each, being full of knowledge, experience, and condescension.

---

(1) Ecclus. vi, 15.

Jesus, as the Sovereign Master of all forces, disposes of all creatures and of all help, and nothing can oppose His all-powerful action. He is faithful during life and, when death draws near, His fidelity in time is changed into eternal fidelity, over which time in its ravages has no power.

From the moment that God created us in pure love, His fidelity encompassed us with His promises of eternal life, for He created us to His own image and likeness in order to make us live forever of His own life and to enjoy His endless happiness. When revolt and ingratitude separated us from God, His fidelity became the mercy which called us all to His Heart that He might create us anew, sweeten our yoke, and lighten our burden. He redeemed us at the price of His Blood, engaged to feed us every day with His own Flesh, and to abandon us never. It is His fidelity that brings Him to our bedside when death and Satan assault our life of body and soul. He comes to reassure us in the throes of our last agony, and He says to us: " May the Body of Christ guard thy soul to eternal life! " Lastly, His fidelity judges us and, if we have been faithful, pronounces over us these words of supreme love, which will introduce us into the peace of beatitude: "Come, ye blessed of the Father. Possess the kingdom that has been prepared for you from all eternity!"

Can we ever magnify as It deserves the Heart of the faithful Christ, we who are the creation, the redemption, the only solicitude of His fidelity: "*Vir fidelis multum laudabitur?*—A faithful man shall be much praised?" (1)

"My heart is so passionately enamored of men that, not being able to contain in Itself the flames of Its ardent charity, It must of necessity spread them around by thy means. It must manifest Itself to them in order to enrich them with Its precious treasures, whose sanctifying and necessary graces will withdraw them from the abyss of perdition.' (Words of Our Lord to Blessed Margaret Mary.)

### REPARATION.

The purest and most abundant source of contrition is, without doubt, the love of God and of His Son, Our Lord Jesus Christ. Whoever can rouse in his soul the sentiment of the infinite loveliness of God, which his

---

(1)  Prov. xxviii, 20.

sins have despised by preferring to it the very limited charms of the creature; whoever has comprehended with what love God has loved him, whether in creating him or in filling his life with His benefits, whoever seizes the mystery of Jesus' dying for him and of making Himself his Eucharist; whoever beholds himself still loved, protected, called to pardon, in spite of his tepidity and malice, in spite of the number of his sins, must feel his heart rent with sorrow and abased with salutary shame. He must be filled with love for this God of mercy, he must return to Him by a sincere and lasting conversion, a conversion that can be effected by perfect love alone.

Nothing can so powerfully enkindle this flame of moral resurrection as the sight of the fidelity of the merciful Friend making Himself for those that He has not ceased to love, in spite of their wanderings, "*the medicine* of life and immortality," which raises up from the dead and cures all wounds: "*Amicus fidelis medicamentum vitae et immortalitatis.*" When fidelity is exercised toward a being who is unfaithfulness personified, it shows itself magnanimous and sublime—sin being, in the mind, only a want of faith in the divine word which orders or prohibits, a want of confidence in the word that promises the recompense, of fear for the word that threatens chastisements; in the heart, only ingratitude and forgetfulness of the Sovereign Benefactor; and in the will, only the refusal of obedience and a revolt against divine authority. It is toward this unfaithful one that the faithful Heart exercises Its invincible fidelity by pardoning him, supporting him, and reinstating him in all the goods that he had forfeited! It is here, too, that fidelity manifests its sovereign goodness, for it comes to the succor of a being condemned to the most dreadful punishments both in time and in eternity, and in the absolute impossibility of freeing himself or even of lessening the evils that encompass him, either by his own efforts or those of any other creature. God alone can remit sin and raise from spiritual death, which surely leads to eternal death if, faithful to its need of pardoning and to the law that He has deigned to make for Himself, His mercy does not intervene: " *Amicus fidelis medicamentum vitae et immortalitatis—*A faithful friend is the medicine of life and immortality."

The Gospel abounds in touching examples of this ministry of merciful fidelity, because the Gospel is the history of the Son of God made Man to save men from their sins. St. Peter is a perfect example of it. Jesus is faithful to warn him of the danger that he runs by his presumption; faithful to pray that his faith may not fail, since Satan demanded to sift him like wheat; faithful to exhort him to vigilance and to prayer in order to strengthen him against approaching temptation. And as soon as Peter, forgetful of these warnings, had fallen into the unfaithfulness of the triple denial, the faithful Friend, though in the midst of His own sufferings, endeavored to catch his eye, to cast upon him a look of tender reproach and infinite clemency, which revived faith in the heart of the poor renegade, and drew from his eyes torrents of reparative tears. Then, after His Resurrection, faithful to render to Peter the rights with which He had honored him, Jesus appeared to him first before all the others, and drew from him in the presence of his fellow-disciples the triple confession of faithful love, which forever effaced the remembrance of his former infidelity.

To sinners at all times, the Saviour has assured the fidelity of His pardon by instituting in the daily effusion of His Blood, the Sacrament that remits all sin: *" Hic est Sanguis meus  .    .   in remissionem peccatorum*—This is My Blood        for the remission of sins."

It was the merciful fidelity of the Sacred Heart that permitted St. John, who knew all the secrets of the Heart upon which he had reposed, to write these consoling and re-assuring words for us poor sinners:  " My little children, these things I write to you that you may not sin.  But if any man sin, we have an advocate with the Father, Jesus Christ the Just.  And He is the propitiation for our sins, and not for ours only, but also for those of the whole world " (1).

" It desires to draw many souls from eternal perdition, for this Divine Heart is like a fortress and a secure asylum for all poor sinners who wish to take refuge therein, in order to shun Divine Justice in Its just anger which, like an impetuous torrent, would drown with their sins those sinners who excite the divine wrath."  (Words of Our Lord to Blessed Margaret Mary.)

---

(1)  I John ii, 1.

PETITION.

The first means of securing for one's self the divine fidelity is earnestly to demand it of the grace of God, for " a faithful friend is a gift from God to them that fear Him and pray to Him: *Amicus fidelis . et qui metuant Dominum inveniunt illum."* God loves whom He pleases, and gives Himself to whom He pleases. His choice is free, and we have nothing in us that can merit it. *" Fidelis Deus . per quem vocati estis in societatem Filii ejus Jesu*—God is faithful: by whom you are called unto the fellowship of His Son Jesus Christ Our Lord "(1). To those that He had drawn around Him in the closest, the most familiar, the most tender of friendships, the Divine Master said: " It is not you who have chosen Me. By the dulness of your intellect, the narrowness of your heart, the impurity of your soul, you were incapable of doing so; and again, even when become man such as you are, I am by My divine filiation above your reach: *Non vos me elegistis.* But it pleased Me to single you out from the multitude and to bow

---

(1) I Cor. i, 9.

down of My own accord to you, to instruct
you, to purify and enrich you in order to
elevate you to Me.    It is, then, I who have
chosen you:    *Sed ego elegi vos.*    Remain
in Me, remain in My love which has made
you My friends, and never cease to deserve
by your humility and fidelity the continuation of it:    *Manete in me, manete in dilectione mea."*

The second means of securely enjoying
the fidelity of Jesus is to believe in Him
firmly, confidently, lovingly, in submission
and abandonment to His guidance. *" Cre-
ditis in Deum?   Et in me credite."* Ye believe in God, did He say to His Apostles, in
His wisdom, in His truth, in His power, in
His goodness?   Well then, believe in Me in
the same manner: *Et in me credite!* This
is the condition that He laid down for answering all those that demand of Him
miracles of cure or conversion: *" Credis in
Filium Dei? "* And He predicted to Nico-
demus that the miracles which they should
see, would be great in proportion to their
faith.

There is question now of believing in the
fidelity of the Heart of Jesus.   First, to believe that His help will never fail, especi-

ally in things necessary to our salvation, such as to shun sin, to resist temptations, to fulfil our duties; for " He is faithful, and He will not permit us to be tempted above our strength." Still more, He will turn our temptations to our profit, and make us find in them strength to resist even to the end: " *Fidelis Deus est qui non patietur vos tentari supra id quod potestis, sed faciet cum tentatione proventum, ut possitis sustinere*—God is faithful, who will not suffer you to be tempted above that which you are able: but will make also with temptation issue, that you may be able to bear it "(1). We must believe, also, that He will never fail to assist us in our trials, of what kind soever they may be. He will either deliver us from them or He will give us the strength to accept them, provided that, being in a state of grace, we implore His help with confidence, humility, and perseverance. He has even engaged Himself thereto by oath: " *Si manseritis in me, quodcumque volueritis petetis, et fiet vobis*—If you abide in Me, and My words abide in you, you shall ask whatever you will, and it shall be done unto

---

(1) I Cor. x, 13.

you "(1).   Lastly, we must believe in the eternal justifications of His fidelity, and that He has in reserve for us heavenly rewards that infinitely surpass all the riches of which, in spite of our confidence in Him and all our prayers, we have, by His permission, been deprived here below.   Is it not for this reason that He can without irony say to us that the poor, the afflicted, the persecuted are happy here below, since poverty, sufferings and tears assure them infallibly the kingdom of Heaven, which is the possession of the infinite God?

Let us, then, believe unreservedly and unhesitatingly in the fidelity of the Heart of our Friend.   Let us abandon ourselves to it, knowing that, according to His word, " the will of the Father is that whosoever believes in Him shall suffer neither hunger nor thirst, and shall possess life everlasting !(2)

" When I present my little requests to my Divine Master, above all those which appear difficult to obtain, it seems to me that I hear these words: ' Dost thou believe

---

(1) John xv, 7.
(2) John vi, 35, 40.

that I can do it? If thou dost believe, thou shalt see the power of My Heart in the magnificence of My love!' And again, seeing the progress of what I had so much desired, He said to me: 'Did I not tell thee that, if thou wouldst believe, thou shouldst see thy desires accomplished?'" (Words of Our Lord to Blessed Margaret Mary.)

Pray that you may have true reverence for the House of God.

Sacred Heart of Jesus, let Thy Kingdom come!

(300 *days' Indulgence.*)

# Twenty=first Day.

## THE SWEETNESS OF THE HEART OF JESUS.

THE Challenge of our dear Sister Novices will be sweetness . . . (1) In order to practise it, they will look upon Our Lord in the Most Blessed Sacrament as their good Master who says to them: " Learn of Me to be meek and humble of heart, otherwise you cannot be loved nor recognized by My Sacred Heart, which will not acknowledge you for Its disciples unless you form yourselves on It by the practice of Its holy maxims." It was thus that Blessed Margaret Mary urged souls on to the imitation of one of the two virtues which the Saviour proposed as the dominant virtues of His Heart. It is this sweetness, this meekness, this gentleness that we are going to bless and adore in Him. It is for it that we shall petition after having deplored the faults into which we have been led by our infidelity to this capital virtue of Christianity.

--------

(1) A *challenge* is an invitation to the practice of some special virtue.

ADORATION.

Meekness is planted in the soul by nature to help to moderate impatience, to conquer wrath, and to repress the desire of vengeance. Grace elevates it, perfects it and, impregnating it with supernatural love, transforms it into the crowning expression of divine charity. It is, then, one of the " fruits of the Holy Spirit " (1), one of those effusions which flow from His personal presence in the just soul, one of those forces which He never ceases to excite and keep alive, in order to manifest His divine life. It is, also, one of those " beatitudes " which rouse to fervor in the practice of virtue and mingle joy with the sacrifices it imposes. Calming the soul against the tumult of anger and the movements of rancor, so easily raised, it inclines it to goodness and benevolence, to patience and the pardon of injuries. Like oil on the troubled sea, which stills the angry waves, meekness mingles with our relations with one another and sweetens them. It shows itself in the benevolent glance and smile, in the affable word, in the preventing salu-

---

(1)   Gal. v, 23.

tation, in the moderate gesture and the modest attitude, in amiable condescension toward all, especially the lowly. It is, indeed, a noble, beneficent, and beautiful virtue, the one among all others especially pleasing to God, the one that conquers men's hearts: " *Quod beneplacitum est ei, fides et mansuetudo* "(1).

But it is in Thy Heart that it appears in all its enchanting beauty, O sweet Jesus! Thou hast a good right to call us all to study it therein, to contemplate it as a marvel worthy of adoration and admiration: " *Discite a me quia mitis sum Corde.—* Learn of Me that I am meek and humble of Heart." There lies the infinite sweetness of Thy Divine Nature, which is " Meekness and sweetness in their very essence: *Quoniam tu Domine suavis et mitis es* "(2). It is the entire plenitude of sweetness which " the most sweet Spirit of God "(3) willed to create in heaven and upon earth, and which He laid up in Thy Heart: " *Spiritus Domini super me, eo*

---

(1) Ecclus. i, 35.   Ps. xxxvi, 11.
(2) Joel ii, 13.
(3) Wisd. xii, 1.

*quod unxerit me*" (1). There is contained the sweetness that Thou didst will to practise with all Thy Heart in order to accomplish Thy mission of servant of God and Saviour of men. It is the fruit of Thy experience of our miseries and the expression of Thy compassion for our innumerable evils: "*In eo enim in quo passus est ipse et tentatus, potens est et eis qui tentotus desirderabilis*" (3).

The sweetness that issues from Thy Heart so profoundly penetrates all Thy powers, clothes Thy whole being with such charms that, making of Thee the Incarnate Sweetness, the Sweetness poured out, it renders Thee perfectly amiable and desirable: "*Guttur Dilecti mei suavissimum, et totus desirderabilis*" (3).

It is not to be wondered at, therefore, that the Sacrament which has issued from the Heart of Jesus as the ripe fruit of His most tender love and which maintains Jesus Himself in the truth of His two natures and in the experience of our miseries, contains sweetness in its every form: "*Panem*

---

(1) Is. lxi, 1.
(2) Heb. ii, 18.
(3) Cant. v, 6.

*in se habentem omnis saporis suavitatem,"*
and should be the convincing demonstration
of the sweetness of God and of His Son
Jesus: *"Substantia tua dulcedinem tuam
quam in filios habes ostendebat"* (1).

Lord, I will approach Thy Sacrament, I
will penetrate even to Thy Heart, I will
plunge therein! I will eat It, and I shall be
nourished by It in truth. After having
tasted Its honey on my lips: *"Fructus ejus
dulcis gutturi meo"* (2), I shall live on
the ever present thought of Thy supera-
bundant sweetness: *"Memoriam abun-
dantiæ suavitatis tuæ eructabunt"* (3).

### THANKSGIVING.

How well it is for us that Jesus, desiring
to submit us to His empire, to instruct us
in His doctrine, and to direct us in the
ways which lead to God, has founded all
His rights on the sweetness of His Heart,
and placed in It the chief means of leading
us to Himself: *"Discite a me quia mitis
sum Corde:* Come to My school and tread
in My footsteps, because I  am meek of

---

(1) Wisd. xvi, 20, 21.
(2) Cant. ii, 3.
(3) Ps. cxliv, 7.

Heart. My yoke is sweet, and light is the burden that I shall place on your shoulders: *Jugum enim meum suave est et onus meum leve.*"

Experience teaches, and reason confirms the truth that, though we may conquer by violence, we can reign only by sweetness. The human will is such that it may, indeed, bend if we gain it and yield unreservedly; but it becomes inflexible when force is exerted against it. Violence rouses resistance and revolt. The Wise Man tells us this: "*Verbum dulce multiplicat amicos et lingua eucharis in bono homine abundat*—A sweet word multiplieth friends and a gracious tongue in a good man aboundeth" (1).

Moses and David, the great leaders chosen by God for His well-beloved people, were men so gentle of character that they faithfully practised sweetness in the government of men, and made it the principal factor of their own sanctification: "*In fide et bonitate ipsius (Moysis), sanctum fecit illum*" (2).

It was under the character of sweetness

---

(1) Ecclus. vi, 5.
(2) Ibid. xlv, 4.

that Jesus presented Himself to the world over which He sought to reign: "*Ecce Rex tuus venit tibi mansuetus*"(1). It was under the charms of the sweetest Infant that He appeared: "*Benignitas et humanitas apparuit Salvatoris nostri Dei*"(2). And the first time that He addressed the multitude, He said to them: "The Spirit of sweetness has descended upon Me, and hath anointed Me. It has sent Me to announce glad tidings to the poor, to heal the contrite of heart, to deliver the captive, to give sight to the blind, and to restore broken members. I come to preach the great pardon of God, to promise the day of compensation to the oppressed, to restore the exile to his country, to console all who weep, and to transform the whole world into a just and victorious people, from whom will rise to the Lord a concert of praise and glorification"(3). And the title which proclaims the sweetness, the condescension, the solicitous and devoted attention of His government, is a title of supreme goodness: "I have pity on this

---

(1) Zach. ix, 9.
(2) Tit. iii, 4.
(3) Is. lxi, 1.

multitude, which is like sheep without a shepherd. I am the good Shepherd. I know my sheep. I call each one by his name, and I give My life for them!"

The same sweetness inspires every action of the Eucharist over the conduct of our souls. This action consists in making them live of the divine and supernatural life, in making them advance in it unceasingly, until it leads them to the goal of eternal life, to perfect resemblance with God. It meets weakness, opposition, treason in our vicious nature instinctively borne to evil and rebellious of sacrifice. This it is that renders the action of grace difficult, laborious, slow, and uncertain. Now, the Eucharistic Christ exercises it with infinite sweetness, with marvellous pliancy to the faculties, as well as to the needs of all. He shows touching condescension to our weakness, heroic patience in supporting our hesitancy and slowness, indefatigable longanimity in pardoning us, raising us up, incessantly recommencing the same old task, so obstinately compromised by our frivolity and tepidity. Nothing discourages Him, nothing exasperates Him, nothing disturbs His equanimity or sweet benevolence. Still more in order to encourage us while elevating us, He transforms every obedience, every effort, every act of virtue into acts of love, that noble and sublime virtue, the queen of all virtues. He traverses the ages, presenting Himself to all men, saying to them as He reveals to them His Heart: " Come to Me, all ye who labor, and I will refresh you. Abide in Me, abide in My love, for you are no longer strangers or servants, but most dear friends: *Manete in dilectione mea!"*

O Christ, infinitely good at Heart, be Thou blessed for treating my misery with so much sweetness: *" Parasti in dulcedine tua pauperi, Deus!"* (1).

### REPARATION.

Sweetness in all its plenitude has been stored up in the Heart of Jesus. The Man-God is constantly producing most perfect and meritorious acts of it, in order to offer to God reparation for the dreadful sin of wrath with its retinue of disputes, vengeance, homicide, and bloody wars.

---

(1) Ps. lxvii, 11.

Anger is one of the principal forms of pride, which suffers no yoke, and of egotism, which will endure no opposition. The Lord holds pride in horror. Anger is one of the outward expressions of hatred, and it kills in the soul charity for the neighbor. He who is in hatred is in death. Anger, in fine, inspires vengeance, which usurps the rights of Him who has said: *" Mihi vindicta, ego retribuam "* (1). It is the mother of despair, whither it so quickly draws its blind victims, and its outbursts never fail to scandalize souls. By every title, therefore, it is one of the seven capital sins, a deadly sin by its very nature. The most sweet Saviour condemns to eternal judgment " him who is angry against his brother and who injures him in his wrath: *Ego dico vobis quia omnis qui irascitur fratri suo, reus erit gehennæ ignis "* (2). We understand, in effect, that the most just anger of God arms itself against the wrath of man always unjust, since all men are equal by origin. by sin, and by their destiny, in spite of the accidental differences that distinguish them during life.

---

(1)  Rom. xii, 19.
(2)  Matt. v, 22.

It was to expiate the crime of human wrath and to appease the holy anger of God by lovingly undergoing its vengeance, that the Son of God became incarnate. This double design condemned Him to appear as a victim and to undergo its terrible destiny. For that purpose, it was absolutely necessary that the Christ should be meek, invincibly sweet. We cannot imagine an expiatory victim, freely offered, anything else. From the moment that He offered Himself to satisfy outraged Majesty, despised Sovereignty, Justice aggrieved, Love unknown, He had silently and intrepidly to bear the burden even to the end with the same generous love. It is this sweetness in lovingly enduring that gives to the sacrifice the savory odor which renders it so agreeable to the Lord: " *Odor suavissimus, victimæ Domini* "(1). The victim *par excellence* of the sacrifices instituted by the Lord was a lamb.

Jesus is the Lamb of God, who comes to take away the sins of the world. Sheep revolted against the Eternal Shepherd, we were all wandering through the ways of

---

(1) Exod. xxii, 18.

evil and misfortune when it pleased God to charge His Son with our iniquities. He consented to be offered for us without opening His mouth to ask an explanation, plead His justification, or utter a cry of sorrow. He was led to death as a lamb to the slaughter, and He was silent as a lamb in the hands of him who shears it for the sacrifice(1). How gentle He was under the inexorable severity of His Father during His Passion! How sweet to those that made Him suffer!—to Judas who betrayed Him, to Peter who denied Him, to the Apostles who abandoned Him, to the judges who condemned Him, to the executioners who tortured Him! When, at last, He broke silence, it was because His Heart could no longer contain the excess of Its sweetness. His pity for all who caused His death forced Him to plead their pardon with His Father: *" Pater, dimitte illis, non enim sciunt quid faciunt!*—Father, forgive them, for they know not what they do! "

This sweetness in enduring everything, so necessary for a victim, follows the Eucharistic Lamb into the Sacrament in which

(1) Is. liii, 19.

He incessantly renews the sacrifice of His Passion and death. It is manifested in the invincible patience with which He there supports the injuries which from all sides attack Him in the weakness, inert and incapable of resistance, of His sacramental state.

What does He endure? Irreverence, frivolity, culpable negligence in the manner of treating with Him,—irreverence in the choice and use of things improper for His worship, manifesting rather the little esteem they have of Him than the respect and gratitude they owe Him. And the secret treason of sacrilegious Consecration and Communions (of which He alone knows all the outrage and bitterness) are joined to public profanation, to blasphemies and mockeries, to the violence of persecution which chases Him from His abodes as a malefactor who has no rights, and against whom every form of outrage is permitted!

Jesus sees these injuries. He experiences all their horror, and He feels against their authors the most just wrath and the most legitimate vengeance. But His incredible sweetness restrains Him, leads Him to accept all in order to perpetuate before His Father His sacrifice of expiation, and to gain our hearts by showing us what He is capable of enduring for our sake. He is always the " Lamb " of whom St. Peter says, " Who did no sin, neither was guile found in His mouth. Who, when He was reviled, did not revile; when He suffered, He threatened not ; but delivered Himself to him that judged Him unjustly. Who His own self bore our sins in His body upon the tree: that we being dead to sins, should live to justice by whose stripes you were healed. For you were as sheep going astray: but you are now converted to the shepherd and bishop of your souls. For Christ also suffered for us, leaving you an example that you should follow His footsteps " (1).

### PETITION.

" *Memento, Domine, David et omnis mansuetudinis ejus!*—O Lord, remember David and all his meekness! " (2) It is through the meekness of Thy Christ so perfect, so meritorious, and so agreeable in Thy eyes, that I supplicate Thee, O God, Thou who dost " receive only the prayer of

---

(1) I Peter ii, 20-24.
(2) Ps. cxxxi, 1.

the meek," that is, of those that overcome anger and suffer in patience: "*Suscipiens mansuetos Dominus*"(1). We know that "*Non enim superbit ab initio placuerunt tibi, Domine, sed humilium et mansuetorum semper tibi placuit deprecatio*—Nor from the beginning have the proud been acceptable to Thee; but the prayer of the humble and the meek hath always pleased Thee "(2). It is an abundant communication of the meekness of His Heart that I implore of Thee, O Father, for I have so much need of it in all my works and toward all with whom I deal! St. Thomas, the great interpreter of Thy thoughts, says very justly: "*Mansuetudo est bonitas cujuslibet ad quemlibet*—Meekness obliges us to be all to all "(3).

It is toward my neighbor, toward every neighbor, in whatever relation I may stand to him, whether as superior, inferior, or equal, that meekness ought to dominate my sentiments and their expression, above all, if I feel a natural antipathy toward him, or if he has offended me. Courtesy, affability,

---

(1) Ps. cxlvi, 6.
(2) Judith ix, 16.
(3) 2a 2æ, q. cxlvii, a. 1.

support, sincere pardon, forgetfulness of injury, kindness testified,—these are the duties of Thy exquisite and sanctifying sweetness, O my God, and I should imitate them perseveringly. "*Sectare charitatem, patientiam, mansuetudinem*—In charity, in long-suffering, in sweetness "(1). All who are by nature or by grace my brethren in the charity of Thy Heart have a right to expect this from me: " *Omnem ostendentes mansuetudinem ad omnes*—Showing all mildness toward all men "(2).

It is plain to me that my duty is to be meek, not with a soft or effeminate sweetness, but with that which will lead me to act wisely, to shun impatience, anger, exasperation, which rouse in my soul agitation and discouragement. "*Fili, in mansuetudine serva animam tuam*—My son, keep thy soul in meekness "(3). "Guard me, then, O my God, by the penetrating power of Thy infinite sweetness, against impatience which obstacles so easily produce in me when my mind is gloomy and my heart is dry, when I am laboring under fatigue and sickness,

---

(1) I Tim. 11.
(2) Tit. iii, 2.
(3) Ecclus. x, 31.

disqualifications and ignorance, difficulties
in the prosecution of good and the overcoming of defects, and the importunity of temptation.   Guard me, above all, when my efforts are useless, my hopes frustrated, when
failure attends all my undertakings, when
humiliation wears me out.   Grant me grace
even then to persevere meekly in the labor
of my sanctification:   '*In mansuetudine
opera tua perfice*—Do thy work in meekness'(1), and to redouble supernatural
sweetness in the ministry confided to me:
'*Deo ministros in suavitate, in Spiritu
Sancto*—In   sweetness   in   the   Holy
Ghost'"(2).

And toward Thyself, O my Sovereign
Lord, against Thy august rights and Thy
paternal conduct over me, my pride dares
impatiently rise up to question Thee, to
blame, and even to condemn, as if Thou
didst owe me anything else than the chastisements of Thy just anger—ah! grant that
I may be meek, patient, silent, always grateful, always content and smiling!   Yes, may
I so comport myself under the pressure of

---

(1)  Ibid. iii, 19.
(2)  II Cor. vi, 6.

Thy will and toward all the instruments that manifest it to me, however much they may contradict my own ideas, however much they interfere with my own independence and pleasure. I know well, my God, that Thou dost hear, help, and save only those that are supple and docile under Thy almighty hand, who bend to Thy good pleasure, which is ever just, wise, and beneficent in whatever form it may appear : " *Quia beneplacitum est Domino in populo suo, et exaltabit mansuetos in salutem*—For the Lord is well pleased with His people: and He will exalt the meek unto salvation ! "(1)

" If you wish to be a disciple of the Sacred Heart of Jesus, you must become meek and humble like Him:—meek to support the annoyances, humors, and chagrin of your neighbor, without vexing yourself over the little contradictions that they may cause you ; but, on the contrary, performing for him whatever services you can, for this is the true means by which to gain the good graces of the Sacred Heart. You must be sweet in order not to be disquieted in events

---

(1) Ps. cxlix, 4.

opposed to your inclinations, but also even in the faults you may commit. Still more, you must not excuse yourself, since our adorable Master did not do so in His Passion. Rejoice when you are forgotten and despised, for that is the true means of making the amiable Heart of Jesus reign in ours. Let us humble ourselves and allow ourselves to be humbled." (*Words of Blessed Margaret Mary.*)

Beg Our Eucharistic Lord to fill your heart with love for your neighbor.

Our Lady of the Cenacle, pray for us.
(50 *days' Indulgence.*)

# Twenty-second Day.

## THE SACRED HEART AND THE ANGELS.

THE angels are the élite subjects of the kingdom of the Sacred Heart. Created by a love of preference, which made them pure spirits after the image of God, who is a spirit; prevented by love, which preserved them from the fall into which Lucifer precipitated the unfaithful legions; absorbed in the love of the Beatific Vision,—by all these titles they belong most intimately to the Sacred Heart, the symbol of divine love. To make some return to that Sacred Heart, they love and adore It, they celebrate It, and eagerly fulfil all Its desires in the government of creation. Our duty, not less than our privilege, is to unite with the angels in loving more ardently and serving more perfectly the Sacred Heart according to Its own demand of Blessed Margaret Mary: "The Divine Heart desires that we maintain special union with the angels, who are particularly destined to love, honor, and praise It in the divine Sacrament of Love in order that, being associated with them, they may in His Divine Presence plead for us."

### ADORATION.

Though never absent from the throne of the Heavenly Lamb, the angels press around the Eucharistic tabernacles, one of their chief functions being to adore the Heart of Jesus hidden under the sacramental veils.

As soon as the Lord had resolved to place His Heart prophetically on the Ark of the Covenant: *"Et erit Cor meum ibi cunctis diebus*—And my Heart will remain there perpetually "* (1), He ordered Moses " to cast two cherubim of beaten gold, which he set on the two sides of the propitiatory, spreading their wings, and covering the propitiatory, and looking one towards the other, and towards it." In our day, He orders the innumerable choirs of blessed spirits to adore Him really present and living in the Holy of Holies, the Humanity of the Word, hidden under the form of the Sacrament: *Cum iterum introducit Primogenitum in orbem terrae dicit. Et adorent eum omnes angeli dei*—And again,

---

(1)  II. Par. vii, 16.

when he bringeth in the first-begotten into the world, he saith: *And let all the angels of God adore him*(1).

They adore Him in the morning of their creation when, revealing to them the " Sacrament of His will and of His love," the Father showed them His only Son lying in a crib, clothed with the flesh of sinful man. Stupefied with wonder, they contemplate Him abased below themselves by the inferiority of His corporal nature: " *Qui modico quam angeli minoratus est*—Who was made a little lower than the angels "(2). But they recognize at the same time that the human Heart of their Creator, deified by His personal union with the Word, is as much superior to them as God is to the creature; therefore, they adore It humbly, for It was the Heart of Him to whom the Father said from all eternity: " Thou art my Son! Thy throne, O God, is forever and ever: a sceptre of justice is the sceptre of Thy Kingdom "(3).

They discover Him now still more abased in the annihilations of the sacramental state.

(1) Heb. i, 6.
(2) Heb. ii, 9.
(3) Heb. i, 8.

He has neither form nor movement nor warmth to reveal His Presence. He is, as it were, buried in the dust of the tomb. And yet, It is the immortal Heart of God resuscitated, the furnace of life and love, the ocean of all joy, the source of every good for heaven and earth! They adore It, and unreservedly devote themselves to Its service. The cherubim extend their wings over Its sacramental weakness to protect It, while fixing their eyes upon It to contemplate all the wonders that It contains. Nothing can separate them from Its presence, except Its own will and the execution of Its orders.

The chief of these true adorers, inaccessible to sleep or distraction is, without doubt, the Archangel St. Michael, who in heaven secured to the Word the adoration of the faithful angels. In contemplating the splendor of the divine nature in the Sacred Heart and the beauties of Its human nature, Its sanctity, Its love, Its magnificent works concealed under humility still more resplendent, he forever repeats to It, and the surrounding angels take up the refrain: " *Quis ut Deus?*—Who is like to God?" It is the homage of adoration, but powerless to express all that it feels. What pure spirit, however holy or mighty, is comparable to the Heart of God made man? Who deserves to be loved, served, and glorified as He?

How perfect is this adoration of the angelic spirits in whom is reflected the splendor of the Vision! They overflow with beatific love. Neither in the weight of the senses, nor in the resistance of the least egoism, nor in the illusion of the slightest shade of pride, do they encounter an obstacle to their adoration in spirit and in truth. Let us, then, unite with them to adore the Sacred Heart. Let us offer the love, submission, purity, and humility of their adoration. They invite us to adore with them, and the Sacred Heart approves it, finding therein glory and satisfaction.

"The Adorable Heart of my Jesus was shown to me," says Blessed Margaret Mary, "more brilliant than the sun. It was in the midst of the flames of His pure love, and surrounded by seraphim, who sang in ravishing harmony:

' Love triumphs, love enjoys;
The love of the Sacred Heart gladdens!'

" The blessed spirits invited me to join with them in praising the amiable Heart, but I dared not do it. Then they told me that they had come to unite with me in rendering It a continual homage of love, adoration, and praise, and at the same time they wrote this association in the Sacred Heart, in letters of gold and ineffaceable characters of love."

### THANKSGIVING.

Another function of the angels that stand before the face of God is to chant His praises, to bless Him and magnify Him in the joy of a gratitude always new. " All the angels," says St. John, " stand around the throne, singing in a loud voice: Amen! benediction and thanksgiving to our God forever and ever! Amen!" And to this canticle to the Divinity, they added praise to the Humanity of the Incarnate Word: " The Lamb that was slain is worthy to receive power and divinity and wisdom and strength and honor and glory and benediction!"

They owe to love and, consequently, to the Sacred Heart, the gift of their sublime nature, the privilege of their magnificent destiny, the grace of their perseverance in good and their victory over Lucifer—in fine, the glory and the beatitude of their recompense. All these benefits were granted them through the merits of the Word Incarnate, consequently, in view of the Adorable Heart of their Chief, through the merits of the love with which He deigned to love them, and of the suffering which He embraced in order to obtain for them eternal salvation. They experienced ineffable delights on receiving from the depths in which was hidden the Heart of their God illuminations unknown to them, and on feeling themselves inundated with joys springing from its love, for they clearly understood with what love the Sacred Heart was animated for them. They magnified It, also, for having made Itself the Bread of the viator, and for all the benefits which that good Heart never ceases to scatter among men in order to lead them to eat with themselves the Bread of Heaven at the eternal table. Their gratitude is pure, full, overflowing, disinterested. It binds them by irrevocable bonds to the liberal Heart from which they constantly behold flowing to them the plenitude of good.

The Archangel Gabriel leads the choir of thanksgiving, because he was the messenger of substantial grace, when he announced to Mary the inexpressible Gift of the Incarnation. It was he who placed upon her lips the canticle of gratitude *par excellence*, the *Magnificat*.

Let us unite in the *Alleluia*, chanted night and day by the angels around the Sacred Heart, and thus offer to It our thanksgivings, also. Let the first act of our gratitude be for the supremely loving thought of the Heart of the best of fathers in giving each of us one of His angels to conduct us, to guard us, to assist and console us. Ah! He well knew that we are weak, lonely, exposed, and unhappy! Let us, then, bless It for all the benefits that come to us through the devoted and vigilant protection of our angel guardians. They are for us one of the best gifts of the Sacred Heart.

" Once when I was in great sorrow," says Blessed Margaret Mary, " Our Lord came to console me, saying: ' My daughter, be not sad, for I am going to give thee a guardian who will accompany thee everywhere and hinder thy enemy from prevailing against thee. All the faults into which the latter will, by his suggestions, try to make thee fall, will turn to his own confusion.' This favor gave me such strength that it seemed to me that I had nothing to fear, for the faithful guardian of my soul assisted me so lovingly that he freed me from all my pains. Once he said to me: ' I want to tell thee who I am that thou mayst know the love thy Spouse has for thee. I am one of those that are nearest the throne of the Divine Majesty and participate most fully in the ardors of the Sacred Heart of Jesus Christ. My intention is to communicate them to thee in as great abundance as thou wilt be capable of receiving them.' "

### REPARATION.

The angels, pure spirits, established in beatitude, can not suffer. If Holy Scripture represents them uttering cries and weeping bitterly at sight of the multiplied disasters caused by the King of Assyria, *" Ecce vivendes clamabunt foris, angeli pacis amare flebunt*—Behold they that see shall cry without, the angels of peace shall weep bitterly " (1), it is to express the ar-

---

(1) Is. xxxiii, 7.

dor of their love and the tenderness of their compassion. They feel for us in the same way that God Himself pities us, namely, by a keen sense of our miseries, by assisting us powerfully, their own happiness in the meantime experiencing no diminution. No suffering can attack their incorporeal and glorified nature.

It is to their Adorable Chief, abased so far below them by the sufferings which in this life made up the condition of His existence, that their pity is first extended. They follow Him from the Crib to Calvary to strengthen Him, to sustain and console His Heart, into whch flow torrents of afflictions. They warmed Him with their breath on that cold December night of His birth. They extended over His Mother and Himself the shelter of their wings during their journey into exile through the sands of Egypt, and under the scorching sun. For forty days they were with Him in the desert ready to serve Him and to give Him the bread for which He hungered when Satan dared to insult Him by temptation. They strengthened Him in the terrors and the sweat of the bloody Agony when, falling prostrate on the ground, He implored His

Father to remove from Him the chalice of His wrath. They rushed in impatient legions to exterminate His enemies when the hideous troops went out to seize Him. But being restrained by His own mighty will, they followed the sacred Victim, unjustly condemned and ignominiously treated, from the prætorium to Golgotha, weeping over Him tears hot as their love. To drown the cries of blasphemy, they loudly proclaimed His praise. They encouraged Him to continue His heroic sacrifice, helping Him to walk, and supporting Him on the cross in His last agony. It was by such means that they eagerly lightened the supreme sorrow which the public abandonment of His Father inflicted on the faithful Heart of Jesus. It was to show their indignation that the angels who govern the world veiled the sun, shook the earth, and rent the rocks: *" Videntes clamabunt et angeli pacis amare flebunt!"*

Can it be supposed that the cherubim and seraphim, intrusted with the guardianship of the tabernacles and consecrated to the service of the Eucharistic Christ, would not weep over the neglected solitude in which He is left by those for whose salvation

He remains there? Will not their tears flow over the lack of zeal and fidelity, over the coldness and irreverence of even His friends? Will they not mourn over the outrages and profanation of which He is the victim, since He has embraced that state of feebleness and silence in order more surely to attach hearts to Him by the bonds of pity?—"*Ecce videntes angeli pacis amare flebunt!*"

The holy angels call us to make reparation in union with them. It is from this union of reparation that the Divine Heart, oppressed by man's deception, weighed down by bitterness and humiliations, looks for satisfaction and consolation. "The Divine Heart," says Blessed Margaret Mary, " seems to desire that we should have special union with the devotion of the holy angels, who are particularly destined to love, honor, and praise It in the divine Sacrament of Love. The reason of this is that, being united and associated with them, they may supply for us before His Divine Presence, as well to render Him our homage as to love Him for us and for all those who love Him not, and to repair the irreverences that we commit.

While compassionating the Heart saturated with opprobrium and broken by our crimes, the holy angels earnestly endeavor to cure us of the evils with which sin weighs down its miserable victims. The most efficacious remedy that they employ is to inspire a great devotion to the Sacred Heart, received and eaten under the veil of the Sacrament. As the Archangel Raphael, the admirable physician sent from heaven, ordered the young Tobias to take the heart of the fish that he had caught, promising him that it would be for him a necessary and very opportune remedy: *" Cor ejus retone tibi: sunt enim haec necessaria ad medicamenta utiliter*—Lay up his heart . for these are necessary for useful medicines "* (1). When, in effect, Tobias had burned a part of the fish's liver in the house of his fiancée, he put to flight the demon that had infested it and, by anointing the eyes of his aged father, restored to him his sight. And thus the Heart of the Divine Fish, the Sacred *Ichthus,* brought by Communion in contact with our heart, chases from it the demon, and dissipates the blindness of pride

(1) Tob. vi, 5.

and the illusions of the passions which drag down to sin. It is the remedy of immortality, absolutely necessary to preserve from death. It is the leaven of resurrection which raises from every fall. It is the antidote of sin, possessed of all virtues, whether to preserve or to deliver. Raphael and the holy angels that have charge of our souls urge us to use it assiduously: *"Cor ejus repone tibi!"*

### PETITION.

By nature and by vocation, the holy angels are the ministers of prayer, the Christian's powerful intercessors before God.

Holy Scripture shows them to us standing or prostrate, golden censer in hand, sending up to Him the sweet-scented fumes of their uninterrupted prayer. Jacob saw them untiringly ascending and descending the mysterious ladder which rested on the earth and reached to heaven, carrying up to God the prayers of men and bringing back to them His gifts. And the Divine Master, specifying this ministry of the angelic spirits, said: "Amen, amen, I say to you, you shall see the heavens opened, and the angels of God ascending and descending upon the Son of Man" (1). They are indefatigable messengers between His Heart and those that He has resolved to save.

Lastly, the Church in the liturgy of the Holy Mass, speaks of an angel who assists the priest and, after the Consecration of the Sacred Mysteries, she says: "We most humbly beseech Thee, Almighty God, command these things to be carried by the hands of Thy angel to Thy altar on high in the sight of Thy Divine Majesty—*Jube haec perferri per manus sancti angeli tui in sublime altare tuum in conspectu divinae Majestatis tuae.*" Is it the angel guardian of the officiating priest that is named here? Is it the angelic custodian of the temple and the altar? Is it an angel specially deputed by God for the service of the Holy Sacrifices? Or perhaps it is St. Michael, whom the Church invokes by name in the offertory of the Mass for the dead. The angels constantly exercise their mediation between the Eucharistic Christ and those whom He nourishes with His Flesh after having sanctified them with the oblation

---

(1) John i, 51.

of His Blood. "Since the day that this altar was consecrated, I have obeyed the order to remain always near it," said an angel to a holy priest who saw him standing near the altar during the celebration of the Holy Mysteries: "*Ex quo sanctificatum est altare istud, ego jugiter illi adstare jussus sum.*"

Who can express the perfection and efficacy of angelic prayer? The inebriating perfume that it exhales before God is composed of the odors of stainless purity, ardent love, most profound devotion, unwavering fidelity, and unbounded loyalty to the divine will. The angels are the friends of God and, after Mary and Joseph, the beings most dear to the Heart of Jesus. What can It refuse them? They love us. They are entirely devoted to us. Having the care of our interests and responsible for our salvation, they know our real needs, they are aware of the designs of God over us. They are powerful, they are prudent, they are faithful. Their prayer is ardent and continuous. Nothing distracts it, nothing discourages it, not even our obstinacy in not profiting by it. What may we not expect from their intercession?

It is our duty to secure their concurrence when we pray, uniting our prayer to theirs, offering its perfection and merits to supply for the defects of our own. Like the Psalmist, let us say: *"In conspectu angelorum psallam tibi*—I will sing praise to thee in the sight of the angels"*(1). St. Ephrem says: " Be like an angel during the time of prayer. Try to make it so pure, so holy, so faultless that, when the angels and the archangels see it coming from your heart, they may joyfully hasten to receive it and present it to God, embellished with their own immaculate purity. During your hour of prayer remain united to God like the cherubim and seraphim."

Let us, then, constantly and confidently make use of the ministry of the angels with the Sacred Heart. They desire to promote our joy, and they have no greater longing themselves than that we should know and love that blessed Heart. " One day," says Blessed Margaret Mary, " I saw the amiable Heart of Jesus on a throne of flames, Its Wound shedding around rays so ardent and so luminous that the whole vicinity was

---

(1) Ps. cxxxvii, 1.

heated and lighted up. The daughters of the Visitation appeared in this place, each holding a heart in her hand. They approached to present to the Divine Heart those that they held. Some, when they touched the Sacred Wound, became beautiful, lovely, and shining like stars; others turned black and horrible. There were several whose names remained inscribed in golden characters in the Sacred Heart, into which they glided and abyssed themselves on all sides with avidity and pleasure, exclaiming: 'It is in this abyss of love that we find our dwelling and our rest forever!' They were the hearts of those that have labored most to make that of our Divine Master known and loved."

Beg the angels of the tabernacle to increase your love for the Eucharist.

May the Sacred Heart of Jesus be loved everywhere!

(100 *days' indulgence.*)

# Twenty=third Day.

## THE SACRED HEART AND PURGATORY.

SUBJECT.—Central star of the supernatural world, the Sacred Heart is the light and life of all devotions. If we wish more clearly to comprehend the doctrinal truth of each one of them and cause their sanctifying virtues to gush forth more abundantly, we must expose them to the radiance of the Sacred Heart, namely, to the love of Our Lord. This is what we shall now proceed to do with regard to devotion to the souls in purgatory.

In revealing His Heart, the adorable Head of the Church Suffering desired to renew the devotion of the Faithful to the dear captives of fire and ardent longing. He consecrated to their service the confidante(1) of His most secret desires. He showed in His Heart the inexhaustible treasure of help necessary for their relief and deliverance. It is remarkable that the first time the Sacred

---

(1) Blessed Margaret Mary.

Heart was honored by the novices of Paray, kneeling around their holy mistress before a little pen-and-ink picture of the Adorable Heart, after " an act of reparation and of consecration, canticles, and prayers, followed by a prolonged adoration in silence to render homage to the Sacred Heart, Blessed Margaret Mary animated those first disciples of hers to devote the rest of the day to prayer for the souls in purgatory." Inspired by this example, let us reanimate our charity toward the souls suffering in the flame of the Sacred Heart.

### ADORATION.

While professing the doctrine of purgatory with the Catholic Church, let us adore under the feeble covering of the Sacrament the Creator of purgatory and the Head of the Church Suffering. It is from the meeting in the Sacred Heart " of mercy and truth," and from the kiss there exchanged between " justice and peace " that this institution, terrible yet full of condescending love, was born. Purgatory punishes by tortures unknown to earth the slightest remains of stains or debts of sin, and while punishing, purifies and delivers the soul from those stains. By a merciful reprieve, it permits the soul to finish the preparation required before taking its place in the eternal festival of the Lamb without stain.

Sanctity and Justice enkindle the fire that sensibly devours and the desire that spiritually consumes. The soul is plunged therein as long as there remains a stain of sin to efface, a farthing of debt to pay. Oh, how terrible are the sanctity and justice of the Sacred Heart, and what awful light the fire of purgatory projects upon them! Perhaps, we limit our view of the Sacred Heart to seeing in It only Its character of goodness, the pity and tenderness of Its love, because we have so much need of them. But what would be that love if it were not so holy as to be unable to unite itself to any alloy, so just as not to seek at any cost to satisfy the rights of God?

Purgatory makes these perfections of the Sacred Heart shine forth in all their splendor. It shows It to us as holy, as just as It is loving. But it is very true that there, as everywhere else, love rules and that " Its mercies are above all Its works."

The Sacred Heart constantly operates therein the work of Redemption, effecting by the merits of Its Passion and death, renewed upon the Eucharistic altar, the purification from their faults and the liberation from their debts of the dear captives. The sweet Shepherd of the Sacrament watches over this low region of His empire. He sheds light upon the darkness that envelops it, He pours waves of refreshment upon the fires that devour it, He penetrates it with an atmosphere of peace and of silent resignation. He keeps alive therein love and hope: a love that no sin can kill, a hope assured of its recompense. He lives there, and the dear souls, tortured beyond all expression, live there, notwithstanding, of His life and for His glory. Let us adore Him with them: "*Regem cui omnia vivunt, venite adoremus!* —Come, let us adore the King from whom all things live!"(1)

The Divine Master revealed the ties that bind purgatory to the Eucharist by permitting Blessed Margaret Mary, the confidante of His Heart, to receive when in His Presence, either on the night of Holy Thursday or on the feast of Corpus Christi, a revelation concerning the sufferings of those

---

(1) *Invit. Off. Defunctorum.*

souls. "One Holy Thursday night, when praying before the Blessed Sacrament for a certain soul, Our Lord showed it to her under the foot of the chalice in which He reposed, and where this dear soul was finishing its purgatory. It was then that the Heart of all pity asked her to abandon herself to It without reserve that It might give her to those dear suffering souls to do for them all the good that she could."

### THANKSGIVING.

However terrifying the sight of the exactions of that Sanctity which purifies souls in material fire and in the fire of unquenchable desires, it is not less true that the thought which presided over the creation of purgatory is one of supreme mercy. Our thanksgiving in time and in eternity will not suffice to praise it as it merits.

The normal time of trial is the measure of life granted to each one on this earth. The divine munificence has filled it with precious gifts, the providence of the Redeemer has supplied it with powerful institutions, and He shares it in person with us, leading us, feeding us, and raising us constantly from our faults. It seems, indeed, however little our fidelity, that eternal recompense awaits us. In every case Justice and Mercy would appear well justified to judge definitely on that last evening of life, " on which ends the day, after which we can no longer labor." And this judgment would be heaven for those that have here below washed their robe from every stain in the Blood of the Lamb, and hell for those others whom a stain, however slight, renders unworthy. If it had pleased the Lord, the Sovereign Master of His gifts, that it should be so, it would have been well done, and no one would have a right to demand of Him a reason.

But His mercy, which has guarded every moment of our life, wishes to survive that life and make itself felt even in the tomb, vivifying the dead, and making the dust germinate. So, it gives to all souls who do not die radically separated from Jesus Christ by mortal sin, a place to rest the foot in order not to fall into the abyss at the instant of perilous passage, an assured means of washing away the last remains of imperfection, a legal sum to discharge the whole temporal debt of their sins, a reprieve in which to finish their preparation for heaven. And this is purgatory! Whoever falls into it is sure of going to heaven.

And truly, were the fire still more fierce and the privation of the sight of God still more painful; were the period of this double punishment to last for ages, is it not clear that such a reprieve, to which we have no right, and a resumption of life so unheard-of, are an admirable and miraculous superaddition of God's mercy, the masterpiece of pity devised by the Heart of Our Saviour? For if every soul receives all and even more than is necessary to merit immediate entrance into heaven; if that is the only end at which the Saviour is aiming by His gifts and assistance, how many, in reality, render themselves worthy of it? One chosen one, alas! only one chosen one! *"Multi vocati pauci vero electi*—Many are called, but few chosen." The mass of Christians are saved, thanks only to the merciful reprieve of purgatory: *"Ipse salvus erit, sic tamen quasi per ignen*—He shall be saved, yet so as by fire "(1).

Those flames from which we cannot es-

---

(1) I Cor. iii, 15.

cape are absolutely necessary to produce the worthy fruits of penance demanded by our sins. This cruel privation of the possession of the Infinite Beauty, whom we have met and whom we should possess as soon as we quit this earth, makes us long for God, thus giving to love the satisfaction which we refused during life, and which alone merits the possession of God in heaven. Now, nothing appears too much to those dear souls. They see clearly now, and not content with accepting their pains, they bless them as the precious instruments of the least deserved and the most efficacious of mercies.

With them let us bless the Sacred Heart. Not satisfied with having gratuitously accorded them the grace of dying in Its love, which grace, in a certain way, no one can merit, It received them after their death that they might not fall into the eternal abyss: " *In Christo quiescentibus.*"

Jesus shelters them in the asylum of His Heart, living and full of hope, although hiding from them His glorious countenance and allowing them to be overwhelmned by incomprehensible sufferings. But He helps them by so many graces, by pure and generous love, by such strength, humility, and resignation, that they taste the certainty of reposing in His Heart.

Jesus loves them as the members of His Body, as flesh of His Flesh. He loves them as His children by whom He is loved in return with sovereign love indissolubly fixed on Himself. For although their love for Him is not without imperfection and deficiency, it is substantially the living and immortal love which unites them to Jesus and permits Him to live and abide in them.

And these dear souls see the love of Jesus for them. They are certain of it. They understand that new hope sprang up in their breast when the Sacred Heart, in manifesting Itself on earth, revealed to them, also, the treasures of love hidden up to that time, and with which It deigned to fill the Church in these latter days. They know that, if the tide overflows on earth, its salutary inundation must extend to the low regions in which they dwell. We read in the writings of Blessed Margaret Mary: "If you knew with what eagerness these poor souls implore this new remedy, so excellent for their sufferings! For it is thus they call the devotion to the Divine Heart."

### REPARATION.

Few considerations are so efficacious as that of purgatory for giving a clear understanding of the malice of sin, the injury it does to God, the wound that it inflicts on the Heart of Jesus, the prejudice that it brings to the soul. It arouses, in consequence, hatred for that sovereign evil, and impels to works of penance. Considering the Saviour's love for the souls in purgatory and their love for Him, how comprehend the horror, the depth, the duration of their torments simply to expiate small stains, the remains of sin, the temporal debts due to sin, except by admitting that the least fault is the greatest of evils, and that to preserve its stain is the greatest of misfortunes? We have only to open the book of the *Revelations of the Sacred Heart* to see with what severity that Heart of goodness and pity punishes after this life the voluntary faults of Its friends, and their neglect to purify themselves from them when on this earth, where It was holding open to them the sources of salutary expiation: " *In die erit fons patens habitantibus Jerusalem in ablutionem peccatoris*—In that day there shall be a fountain open to the inhabitants of Jerusalem for the washing of the sinner "(1).

The following revelation, touching their physical pains, shows that they differ little from those of hell itself:

"Once," says Blessed Margaret Mary, "I saw in a dream one of our Sisters who had been dead for some time. She told me that she was suffering much in purgatory. I awoke at these words, and so full of pain that it seemed to me that she had impressed her own upon me. My whole body was so bruised that it was painful to me to move. She gave me no peace, but constantly repeated to me: 'Pray to God for me. Offer Him your sufferings in union with those of Jesus Christ to relieve mine!'

"Approaching my bed, she said to me: 'You are taking your ease in bed. Look where I am lying on a bed of flames, on which I am suffering intolerable evils.'— And showing me that horrible bed, which makes me tremble whenever I think of it, with its sharp fiery spikes which pierced the flesh, she told me that it was for her in-

(1) Zach. xiii, 1.

fidelities to God and her negligence in the observance of her Rules.

" ' They tear my heart with red-hot iron combs,—and that is my most cruel suffering,—for the thoughts of murmuring and disapprobation that I entertained against my superioress. My tongue is eaten by vermin in punishment of my words against charity, and my whole mouth is ulcerated for my little attention to silence.'

" ' Oh, that all souls consecrated to God could see me in this torment! If I could make them feel the greatness of my pains and those that are prepared for religious who live carelessly in their vocation, doubtless, they would walk with renewed ardor in the way of exact observance. They would take good care not to fall into the defects that make me suffer so much!'— On another occasion, when they wanted to give me some remedies, that soul said to me: ' They are thoughtful to relieve you in your misery, but no one thinks of alleviating mine!'

" Another time, as I was before the Blessed Sacrament on the days of Its feast, a soul all on fire suddenly presented itself before me. The heat that came from it so penetrated me that I, too, seemed to be burning. The pitiable state of the soul gave me to understand that it was in purgatory, and forced from me an abundance of tears. It told me that it was the soul of a Benedictine monk, who had once heard my confession and ordered me to receive Holy Communion. In consideration of this, God had permitted him to address himself to me to obtain relief in his suffering. He asked me for all that I could do and suffer during three months, and he gave me three reasons for his great sufferings. The first was, because he had preferred his own interest to the glory of God, by too great attachment to his reputation; the second was his want of charity toward his brethren; and the third, the too natural affection he had had for creatures, and the too great testimony he had given of it in his spiritual conversations with them, which displeased God much. It would be difficult to express what I had to suffer during those three months. That soul never quitted me and, on the side where he was, it seemed to me to see him all on fire, and with pains so acute that I was forced to groan and weep almost continually."

The Blessed Sister again wrote: " I beg some special help for our poor Sister N———, for whom I have been offering since the new year all that I could do and suffer. She gave me no repose until I had made her the promise to do penance for her. She told me that she was suffering much, especially for three things: the first was for her too great delicacy and bodily indulgence; the second was for tale-bearing and failures in charity; and the third for certain petty points of ambition."

Blessed Margaret Mary, the dear confidante, entering into the desires of the Sacred Heart, offered herself as a victim to Divine Justice in behalf of the poor souls, and the Sacred Heart immolated her without pity to Its requirements. She said of this: " It seems to me that everything serves as an instrument for Divine Justice to torment me. Nothing makes me suffer more than this sanctity of justice. It is a torment which seeks as a remedy only crosses, humiliations, sorrows, pains of all kinds, under which I would succumb a thousand times, if His goodness did not sustain me in an extraordinary manner."

### PETITION.

The solicitous love which fills the Heart of the Divine Shepherd for the suffering portion of His flock, and the eminent dignity to which He raises the least of the children of men by calling them to co-operate by an active ministry in the work of Redemption, give us to understand that nothing enters more fully into His desires than to offer one's self to plead for and to satisfy for the souls in purgatory. The increase of love for God, which is the necessary fruit of devotion to the Sacred Heart well understood, ought to be accompanied by an increase of charity for the dear neighbor so needy and so deserving of pity. Blessed Margaret Mary says: " I abandoned myself to the direction and the conduct of the Sacred Heart, which has deigned to do me this charity. And It often gives Its poor victim to the souls in purgatory to help them and to satisfy Divine Justice. At such times I endure a pain almost like their own, finding rest neither day nor night."

The Sacred Heart made known to her two efficacious means for the relief of the dear souls: prayer, and acts done in union with Its own.

First, prayer of every form, but above all sacramental prayer, namely, the Holy Mass, the full application of the death and merits of Jesus. The Saviour said: "These poor souls especially implore Masses in honor of the Sacred Heart." Secondly, Holy Communion, which renders the soul so pleasing to Jesus and so powerful over His Heart. "A deceased religious bids me apply to you, my dear Mother, for a general Communion," wrote Blessed Margaret Mary to a certain superioress. Thirdly, adoration of the Blessed Sacrament, for it was when the Blessed Sister prolonged her prayer at the foot of the tabernacle that the suffering souls surrounded her, imploring her intercession.

The virtues indicated by the Sacred Heart or by the souls in purgatory themselves as the most efficacious are purity, charity, mortification, and humility. These virtues Blessed Margaret Mary begged her Sisters to practise in union with the Sacred Heart, and in the Sacred Heart Itself with the soul turned toward the Blessed Sacrament. "The first thing in the morning, place yourself in the Sacred Heart, consecrating yourself entirely to It with all that you shall think and say. Offer to Jesus in the Blessed Sacrament all the Holy Masses that shall be celebrated throughout the Holy Church, which you will beg your good angel to hear and offer to God to appease His justice.

"In the evening, make a little turn through purgatory in company with the Sacred Heart, consecrating to It all that you shall have done, begging It to apply its merits to those holy suffering souls. At the same time, implore them to make use of their power to obtain for you the grace to live and die in love and fidelity to the Sacred Heart by unresistingly corresponding to Its desires in your regard."

To encourage devoton and stimulate zeal, she used to say, smilingly: "Let us think of our good friends and ask Our Lord's mercy for them. They will not forget us!"

The following prayer to the Sacred Heart, indulgenced by Leo XIII, of blessed memory, proves how good it is to invoke that dear Heart for the souls in purgatory:

"*O divinum Cor Jesu, praesta, quaeso, animabus purgantibus requiem aeternam, hodie morituris gratiam finalem, peccatoribus veram poenitentiam, paganis fidei lucem, mihi meisque omnibus tuam benedictionem. Tibi ergo, Cor Jesu piissimum, omnes has animas commendo et pro ipsis tibi offero omnia tua merita, una cum meritis Beatissimae Matris tuae, omniumque sanctorum et angelorum; atque omnibus missarum sacrificiis, sacris communionibus, orationibus et bonis operibus, quae hodie in toto chrstianorum orbe peraguntur.*—O Divine Heart of Jesus, grant, I conjure Thee, eternal rest to the souls in purgatory! To those that will die today, grant the final grace; to sinners, true contrition; to pagans, the light of faith; to me and mine, Thy blessing! To Thee, O most merciful Heart of Jesus, I commend all these souls, and for them I offer to Thee Thy own sacred merits along with those of Thy Blessed Mother, of all the angels and saints, together with all the Masses, Holy Communions, prayers, and good works which shall be performed today throughout the whole Christian world!"

By a Brief of March 13, 1901, Leo XIII accorded to all who recite this prayer *one hundred days'* Indulgence, once a day, applicable to the souls in purgatory.

Beg Our Lord to increase your devotion toward the Holy Souls in purgatory.

Let us adore, thank, supplicate, and console with Mary Immaculate the most sacred and beloved Eucharistic Heart of Jesus.

(200 *days' Indulgence.*)

# Twenty=fourth Day.

## " BEHOLD THIS HEART."

THE heart of Jesus is the origin of the Eucharist, because His love alone, attaining supreme power, inspired the Saviour on the last night of His earthly life to make to His own, whom He could not resolve to leave, this gift of Himself. For this reason, the Sacred Heart may be called the Eucharistic Heart, that is, the Heart which gives us the Eucharist. But still more: if we consider It as present, living and acting, loving us, immolating Itself for us in sacrifice, giving Itself to us in Communion, in the Christ veiled by the sacramental signs, it is, then, the Sacred Heart which by incessantly renewing, perpetuates the love and the gift of the Eucharist.

It is under this aspect that we shall render to It our homage in the present adoration. The Heart of the Eucharistic Christ in Its truth and Its life is the object of our adoration. In Its love and Its benefits, It is the object of our thanksgiving. In the offences inflicted upon It by the ingratitude of men, It is the object of our reparation. In the power of Its untiring intercession, It is the object of our petitions.

We shall reflect on the grand revelation of the Sacred Heart: "Behold this Heart that has so loved men!—In return I receive, for the most part, only ingratitude—Do thou, at least, try to console Me by making Me some return!"

### ADORATION.

"Behold this Heart that has so loved men!" said the Saviour, showing His Heart to Blessed Margaret Mary. The Blessed Sister tells us: "One day, the Blessed Sacrament being exposed, Jesus Christ, my sweet Saviour, appeared before me sparkling with glory, His five wounds brilliant as five suns. From His Sacred Humanity shot forth flames on all sides, but more than all from His adorable breast, which looked like a furnace. Opening it, He disclosed to me His loving and lovable Heart, the living source of those flames."

In this way does the Sacred Heart present Itself to the adoration of His creatures: in the breast of Christ really present under the Sacramental veils. It is the furnace of the glorified life lived by the Sacred Humanity in the Sacrament, and of the life of grace that It pours into souls by the Eucharist. All this is clearly signified by the flames issuing from the Sacred Heart, which transform the breast of Christ into a glowing furnace, and which shine like suns in the wounds of His hands and feet.

It is, indeed, true that, in virtue of the sacramental state, to which It is reduced by Consecration, the Sacred Heart, as is the whole Body of Christ, is, as it were, annihilated, without extent, without form, without physical communication with the outward world. But, again, like the Eucharistic Body, It retains the integrity of Its substance and intrinsic life. And because in man the heart is the symbol, as well as the principal organ, of life, the Divine Master by showing His Heart, proclaims that He is living in the Eucharst; and that His mode of material existence does not prevent His being a human composite, resulting from a soul and a body personally united to the Word, who deifies them, and re-unites them by immortal resurrection never again to be separated by death.

No manifestation could better reply to Protestant heresy, which pretends that the Eucharist is only the symbol of Christ's Body, but not the Body itself. By showing His Heart in His breast, by showing It glowing like a brazier, Christ declares the integral reality of His Body and the truth of His corporal life, for a living heart means a living body. He proclaims the truth of His mortal life, for the human heart can beat only under the impulse of a human soul. He manifests the truth of His divine life, for never would the Body and Soul of Christ have existed if not borne by the Word. Whoever sees the living Heart of the Christ, sees the sanctuary in which resides the Word Incarnate, deifying the Sacred Humanity of Jesus and causing It to live personally of the life of God Himself.

But as life necessarily manifests itself by action, the Heart of Christ revealed in the Sacrament, reminds us that, under the appearance of death, the Eucharistic Christ operates, acts, spreads abroad the radiance of life. His is the life of a creature the most submissive to the Creator, the life of a servant the most devoted to his master, the life of a son the most loving toward his father, the life of a priest the most faithful, of a religious the most holy in view of the majesty and sanctity of the Most High. His is a life of all the virtues in their most intense perfection. They arrest and fix upon themselves the complacency of God, they form the infinite delight of God.

The Sacred Heart is, at the same time, the furnace whence spreads the life of grace throughout the whole Church and in each individual soul, for it is from the plenitude of Jesus that we receive everything, and grace for grace—*De plenitudine ejus omnes accepimus, et gratiam pro gratia*(1). For the Church it means unity in hierarchy and fraternity, universal expansion, uninterrupted duration which no obstacle can break, together with sanctity of doctrine, Sacraments and morals. For souls, it means all the grace of the most diverse states, of all virtues, of all duties, all progress in good, all the holy deaths that open the way to the perfect life of God in heaven. All these beautiful forms of grace, these beams so luminous, these beneficent and triumphant forces of life, flow forth

(1) John i, 16.

abundantly in copious, inexhaustible streams from the Eucharistic Heart of Jesus. They are all only manifestations of the eternal life, of which the Eucharist is the Bread.

" Behold this Heart! "

Behold the Heart *par excellence,* the unique Heart, the Heart of Jesus and our Heart, also, which the living Sacrament of Jesus offers to us that we may acknowledge, adore, and exalt It with piety, attention, and fidelity : " *Omni custodia serva Cor tuum; quia ex ipso vita procedit*—With all watchfulness keep thy Heart, because life issueth out from It "(1).

### THANKSGIVING.

" Behold this Heart which has so loved men that It has spared nothing, even to exhausting and consuming Itself, in order to testify to them Its love ! "

The Heart of the Saviour in the Sacrament is the object of our thanksgiving as well as of our adoration; for if the heart is the furnace of life, it is, also, the source of love and of all the benefits that manifest it.

(1) Prov. iv, 23.

And as " from the *heart* of a good man
cometh forth good things, new and old :
*Bonus homo de bono thesauro profert bona,
nova, et vetera* "(1), so is the Heart of
Christ in the Sacrament the ever open
source whence flow forth the goods new and
old, brought to the world by the Redeemer.

The memorial of ancient benefits, His
Heart repeats to us that God so loved the
world as to give to it His only Son in the
Incarnation. It tells us that this Son, although we were His enemies, after having
lavished upon us all the treasures of His
prayers and virtues, His teaching and beneficent power, His pity and mercy, loved
us so far as to deliver Himself to death. It
tells us, again, that having loved us to that
extreme, He willed to love us to the end,
by giving Himself to us in the Eucharist
before returning to His Father.

These ancient loves His Heart incessantly
renews for us in the Sacrament, since the
Sacrifice that Jesus daily offers, is the perfect reproduction of His death as Redeemer. Communion gives to every soul
the Flesh and Blood, the life, the strength,

---

(1) Matt. xii, 35.

and consolation that He imparted to His Apostles at the Last Supper. The abiding Presence in the tabernacle is the prolongation of His beneficent and protecting Presence among men when dwelling corporally in their midst.

Lastly, His Heart in revealing itself surrounded by flames in the Sacrament, tells us that He there loves us with an actual and personal love, which no ingratitude can extinguish. It declares that It longs to communicate Itself, to give Itself to every soul. Every Host is a burning brand meant to enkindle a fire of gratitude, fidelity, and generosity in the hearts of all men.

The Sacred Heart is the Eucharistic Christ's reply to Jansenism, which aims at restraining man by fear and crushing in him every spark of love and confidence, by representing so exclusively the holiness and majesty of the Saviour as to render Him inaccessible to human weakness and misery. "My Divine Heart is so passionately enamored of men that, no longer able to restrain the flame of Its burning charity, It must needs allow them to spread abroad. It must manifest them in order to enrich men with these precious treasures." And the

Son of God, who had need of nothing nor of any one, deigned to utter this ineffable desire: " I ardently thirst to be loved by men in the Sacrament of My love! "

### REPARATION.

" Behold this Heart that has so loved men! In return, I receive for the most part only ingratitude and forgetfulness. That grieves Me more than all I suffered in My Passion. If they would make Me some return of love, I should esteem as little all I have done for them, and I should wish, were it possible, to do more. But by coldness and rebuffs they meet My eagerness to do them good! Do thou, at least, console Me by supplying for their ingratitude as much as thou canst."

The Divine Saviour proposes His Heart in the Sacrament as the object of our reparation, because, in reality, it is that Heart that is struck by all the sins of mankind. It is the direct object of all sins formally committed against the Eucharist, such as irreverence, sacrilegious Masses and Communions, profanation, the violation of the day consecrated to the Eucharistic Sacrifice, and the contempt of the Paschal precept. It is the object of the ingratitude shown Its ardent and eager love in the Eucharist by the tepidity, the coldness and indifference, the disrelish and abandonment with which we too frequently respond to Its advances.

But every mortal sin being a sin of ingratitude toward God, which extinguishes in the soul the love that the creature owes his Creator, every mortal sin is a sin against the Heart burning with love in the Eucharist. Mortal sin is so much the more dreadful as this Sacrament is the sign, the memorial, the most eloquent proclamation of all the love that Christ had and still has for mankind. To repel Its love is, then, to repel the Heart of the Eucharistic Christ. To extinguish love in the soul of a Christian, a member of Jesus, would be to crush life out of the Heart of the Saviour Himself, if such a thing could be done. But most certainly, it was of those blows that He died upon the Cross. Every sin attacks the life of the Sacred Heart.

Again, all the less grave sins, venial sin, the habit of venial sin, affection to venial sin, and tepidity. which results from it without actually killing love, weaken its life.

They enfeeble its action, tarnish its brilliancy, dull its sentiment, render it, in fine, so heavy and languishing, so disagreeable and repulsive, that the Sacred Heart cannot support such a soul, but threatens to cast it forth.

It is, indeed, to the Sacred Heart, the Sacramental Victim of the sins of mankind, that reparation ought to be directed as to its first and immediate object. The Saviour Himself calls for it in behalf of " sinners, to obtain mercy for them; and for tepid souls who continue to inflict upon Him the bitterness that He experienced from the sleep of the Apostles during His agony. The reparation of the devout can alleviate that bitterness."

Which are the chief means of reparation? Holy Communion, most fervent and frequent; the Holy Hour, or that of adoration, in which we keep Him company; the worship of His Sacred Heart and the spread of Its reign; but, above all, love, love grateful for Its benefits, compassionate for Its humiliations, penitent and filled with those generous expiations that It sighs for: " Do thou, at least, try to console Me by making Me some return! "

PETITION.

" My Heart shall remain there forever—
*Et erit Cor meum ibi cunctis diebus*" said
the Lord when He accepted as a house of
prayer the Temple which Solomon had built
to Him (1). He gave this prophetic image
of His Heart to excite confidence in all who
would come to pray there. It was to be, in
advance, a pledge of His watchfulness over
their needs, and of His loving care in providing for them. When revealing His
Heart truly living and always present in the
Sacrament, the Saviour said to Blessed Margaret Mary: " Help shall fail thee only
when power shall fail My Heart." This
shows us how anxiously the Sacred Heart
awaits our prayers in order to answer them.

The Sacred Heart exists for our prayers.
It is the sanctuary in which they find God
personally present, in which they are offered
to Him and heard by Him. The Sacred
Heart is the adorable object which we ought
to invoke confidently, because It is love,
goodness, compassion, riches, providence,
and power.

The Sacred Heart is the assured means

_____

(1) II Par. vii, 16.

of rendering our prayers efficacious, if we offer them through It, for It is the Heart of the Holy Priest, always heard by the Father. That Heart perfects and sanctifies our prayers. It is the Heart of the innocent Victim, who delivered Himself to purchase in advance all the favors that we beg of God in His name.

We must, then, enter into the Sacred Heart and remain there to pray to the Father, to pray to Itself, and to pray through It.

"I have found My Heart that I may pray to my God," said the devout St. Bernard: *"Inveni Cor meum, ut orem Deum meum,* that is, the Heart of my King, of my Father and my Friend Jesus! I shall enter into this Sanctuary, in which Thou dost always answer prayer, O my God, and I shall confidently pour forth my petitions."

Blessed Margaret Mary said: "When you wish to pray, enter into this Sacred Heart as into an oratory, in which you will find wherewith to pay God what you owe Him, by offering Our Lord's prayer to supply for the defects of your own, by · loving God with the love of His Divine Heart, adoring with His adoration, praising with His praise, working with His works, and willing with His will." Behold the infallible means of being favorably heard and of always accomplishing the divine will.

After the Sacred Supper during which He had forever enclosed His Heart in the Eucharistic sanctuary, behind the sacred veil of bread, Our Lord said: " Abide in me. Abide in my love," which words mean: " Abide in My Heart. If ye abide therein, all that ye ask shall be given you. My Father is glorified in granting you all that ye ask in My name."

Let us, then, in all our needs, in every affliction, however desperate, in every necessity of Church or State, let us go with confidence and perseverence to the Heart of the Eucharistic Christ hidden in the depths of the Sacrament. Almighty God will be glorified by all the favors, all the pardon, all the victories that He shall be pleased to grant us: " *Accedet homo ad Cor altum, et exaltabitur Deus!* Man shall come to a deep Heart, and God shall be exalted " (1).

Perform an act of charity in honor of the Eucharistic Heart of Jesus.

Eucharistic Heart of Jesus, have pity on us !

(300 *days' Indulgence.*)

_____
(1)  Ps. lxiii, 7, 8.

# Twenty-fifth Day

## THE HOLY EUCHARIST AND THE SACRED HEART.

### ADORATION.

OUR object in the following pages is, to win for the Holy Eucharist greater love, by showing the adorable Heart of Jesus present in It, living in It, rendering It so loving and so lovable, so powerful and so patient, so worthy of the complacency of Heaven and the desires of earth.

The Holy Eucharist and the Sacred Heart are not, indeed, one and the same, as is sometimes said, and the devotion to the Sacred Heart, closely considered, is found to be distinct from the devotion to the Blessed Sacrament.

The material object of the former is the Heart of Jesus, His Heart of flesh, considered in the triple phase of Its living existence, namely, in Its mortal life, in Its Eucharistic life, in Its glorious life in heaven. Its formal, or moral, object is all the love for us that Jesus has drawn from

His Heart in being born, in living, in instituting the Eucharist, in dying on the Cross, and in ascending to heaven to prepare for us our everlasting abode. The material object of the devotion to the Blessed Sacrament is the Sacred Humanity and, consequently, the whole Adorable Person of Jesus residing in the Eucharist; and its motive is the love that He therein testifies to us, and the remembrance of His Passion, which He recalls to us incessantly by its daily renewal therein.

These two devotions are, consequently, distinct in their object. But they have, nevertheless, points of resemblance so numerous, they so closely support and embrace each other that, in practice, if we desire to attain the perfection of each, we must unite them into a single one.

Souls devout to the Sacred Heart will gain much by always seeking the divine object of their love in the Sacrament which presents It to them present and living, which places It under their eyes, in their hands, and in their breasts. Souls devout to the Holy Eucharist will find immense profit in penetrating beyond the outward appearance of the Sacred Species, in plunging into the

profound secrets of the Sacrament, into the
Adorable Body Itself, in order to discover
therein the Sacred Heart of Jesus, which
makes the Eucharist a living Being, loved
and loving, and leading for God and for us
a life full to overflowing.

To be satisfied with honoring the Sacred
Heart in Its pictures, and not to know how
to find It in Its Eucharistic reality, is to
understand It but little, to neglect the principal objects of the devotion to the Sacred
Heart, namely, Jesus' Heart of flesh actually present among us, and the greatest
proof of His love, the Holy Eucharist. And
not to know how to discover the Heart of
Jesus under the lifeless Species of the Sacrament, is not to comprehend the Eucharist
as It should be comprehended.  If It has
no Heart, if we do not find in It the Heart
of Our Saviour, what can this Sacrament
be for us?   And if we do not habitually
meet there that Heart, how shall we love
It sufficiently to honor and serve It as It
deserves?  Where would be our confidence
to tell It of our needs, our desires, our
troubles?

Whether we have an attraction to the Sacred Heart or to the Holy Eucharist, in

order to receive all the graces that these two devotions offer us, we must reach the Heart of Jesus living in the Blessed Sacrament, we must know and adore It therein, honor It, and unite ourselves to It in Holy Communion.

May the points of doctrine upon which we are going to touch relative to the presence, the action, and effects of the Heart of Jesus in the Eucharist, lead our readers more easily, and with greater fruit to themselves, to that Heart of our God and Saviour become so really ours by His Presence in the Sacrament of the Altar!

It is a dogma of faith that Jesus is living in the Blessed Sacrament in all the integrity of His Sacred Humanity. He is there with His Body, His Blood, His Soul, and His Divinity—*Christus totus!* And He is living, for St. Paul says: "Christ since the day of His resurrection is living, and He shall die no more."—On Easter morn, all the Blood that Jesus had shed during His Passion in Gethsemani, in the praetorium, on the road to Calvary, on the Cross, was gathered into golden vases by the angels eager for that ministry of life.

Thence it was poured into the Heart of Jesus, and when the holy Soul entered into Its august sanctuary, the reanimated Heart of Jesus beat with joy. It sent Its vermilion waves into the arteries, It tinged the Saviour's cheeks discolored by death. It recommenced to pulsate in Jesus' breast with a pulsation that was never more to cease. It animates His glorified Body in the celestial Jerusalem. And when the priest consecrates the Sacred Host, it is Jesus Christ entire, His whole Humanity that the almighty words enclose under the veil of the Sacramental Species. The Saviour's Body possesses therein all its organs, all its members. They are all animated by the Blood which flows from the Heart, and which laves them with its vivifying currents. It is true that Jesus reduces that corporal life to a point, that He withdraws it from our gaze, that it escapes our most earnest researches. It is true that that life is not in communication with any exterior agents, and that for its existence it has need neither of air to breathe, nor space, nor nourishment. This is the profound mystery of the Eucharist, that Christ should be therein entire, but in the manner of substances altogether like unto that of pure spirits. We ought to adore Him in humble and submissive faith. But the darkness in which Jesus shrouds His Humanity in the Blessed Sacrament ought not to make us forget that He is really there in all His truth, in all His integrity, with all His members, all His organs, all the fulness of His life, glorified and immutable.

The seat of that life, the source of the Blood that feeds it, the bond of the Saviour's members, in which shine the marks of the Five Wounds, the centre of that Eucharistic Humanity, is the Heart of Jesus, His Heart of flesh, formed of the most pure blood of Mary. Living, beating, that Heart is in each of the consecrated Hosts on our altars, and in every particle that may be detached from them. The Host is not the Heart alone of Jesus, but without that Heart there would be no Host.

## THANKSGIVING.

The Host is Jesus in the integrity of His Humanity. This Humanity rests upon His Heart from which flows all life, says Holy Scripture, and which is the first organ to live in us and the last to die, accord-

ing to the dictum of scientists. Let us then
study It, study It well. The Sacred Host
is the Adorable Person of Jesus. It is
His Divinity, His Soul, His Body, His
true Body, perfect and entire. Prostrate
before the Host, we may in spirit kiss the
adorable hands and feet of Jesus. We have
a right to aspire even to the " kiss of His
mouth." We may gaze in spirit upon His
divine countenance. His eyes are fixed
upon us, His ears are attentive to our supplications. How, then, could we neglect
His Heart, His sweet Heart, in which took
birth the divine plan of the Eucharist,
which led the Saviour to institute It, to perpetuate for us the Real Presence, which
daily offers us the Bread of our Communion, and which, up to this moment, is inflamed for us with a love infinite, tender,
patient, though, perhaps, saddened and afflicted because of our failure to comprehend His love, His Presence, His truth?

The Heart of Jesus in the Host is both
human and divine, finite and infinite, created
and uncreated; that is to say, in Its nature
and Its origin, It is the Heart of a man,
formed of flesh, but in Its term, It is united
personally to the Word of God. It has be-

come, and It remains the Heart of the Word, at one and the same time the Heart of the Son of God and the Heart of the Son of Mary. The Second Person of the Most Holy Trinity has united Himself to It hypostatically, that is to say, He has made It His member, His organ forever. He has thereby elevated that simple, created, material organ above all spiritual and angelic substances. It is, without any exaggeration, the Heart of God. Its dignity, Its price are literally infinite as a result of that marvellous union with the Word. That Heart, in consequence, performs the infinite operations of the Word Himself, and It deserves the homage due to God alone. By that Heart, the Word loves us with His eternal love; by that Heart, He knows us with His infinite knowledge; by that Heart, He desires us all good. He loves His Father with that Heart. He offers to Him His infinite worship of adoration, praise, prayer, and propitiation. These marvels, these infinite operations, this multiple life is constantly going on in each of the Hosts in our tabernacles, in the profound silence, in the neglected solitude to which, alas! we too often abandon them.

But the Heart of Jesus claims in each of our sanctuaries, under the covering of bread, a divine worship, the worship of supreme adoration of *latria.* We must recognize It as the Heart of Jesus substantially united to the Divine Nature in the Person of the Word. We must contemplate It clothed with the majesty of God Himself, holy with the infinite holiness of God, good with the goodness itself of God, the organ of infinite charity, uncreated life, love, and mercy. We must adore It with the adoration due to God Himself, love It with the absolute love that God alone deserves, and attribute to It, offer to It all praise, human and angelic, and even that which Christ Himself as Man gives to God.

It is at the same time a human Heart, created, formed of Mary's blood. It has a beginning, a growth, and It is now in a state stable and unalterable. As such, It has a past, a history, namely, Its immortal life, first, in the Blessed Sacrament, and next, in the splendor of the saints. Its past life is composed of all that the Word Incarnate did upon earth. It was the Heart of Jesus, the Heart actually present in the Host, that animated the life of Jesus during the nine months that He spent in His Mother's womb. It was that same Heart that beat in His breast when He was born at Bethlehem, which suffered with cold, which shed tears of emotion. It was that Heart which attached Him to His Mother, which was filled with gratitude for her devoted care, and which became the Heart of the best, the most tender of sons. It was in that Heart that flourished the virtues of sweetness, obedience, and humility, which embalmed the life of Mary's hidden and uninterrupted prayer. It was from that Heart that issued all the words of the public ministry of the Saviour, words of truth, of mercy, of pardon, and sometimes words of menace against hypocrites and the obdurate. It was in that Heart the *Pater noster* was. composed. It was that Heart that melted at sight of the moral and physical miseries of the people, that wept over Lazarus and over Jerusalem, Its ungrateful city, that was moved at sight of the afflicted widow of Naim. It was that Heart that suffered the bitter desolation of the Agony in the garden, the cruel shame and sorrow of the abandonment of Its followers, the denial of Peter, and the treason

of Judas.   It was that Heart that was saddened by the sorrows of Mary, and moved
with compassion for the good thief.   And,
finally, it was that Heart that swelled with
Its last pulsation when the Saviour accomplished the grand act of His death.   The
soldier transpierced It with a lance, and the
Sacraments sprang forth from It under the
symbols of blood which nourishes and
water which regenerates.

Such is the history of that Heart and Its
glorious past.   It repudiates no thought, no
act of it, for all in it was love, devotedness,
salvation.   The fruits of that past, It applies to us through the Sacrament.   We
ought to take cognizance of it, and recall it
often to the Heart of Jesus when we adore
It in the Holy Eucharist.   It will help us
better to comprehend the present.   The
mortal life of Jesus is the elucidation of His
Eucharistic life.

### REPARATION.

The Eucharistic life of the Heart of
Jesus commenced at the first Consecration
of the Last Supper.   As soon as He held
Himself in His hands under the species of
bread changed into Himself, the Heart of

Jesus began a new existence. He took the annihilated state of the Sacrament to which He had reduced His Sacred Humanity, and therein is the principle of the Eucharistic, or Sacramental, life of the Saviour present under the species of bread. This life He there continues under our eyes, or rather unknown to us, so profound is His retreat, although we know very distinctly where it is spent, although we can point out His dwelling very precisely, as well as the space that contains it, and several of the laws to which it is subjected.

The life of the Heart of Jesus in the Eucharist is that of a perfect victim and, consequently, of absolute immolation. It is outwardly manifested by no sign, no pulsation, no sound, no movement of the organs, no coloring of the flesh, no vital heat. Nothing! It lives, It beats, It palpitates, It animates the most perfect of lives, but at the same time reduces it to nothing, buries it in inertia and exterior death, in order to transform it into a perfect holocaust of adoration and expiation.

**It is the interior life that belongs to the Priest of the Most High. He knows all the rights of God, all the duties of humanity.**

He assumes the task of harmonizing man's
duties with God's demands, and He offers
in His own name and in the name of all
men a Sacrifice infinite and uninterrupted,
in value worthy of the Divine Majesty, the
Sacrifice of adoration, thanksgiving, reparation, and prayer.    The Heart adores in
the name of all men, and, giving to those
that adore with It whatever may be wanting
to render their adoration worthy of God,
It adores in the place of those that adore
not.    It is the complement, the supplement
of mankind in their duty toward God.    Not
a benefit descends from the overflowing
bosom of Divine Goodness, that that grateful Heart does not see, does not accept as
Its own, does not assume its debt, and discharge it by infinite thanks far superior to
the benefit itself.    Not a sin is committed
that that Heart is not instantly moved, does
not offer Its own love and purity, Its own
Blood in reparation, to appease Divine Justice, and to obtain pardon for the guilty.
Attentive to all the needs of humanity, even
before the beggar has asked his daily bread,
before the afflicted has presented his tears
to the God of all consolation, the Heart of
Jesus, that ever-watchful Sentinel, has ut-

tered the cry of distress. It had prayed, and obtained food for both body and soul. Not a grace comes from the celestial treasury except by It. No prayer rises to the throne of God until it is first laid in the Eucharistic Heart of Jesus, thence to mount, borne upon the wings of the prayer of Jesus Himself, to the bosom of Infinite Goodness.

The Heart of the Eucharistic Christ is, then, the Heart of the Priest, the Advocate, the Mediator with God. Toward us It exercises all the offices of love. It is the heart of a mother, a father, a shepherd, for It nourishes us, protects us, guides us. It has all the tenderness, all the patience of maternal love; It has all the energy of paternal love; and it is as a devoted shepherd that Jesus watches from the tent of the tabernacle over the lambs and the sheep, defending them from the wolves of the world and of hell, reviving them upon His bosom, calling them to follow Him, and leading them to green pastures and clear waters.

The Heart of the Eucharistic Christ is the Heart of a Brother, a Friend, a Spouse. It is the Heart of a Brother, for He has the same Father in heaven, the same Mother on earth as we, God the Father and Mary.

It is the Heart of a Brother, for He is of the same origin, of the same flesh, of the same blood as we. It is the Heart of a Friend, for He became our equal, He discovers to us all His secrets, He shares with us all His riches. He rejoices in our joys, He grieves over our sorrows. He invites us to pour out our innermost thoughts to Him, and He appears to value highly the respectful familiarity of the closest friendship. As soon as He had instituted the Eucharist and had given Himself in the Sacrament, His Heart exclaimed with transport: " I shall henceforth call you My friends, for all that I have received, I have given to you!" It is the Heart of a Spouse who puts all His goods in common, who gives His name, His wealth, His life, His love, and that forever, to all souls who, baptized in His Blood, wish to be united to Him in the sacred espousals of Communion.

There is something more. Not satisfied with living in the tabernacle for His Father and for us, the Heart of Jesus is hungering to communicate Himself, to give Himself to those that He loves. And He loves all, the just whose way is without stain, and poor sinners escaping from the mire of sin and about to enter into the paths of justice. Communion is the supreme miracle, the ripe fruit of the Eucharistic Heart. It would not be sufficient for Him to think of us, to watch over us, to offer Himself for us, if He did not really give Himself to each one. And this prodigy the Eucharistic Heart alone realizes. Communion is the gift of the Heart of Jesus, the incontestable proof of His personal love.

" O Lord, what is man that Thou shouldst treat him so magnificently, shouldst deign to unite Thy Heart with his poor heart? "

Would we contemplate the marvellous effects of this communication of the Heart of Jesus in the Eucharist?—Behold John upon that Heart at the Last Supper. " Happy Apostle," exclaims the Church, " whom we cannot praise too much, envy too much! " In that contact, his soul drank in long draughts of light and truth. He divined the mystery of the Word in the Father's bosom, he read the destinies of the Church, he listened to the sublime inspiration of his Gospel; and as no one knows the Father except by the Son, because the Son lives in His bosom, so no one speaks so well of

the Son as that disciple who rested on His
Heart at Communion in the Cenacle. His
Heart was there filled with love and sweetness. He there learned and tasted the laws
of charity, which he handed down even in
extreme old age by his sweet expression:
" Love one another."

If we cannot presume to such favors,
since we are not of the number of those in
whom Jesus finds a virginal soul, yet, poor
sinners as we are, the Heart of Jesus will
not repulse us. It belongs to us, also. With
the prodigal, let us arise, let us go to It, let
us confess our sins, and they will be par-
doned. But the rags of our misery still
cover us, we still bear the visible marks of
our wandering. Ah! Jesus will not reject
us on that account. Like the father of the
prodigal, He will come out to meet us at
the Communion Table. He will press us to
His Heart, He will not reproach us, for He
has forgotten all our past misdeeds; and by
sweet tears that His loving kindness will
cause us to shed, we shall find our lost peace,
we shall be inundated with joy, we shall
be consoled with the assurance of pardon.
Oh, how good is the Heart of Jesus! It
warms the cold heart, It strengthens it in

Holy Communion, and it looks upon the wanderer's return as the dearest joy of Its life!

Just or sinner, let us all draw near to the Sacrament that gives us the Heart of Jesus for our resting-place, in which we may be restored to health of soul, and taste again the joys of innocence rewarded, or of repentance pleasing to God.

### PETITION.

Lastly, the Heart of Jesus received at the moment of Communion, becomes truly our own, and we can, we ought to make use of It in order to love God, to practise virtue, to embrace sacrifice. That Heart ought to animate our whole supernatural life. It is the realization of the prophecy: " I will take away your heart of stone, and I will give you a heart of flesh," a heart tender and loving. Oh, marvellous change, as true as wonderful! It is a gift, an irrevocable gift that Jesus makes us of His own Heart in Holy Communion. As long as the Eucharistic Species remain in our breast, we really possess Jesus' Heart of flesh. It loves, prays, adores, and wills in us. It is for us to unite our tepid and cowardly, our

blind and egotistical heart to the Heart of
Jesus, to lose it in His, in order to love God,
our Father, in a manner worthy of Him. As
soon as the Sacred Species are consumed,
Jesus' Heart of flesh disappears with the
Sacrament, but Jesus continues to remain
in us spiritually, in order to make us live
of His own life. We remain spiritually
and very really united to His Heart, which
loves, acts, suffers, and merits in us. Our
life led on by His light and receiving His
inspirations, will become truly supernatural.
St. Bernard comprehended the gift of
Jesus' Heart in Communion when he penned
these words of loving confidence: " Since
we have had the happiness to approach the
most sweet Heart of Jesus, and since it is
good to remain in It, let us never separate
from It. How sweet it is to dwell in that
Heart! Infinite treasure, precious pearl, is
the Heart that I have found in Thy most
sacred Body, O Jesus! Who could neglect
such a treasure? Far from doing so, I
will give all that I have, my thoughts, affections, heart, and mind, to purchase It,
and I will abandon myself to Its direction.
That Heart is a temple, a sanctuary, the
Ark of the Covenant, and there it is that

I will go to pray, to adore, to praise the name of the Lord, saying with David: '*I have found my heart in order to pray to my God.*' Yes, I have found, I have possessed myself of the Heart of my King, of my Brother, of my faithful Friend, the Heart of Jesus. What henceforth can prevent me from praying with confidence? My own heart is full of hesitancy, not knowing how to pray, but the Heart of Jesus is now my own: *Cor enim illius meum est.* If Christ is my head, if I am His member, is not all that is His mine, also? It is, then, with Thy Heart, O most sweet Jesus, that Heart which is Thine and mine at one and the same time, that I will pray, for Thou art my God. Suffer my prayers to penetrate into that Sanctuary in which Thou wilt always hear them favorably. Still more, draw me entirely into Thy Heart that I may dwell therein all the days of my life!"

We now know what the Heart of Jesus is in the Eucharist. It is His Heart as true man that therein animates His sacramental life. It is a Heart at once human and divine. It fulfils therein before the Father the duties of a perfect priest and of a victim ever immolated; and with regard to us, It is the Heart of a Mother, of a Brother, a Spouse, and a Friend. Not satisfied with living for us in the tabernacle, He attracts us to Himself and gives Himself to us in Holy Communion. This gift is without repentance. It is made to us that we may live and act supernaturally in Him and by Him. And now, what remains to be said, except to indicate in a few words the duties imposed upon us by the presence and the gift of the Heart of Our Saviour in the Eucharist.

First, we must know It, recognize It explicitly in the Sacrament, penetrate to It in thought, and go to adore It in the tabernacles in which It is loving us and waiting for us. Let us give It our time, much of our time. We cannot better employ it. We must adore It and praise It in all Its greatness, human and divine. We must thank It for all the proofs of love that It has testified to us by the gift of the Eucharist, which It perpetuates upon all our altars at the cost of so great sacrifices, and with so much profit to us.

Secondly, we must have for It love full of heart, true tenderness, and the confidence of a son, a friend, a brother. It is our heart that It craves more than anything else; and *that* we will give It if we sympathize in Its thoughts, Its interests, Its affections. Oh, what great things the Heart of Jesus in the Eucharist desires for the glory of His Father and the salvation of men! He remains in so many tabernacles only to procure that glory, sustain His Church, save sinners, preserve the just, and offer Himself for the poor souls in purgatory. Let us make His interests our own. Let us join our prayers, our love and our works to His sacrifice, to His perpetual apostolate.

Thirdly, let us compassionate that Heart, neglected, despised, abandoned. Doubtless, It is interiorly inundated with unalterable joy, plunged in unalloyed beatitude. But sin and forgetfulness affect It in a divine and inexplicable manner. Its complaints to Blessed Margaret Mary, if we truly loved, we would hear issuing from all the Hosts that we adore behind the golden wall of the tabernacle, or under the crystal of the ostensorium; and above all, from the Host of our Holy Communion, which descends into our breast, begging for our compassion, our tears, our love, our reparation. Oh, may our heart be ever loving to the Heart of Jesus, unknown, humiliated, and wounded by ingratitude!

Fourthly, let us make it our duty to commune with the Heart of Jesus whenever we approach the Holy Table. Let us go beyond appearances. Let us enter into the Eucharistic Body by the Wounded Side, to discover therein the Heart of Our Saviour, the source of His mortal life on earth, of His glorified life in heaven, of His Eucharistic life, the pledge of His perpetual abiding with us, the furnace of all the love that this Adorable Sacrament lavishes upon us.

Then, as the fruit of Communion, let us give to the Heart of Jesus full empire over our heart and our life. Let Him hold the reins of our thoughts, and above all, of our affections. Let us submit to It our desires and our projects that It may approve and bless them. Let all our crosses be faithfully offered to It, that It may alleviate them, sanctify them, and render them meritorious for us and for the whole world.

What shall we say in conclusion? — The Eucharist is Jesus living, Jesus loving,

Jesus kind, Jesus who gives Himself, Jesus who understands us just because, in the Holy Eucharist, is truly and really His Heart. Let us seek and find the Heart of Jesus where It is hidden for us. Let us love It where It loves us, in the most Blessed Sacrament.

Beg our Eucharistic Lord to increase your reverence when in the presence of the Blessed Sacrament.

Eucharistic Heart of Jesus, solace in our exile, give peace to the Church.

(100 *days' Indulgence.*)

# Twenty=sixth Day

## THE HOLY NAME OF JESUS.

### ADORATION.

O JESUS, my adorable Saviour! I pronounce Thy holy name Jesus, and I feel my soul penetrated with respect, love, and adoration for the Divine Person who bears this thrice holy name. I love Thee, O my Saviour, for ennobling our human nature by taking from it Thy Body, Thy Blood, Thy Heart, and Thy Soul with all their admirable faculties! I say to myself: If the name of Jesus is so holy, so terrible that, when pronounced every knee should bow in heaven, on earth, and in hell; if it is so powerful that the first miracle of the New Law, the first miracle of Thy Apostle Peter, was wrought in the name of Jesus of Nazareth, and ever since by the power of the same holy name the saints have performed so many prodigies, what must we think of Him who bears that name of glory and of love? If the name of Jesus is so sweet. so charming that the Church delights

410

in chanting it, and all who love the Saviour thrill with joy when pronouncing it or hearing it pronounced, what shall we say of Him, of Jesus Himself?

Ah! I understand why the name of Jesus is of so much worth and merit, why it is deserving of so much reverence and confidence. It is because Jesus signifies *Saviour* of the world. Now, only a God, a God made Man, has power to save us, as Peter assured the Jews that there was no other name by which we could be saved. *Jesus!* Matchless name, peerless name, sacred name *par excellence,* name truly adorable, because it is the name of our Emmanuel, the name of the good God, present and living among us! To merit this name above every name, Oh, how much our dear Saviour suffered and humbled Himself, becoming, as St. Paul says, obedient unto death and the death of the cross! (1)

Gladly, then, will I cry out with David: *" O Lord, our Lord, how admirable is thy name in the whole earth! From the rising of the sun till the going down of the same, the name of the Lord is worthy of*

---

(1) Philip. ii, 8.

*praise. Young men and maidens: let the old with the younger praise the name of the Lord, for his name alone is exalted. All the nations thou hast made shall come and adore before thee, O Lord: and they shall glorify thy name!"*

Would, O my Jesus, that I could speak and write Thy name in season and out of season, as did St. Paul in his Epistles! Would that I could declare with St. Augustine and St. Bernard that every writing is insipid if I find not there the name of Jesus, that every conversation is wearisome if it does not echo the sound of the holy name of Jesus! Would that, in imitation of St. Bernardine of Siena, I could engrave the name of Jesus in letters of radiant gold on the walls of every public edifice and every private dwelling! Above all, by dint of pronouncing it and chanting it, would that after my death it might be found engraven on my heart, as on that of St. Ignatius of Antioch!

### THANKSGIVING.

The name of Jesus is a name of sweetness and love. If it calls upon me loudly to adore, it commands me not less imperatively to thank. The name of Jesus recalls to me my beloved Saviour, my Sovereign Benefactor, Him to whom I owe all that I am, all that I have, all that I hope for and expect in this world, both in the natural and the supernatural order, and in the next, eternal glory and beatitude.

To pronounce, to hear the name of Jesus, is in itself a grace, a protection. The saints teach charming things on this subject. I love especially to recall what St. Laurence Justinian says of the advantages to be derived from the pious invocation of the name of Jesus (1) : " As often as you piously pronounce this holy name, you taste a certain spiritual sweetness most agreeable, not only in the heart, but also on the lips. This name has a power all its own to rejoice the soul, refresh the spirit, strengthen devotion, and rouse the piety of him who invokes it. If tempted by the demon, oppressed by men, burdened by sadness, worn out by suffering ; if violently agitated by the spirit of blasphemy or despair, struck with terror, or plunged into the agony of doubt, utter the name of Jesus and, at once, light

---

(1) *Sermon on the Circumcision of Our Lord.*

and grace will flow upon you. Yes, in difficult, perilous, terrible moments, at home and abroad, in the desert and on the billows of the sea; in fine, wherever you may be, pronounce the name of the Saviour. Pronounce it not with the lips alone, but from the bottom of the heart, with faith, love, and confidence, for it would serve little merely to spell, as it were, the syllables of the divine name. But if you say, *Lord Jesus!* confessing with mouth and heart that He is truly God and truly man in the unity of one same Person, you will be entirely embalmed with the good odor of Christ and, by virtue of that confession, you will be saved."

Let us now listen to St. Bernard: " The name of Jesus," says he, " is honey to my mouth, music to my ear, jubilation in my heart.    .    Thy name, O Lord, is like oil poured out. Oil enlightens, nourishes, softens. It feeds fire, nourishes the flesh, soothes pain. It is a light, a nourishment, a remedy. And so it is with the name of Jesus."

Here let us give utterance to our sentiments of gratitude, for we have near us in our tabernacles Him who is called Jesus, and we can approach Him, speak to Him, receive Him into our breast, and unite ourselves to Him as closely as we please. O my Jesus, if Thy name is already a light, a nourishment, and a remedy, can I doubt that Thy Body and Blood, Thy Soul and Thy Divinity contained in the Most Blessed Sacrament, are with far greater reason our indefectible light, our supersubstantial nourishment, and the remedy for all the evils of our soul? Moreover, it is Thou Thyself, O well-beloved Saviour, who hast said: *"I am the light of the world." "My Flesh is meat, indeed. I am the living Bread." "I am not come for those that are well, but for the sick."*

*May the name of the Lord be forever blessed, and praised and thanked at every moment be the Most Holy and Most Divine Sacrament!*

### REPARATION.

The name of Jesus has wonderful power to incite us to reparation. There is nothing astonishing in this, since Jesus is the name of our dear Saviour, officially imposed upon Him on the day on which, in His eagerness to save us, He began to shed the first drops of His Precious Blood, namely, the day of His Circumcision. It is in view of this fact that Holy Mother Church places upon the lips of her erring children these words: *" By Thy name, O Lord, have pity on me, for great is my sin! " " Through Thy holy name, O Lord, pardon my sins! "*

To repair the sins committed against the Eucharist, the forgetfulness, the irreverence, the blasphemy, let us love to repeat often the following little act of love and adoration: *Praised be Jesus Christ!* Let us say it when passing before a church, when we see a steeple in the distance, when making the genuflection or the prostration before the Most Blessed Sacrament. Our fathers, the first Christians, when they met, saluted one another with the words: *Praised be Jesus Christ!* Why, at least among devout persons, should we not try to establish this holy custom? Let us say, let us cry out if possible, when we hear a blasphemy: *Praised be Jesus Christ!*—If miscreants claim the right to blaspheme and curse aloud, why should we not enjoy the liberty to bless and adore aloud? In many Christian homes, notably in Catholic Belgium, may be seen on the walls scrolls and placards, bearing in large characters these words, which are constantly repeated: *Praised be Jesus Christ! Forever!*—Ah! here is a tradition which we should not allow to fall into disuse. It would help to repair the evil wrought by so many vile posters stuck on the walls of our cities.

There is another invocation of Thy holy name, O my Jesus, which is reparative in the highest degree. It consists of the three words: "*My Jesus, mercy!*" (1).

Let us love to repeat it in reparation for our sins and for the conversion of sinners.

### PETITION.

*My Jesus, mercy!* It is a cry of reparation and an ardent prayer. St. Leonard of Port-Maurice, that illustrious converter of souls, that great apostle of Italy in the eighteenth century, constituted himself the indefatigable propagator of this short, but powerful, invocation. He used to cry out at the end of his missions: "Ah! my dearly beloved brethren, who will give me a voice of thunder, or rather one of the trum-

---

(1) *This invocation is enriched with an Indulgence of 100 days.*

pets that will resound on the day of the
Last Judgment, and, transported with holy
zeal, I shall ascend to the top of the highest mountains and from there shout with
all my might: 'Erring people, commend
yourselves to God in these or similar words:
*My Jesus, mercy! My Jesus, mercy!'*—
And I give you my word, since Jesus has
given you His before me in His holy Gospel, when He said, *'Ask, and you shall
receive'*—yes, I give you my word, I repeat, if you commend yourselves often to
God by these words, *My Jesus, mercy!* you
will cease to sin, and you will be saved!"

This incredible power of the invocation
of the holy name of Jesus is founded on
the promise of Our Lord Himself.    Hast
Thou not said, O good Master: *Whatsoever you shall ask the Father in My name,
that will I do?*    Has not Thy Apostle written: *Whosoever shall call upon the name
of the Lord shall be saved?*    Behold why
the Church expects all her help from the
Lord who made heaven and earth: *Adju-
torium nostrum in nomine Domini qui fecit
coelum et terram.*—Blessed, then is the
man whose hope is in the name of the
Lord!    Again, if the name alone of Jesus

possesses so great supernatural power, what of His Person Itself, of His Divinity, His Sacred Humanity? What is the power of His Soul, of His Body, and of His Precious Blood? What shall we say of His Heart, that adorable Heart, which the Divine Sacrament places at our disposition, that by It we may render to God all our religious duties, merit all His benefits, and pay our debt of gratitude for them? Yes, when we offer to Almighty God the Sacred Heart of Jesus in the Holy Eucharist, we discharge our debt far beyond its value, since nothing can equal in worth the Holy Eucharist, the Gift above all gifts!

Pray earnestly for the conversion of sinners.

My Jesus, mercy!
(100 *days' Indulgence.*)

# Twenty=seventh Day

## THE SACRED HEART IN THE HOST OF THE REAL PRESENCE.

### ADORATION.

THE Sacred Heart in revealing Itself to St. John as present and living in the Host which the Divine Master presented to His Apostles before giving It to them in Communion, showed him at the same time Its reality, human and divine. It made him understand that, under the appearance of material bread, the Eucharistic Christ was in every sense the Man-God, born of the Father from all eternity and of Mary in time. By the words with which He invested It with the sacramental state, He revealed with what splendors of divine love, with what tenderness of human love, the Saviour willed, by means of His abiding Presence throughout the ages, to love, " His own, " that is, all men now become His brethren by a double right, by nature and by redemption: " *Cum dilexisset suos qui erant in mundo, in finem dilexit eos*—Having loved

420

His own who were in the world, He loved them to the end."

It pleased the Heart of Christ, in His long Eucharistic career, which the universal and obstinate ingratitude of men rendered equal to the most ignominious captivity, to make a brilliant manifestation of His Presence, His life, and His love in the Eucharist. For the benefit of Christianity now grown old, He renewed to a daughter of France the Revelation formerly made to St. John for the early Church. Paray-le-Monial was the Cenacle of the Sacred Heart, as the house of St. John had been the Cenacle of the Eucharist.

"One day, when the Blessed Sacrament was exposed," says that favored daughter, Blessed Margaret Mary, "my good Master presented Himself to me brilliant with glory, His five wounds shining like so many suns. From every part of His Sacred Humanity streamed flames; above all from His adorable breast, which was like a furnace. Opening it, He disclosed to me His Divine Heart, the living source of those flames!"

The special end of this Eucharistic revelation of the Sacred Heart is to manifest the love, the real, the actual love with which

Jesus never ceases to love souls in the Sacrament.

Faith had grown weak and indifference was testified by the contempt and forgetfulness shown the outward sign of the Eucharist. But the Saviour, raising the Eucharistic veils, or rather illuminating them with a radiance more brilliant than that of the sun, shows His Heart with the words: " Behold this Heart which has loved men so much that It has spared nothing, even to exhausting and consuming Itself to testify to them Its love ! "

This love is a real love in His Heart. It is not the mere remembrance of the old love which made Him redeem the world by becoming incarnate and dying for man's salvation, which the burning lamp of His Heart enkindled on the night of the Eucharistic Mystery, ought to recall to an indifferent world. It is the actual love with which He loves it, and through which, after nineteen centuries, He still devotes and consumes Himself daily for it, as He did on the evening of the Last Supper. On that evening He loved " even to the end," that is, without measure. Today behold how He loves without being exhausted or wearied:

"My Divine Heart is so filled with love for men that, no longer able to contain in Itself the flames of Its burning charity, It must of necessity spread them forth by thy means. It must manifest Itself to them in order to enrich them with Its precious treasures which contain the salutary graces necessary to withdraw them from the abyss of perdition."

### THANKSGIVING.

Still more, this love of the Sacred Heart is eager for a return. It feels the need of being comprehended, of being faithfully reciprocated. It suffers from forgetfulness, coldness, ingratitude, and abandonment. "He discovered to me," says Blessed Margaret Mary, "the inexplicable marvels of His pure love, and to what excess it had carried Him, leading Him to love those from whom He received only ingratitude. 'This is to me,' He said, 'more wounding than all that I suffered in My Passion! For, if they made some return for My love I should esteem all that I have done for them as little, and I would wish, if it were possible, to endure still more. But they meet all My eagerness to do them good with coldness and rebuffs.'"

" This is more wounding to Me than all
that I suffered in My Passion! " These
words forcibly proclaim the truth, the reality,
the ardor of the love of Thy Sacred Heart
for us, O adorable Master! Are we to understand from them that Thou dost endure a
real sorrow such as we ourselves sometimes
feel? a grief which lessens or destroys Thy
joy as to its extent, its depth, or its duration? By no means! For all the manifestations of Thy sacramental life are in accordance with the laws upon which it is
founded. Now, since the morning of the
Resurrection joy has forever taken possession of Thy Soul, filling It to overflowing,
without the possibility of its being impaired
or diminished by any cause whatever. It
is like the immortal life that raised Thy
Body from the tomb, excluding from it forever physical suffering, fatigue, or hunger.

But why use expressions that do not cor-
respond to the reality?

Those expressions of suffering in the
Heart of the Eucharistic Christ were true
at the moment in which the Saviour instituted the Sacrament. He was then passible
and subject to all kinds of sufferings. " His
Heart was filled with evils: *Repleta est*

*malis anima mea,"* and the horror that He felt on beholding Judas sacrilegiously participating in the reception of His Body sufficently testifies how much He suffered from the contempt, the outrages, which met His clear-sighted gaze down the coming centuries. In His chalice of the Last Supper, by foreseeing and accepting them, He drank at a single draught all the bitterness and sadness which, until the end of time, are to fall upon Him in His Eucharistic existence. As He receives this ingratitude from those whom He purchased with His Blood and nourished with His Flesh, whom He elevated to the dignity of children of God, nay, even from consecrated virgins and priests of the New Covenant, He can say in all truth that it is *" more wounding to Him than all He endured in His Passion."* These words are rigorously true for the moment of the Eucharistic institution, which in reality embraced all the Holy Masses that were to follow till the end of time. O Master of truth, in the strictest theological sense, Thou wast justified in using them!

" One day," says Blessed Margaret Mary, " the Sacred Heart was represented to me as upon a throne of fire, more brilliant than

the sun and transparent as crystal." Here
we see Its state of fundamental glory. But
now let us see the sufferings of Its institution, the remembrance of which Jesus desires to imprint in our mind: " The wound
that It had received on the cross," the Blessed Sister goes on to say, " was plainly visible. There was a crown of thorns around
the Divine Heart and a cross above It. My
Divine Master gave me to understand that
these instruments of His Passion signified
that from the first moment of Its institution He accepted all the outrages to which
His love for man would expose Him in the
Most Blessed Sacrament."

### REPARATION.

These loving and sorrowful complaints,
O Lord, Thou dost employ also toward us,
to give us some idea of the gravity of our
faults in Thy regard. As we are more alive
to what is actual and present, by telling us
how greatly Thy Heart suffers in the Sacrament, Thou didst wish us to hear these
words: " When I instituted the Eucharist,
My Heart suffered from all the ingratitude
that men would heap upon It in the years to
come. Every time that it was struck by

one of these outrages, It would again have endured as much were that still possible."

It is for this reason that, in the revelation of Paray, which throws so much light on the nature of His love for man in the Eucharist, Jesus so often shows Himself wounded and covered with ignominy.

" Disclosing to me one day," says Blessed Margaret Mary, " His loving Heart all torn and transpierced with blows, He said: ' Behold the wounds I have received from My chosen people! Others are satisfied with striking Me on My person, but these attack My Heart, which has never ceased to love them!'" And again, " He presented Himself to me as the *Ecce Homo*, all bruised and disfigured, saying: 'I have found no one willing to shelter Me in the suffering and pitiable state in which I am!'" She adds: " This sight filled me with so lively a grief that death would have been a thousand times sweeter than to see my Saviour in that state!" The Divine Heart had obtained what It sought by showing Itself under this exterior of suffering, namely, compassion and reparation.

Our Lord's glorious impassibility does not, then, lessen the sufferings caused by

our injuries, which all mount up to the first
moment of His sacramental existence. On
the contrary, it increases the gravity of our
faults by uselessly continuing under our
eyes the perseverance of His invincible love.
O my sweet Master, repeat again the complaint of Thy Heart! I have need of its
frequently striking my heart, until it is
broken with contrition and softened by compassion: "I receive for the most part only
ingratitude, and that is *more wounding to
Me than all that I endured in My Passion!*"

The Revelation of Paray clearly manifests the desire and need of the Sacred
Heart to be loved by men in the Sacrament,
and how sensible It is of the least homage,
of the least attention. This seeking after
affection is akin to Its nature and is a satisfaction to which It has a right, for It has
every title to our love. It is, above all,
the means of making us capable of doing
good. By loving It we fulfil our chief
duty, we find the assured means of easily
accomplishing all others, and we receive the
joy, the consolation, and the foretaste of
beatitude.

Thou wilt say, then, O Heart eager to be
loved: "I thirst ardently to be honored by

men in the Blessed Sacrament, and I find almost no one who tries, according to My desire, to slake My thirst by making Me some return!"

And again Thou wilt say: "If men made Me some return for My love, I should esteem what I have done for them as little, and I would wish, if it were possible, to suffer still more."

### PETITION.

After these appeals, which are made to all mankind, Jesus becomes a suppliant, humbly soliciting, earnestly begging of everyone the smallest testimonies of love. "Do thou, at least," does He say to His servant Blessed Margaret Mary, "give Me the consolation of supplying for their ingratitude as far as thou art able!" And she again assures us: "My Divine Master has told me that He takes special pleasure in being honored under the figure of this Heart of flesh."

Although His glorified state cuts Him off from experiencing suffering, yet He does not deny Himself the joy to be tasted in the marks of love shown Him, or the glory derived from the honors rendered Him. Although plunged in the plenitude of infinite happiness, He still seeks an increase of accidental glory and beatitude in the love, the fidelity, the delicate attentions of men, who belong to His Heart by so many sacred claims.

Sighing for relief and consolation, He continues: " Thou shalt bear Me company in the humble prayer that I offered to My Father in the Garden of Olives. Thou shalt prostrate, thy face to the ground. . in order to alleviate in some degree the bitterness that I then experienced from the desertion of My Apostles, which forced Me to reproach them with not being willing to watch one hour with Me."

That we may not be able to plead inability to love Him as He desires, He infuses into us His own love, and fans it into flame. Still more, He changes our heart, giving us, in order to love Him, His own Heart. " As I represented to Him," says Blessed Margaret Mary, " my powerlessness to love Him, He demanded my heart. I begged Him to take it. He did so, and placed it in His own adorable Heart, in which He showed it to me as a tiny atom being consumed in that burning furnace. Thence withdrawing it like a glowing flame in the shape of a heart, He replaced it in my breast, saying: 'Behold, My beloved, a precious pledge of My love, which shuts up in thy side a little spark of Its fiery flames, to serve thee for a heart and to consume thee till the last moment of thy life.'"

"This favor," says the Blessed Sister's contemporaries, "was renewed the first Friday of every month in this way—the Sacred Heart of Jesus was represented to her as a sun, brilliant with light. Its burning rays shot down upon her heart which, under the influence of so intense a fire, felt as if it were being reduced to ashes. It was especially at these moments her Divine Master instructed her as to what He demanded of her, and discovered to her the secrets of His Heart."

These diverse testimonies from the Revelation of Paray unite in proving to us how truly the Sacred Heart in the Blessed Sacrament actually loves us. It is a love both divine and human, but sincere, intelligent, and sensible. It is a love which pours itself out in infinite effusions upon the world, but which longs to flow without measure into every soul redeemed by Him on the Cross.

Jesus desires to lead every soul to heaven by constituting Himself in the Blessed Sacrament its guide, support, surety, and help at every moment. It is a love that has need of reciprocity, a love that calls for return, that really enjoys receiving it, and that suffers (in the divine manner in which God can suffer from our offences) at seeing itself rejected. It is a lasting, persevering love, that recoils before no obstacle, is wearied by no ingratitude, that no hatred can turn to hate, but which, on the contrary, is changed by sin into mercy and pardon. It is the love faithful among all loves, sweet, compassionate, indulgent, condescending, and patient.

Ah! if we could believe in the truth and sincerity of this love which calls us by our name, reads our most secret thoughts, knows our most private needs, watches over every one of us night and day, follows us step by step, prays and pleads for us incessantly before God, and has no other desire than our good! If we could believe that this love feels itself repaid if we only trust in Him and allow ourselves to be loved by Him! Ah, if we truly believed in His tenderness, devotedness, and fidelity, what a blessed change would come over the conditions of our existence on this earth! No doubt, we should still have sins to shun and defects to reform, difficulties to surmount and sufferings to endure; but we should no longer be alone without guide or support, without Saviour or pastor near us, without Jesus, without God with us, all to us and for us. We should feel ourselves truly and personally loved by the most generous and loving of hearts. And, in truth, what more can man desire upon earth: "*Et a te quid super terram, Deus cordis mei et pars mea Deus in æternum?*—And besides Thee what do I desire upon earth, Thou God of my heart and my portion forever!"

"I find in the Sacred Heart of my Jesus all that is wanting to my own indigence, because It is filled with mercy," says Blessed Margaret Mary. "I have never found a more efficacious remedy in all my afflictions than the Sacred Heart of my Adorable Jesus. There it is that I slumber in peace, that I repose without disquietude. There is nothing so rough or vexatious that it cannot be ameliorated by the sweet Heart of Jesus. The sick and the sinful find in It a safe asylum in which to remain in security. This divine and loving Heart is all my hope, all my refuge.   Its merit is my salvation, my life, my resurrection.   While Its mercy fails me not, I am well provided with merits; for the more powerful It is to save me, the more trust have I in It.

" O most liberal Heart, be Thou all our treasure and sufficiency!

" O Heart most loving and desirable, teach us to love and desire but Thee!

" O Heart most propitious, which dost take so much pleasure in doing us good, grant me wherewith to acquit my debt toward Divine Justice!   I am insolvent, do Thou pray for me!   Repair the evil I have done by the good which Thou hast done!

" And that I may owe everything to Thee, O charitable Heart, receive me at the awful hour of my death!   Hide my soul from the divine wrath! Protect and answer for me! O permit not that I should be deprived of loving Thee eternally!   May I live but by Thee and for Thee!   Be forever my life, my love, and my all!"

Pray for fidelity to the inspirations of grace.

Jesus!   Mary!   Joseph!
(*Indulgence, 7 years and 7 quarantines.*)

# Twenty=eighth Day

## THE EUCHARISTIC HEART, THE PALLADIUM OF THE CHURCH.

THE Eucharistic Heart is the Heart of Jesus Christ in the Eucharist. It is the Heart that inspired the Divine Master to make to the world the gift of the Eucharist. It is the Heart that leads Him to renew this gift every day. Again, it is the Heart immolated with Christ in the august Sacrifice of the Mass. It is the Heart that gives Itself as nourishment in the Communion with the Flesh and Blood of Jesus. Lastly, it is the Heart that is ever present, living and loving, in the breast of Christ abiding in the tabernacle. Toward this Heart so really present, of whose love for us we cannot doubt, which loves us with all the strength of which it is capable, which is so unchangingly faithful to us throughout the long misery of life, we shall, raising wistful eyes and suppliant hands, send up our heartfelt adoration, thanksgiving, reparation, and petitions. May Mary and Joseph, the first who felt the pulsations of this Heart of a

God, hidden in the feeble breast of a new-born Babe, reveal Him to us, make us feel living and loving in our breast, although invisible to our eyes, the Christ hidden under the veils of the Eucharist!

### ADORATION.

" Is it then to be thought," exclaimed Solomon, after bringing the Ark of the Covenant into the oracle of the Temple, erected by his pious and magnificent care, " is it then to be thought that God should dwell upon earth? For if the heaven of heavens cannot contain Thee, how much less this house which I have built? But have regard to the prayer of Thy servant and to his supplications, O Lord, my God, hear the hymn and the prayer which Thy servant prayeth before Thee this day! That Thy eyes may be open upon this house night and day, upon the house of which Thou hast said: My name shall be there!" (1)

" And the Lord appeared to him and said: I have heard thy prayer and thy supplication which thou hast made before Me. I have sanctified this house which thou hast

_____

(1)  III Kings viii, 27.

built to put My name there forever, and
My eyes and My Heart shall be there
always. *Et Cor meum ibi cunctis diebus*" (1).

Solomon did not dare to ask the presence
of the Divine Name in the Temple as a
pledge of protection, as a palladium for the
city and the nation. The Lord Himself
added the promise of a watchful eye and
an attentive ear toward all who would come
there to pray, and still more, He promised
the presence of His Heart. It is very natural that wherever the eyes are the heart
will be also, for without the heart which
gives life, how could the eyes see? The
Lord specified, nevertheless, and promised
that where His name and eyes should be,
there should be His Heart, also, and that
forever. Was not this repetition only an
Oriental redundance attributable to the
translator of the divine revelation? Ah!
we greatly prefer to see in it the intention
of the paternal goodness of God who, wishing to make His Presence as favorable as
possible to man's confidence and prayer,
adapted it to his needs. And the great need

---

(1) Ibid. ix, 3.

of man is to know, to feel himself loved, because he is born for social intercourse of which love is the fundamental good. Now, the most expressive symbol of love is the heart. As the sensible, though mysterious, Presence of God in the propitiatory was the figure of the real and personal Presence of the God-made Man in our Eucharistic tabernacles, we see again in this word the intention of formally arresting the eyes, the piety, the confidence, and the prayers of Christians upon the Heart of Jesus Christ, although His eyes be open to our presence, His ears attentive to our supplications, and His hands with their stigmata of love extended toward us to receive and hold us fast.

I understand Thee, O my God, my good Father, become my Brother and my Friend by making Thyself man like to me! Thou art present there for me, but knowing how material I am, how little given to spiritual things, how I shrink from mystery if too profound, how silence and inaction chill me, how the chastisements I have deserved for my sins make me afraid of Thee, and how much my inborn self-love renders me diffident, timid, and pusillanimous, Thou hast concentrated all my attention on Thy Heart. Knowing me well, for Thou hast created me and re-created me by redeeming me, having for over thirty years had experience of the miseries of my state, Thou hast given me Thy Heart, because It proclaims Thy own human life, personal and actual; because It tells of Thy goodness, benevolence, devotedness, patience, and mercy; because It excites sympathy, invites confidence, favors familiarity, encourages repentant and humiliating avowals. Ah! mayst Thou be blessed for having so well understood me and for having summed up everything in Thy Heart in order to reveal Thyself to me in the mystery of Thy prophetic Presence in the ancient Temple, the anticipation, the shadow already so pronounced of Thy Real Presence in the Sacrament of our altars!

Blessed Margaret Mary, in the light of the Sacred Heart, admirably understood the Real Presence of God in the Eucharist. "When only four years old, she felt so powerfully attracted to the church that, very far from becoming weary when in its sacred precincts, she knew no pleasure in life equal to remaining there a long time, and never left it but with regret. As she had the happiness to dwell not far from a church, she frequently visited it. There she would kneel, her hands joined, thinking only of the first questions of her catechism, such as are taught to children when they are just beginning to learn. She believed God more really present in the church than elsewhere, because she had been instructed according to her childish capacity that Jesus Christ, God and Man, abides Body and Soul in the Most Blessed Sacrament of the altar. She believed this truth simply, and she was satisfied in the Presence of Him who from that time took possession of her loving heart."

"The Divine Goodness kept me so occupied in His holy Presence," she tells us, "that I could have passed whole days before the Most Blessed Sacrament." When she was not to be found in the house, they went to look for her in the church, and there she was sure to be. From that time she lost all relish for vocal prayers, which it was impossible for her to make before the Blessed Sacrament. She felt so strongly attracted by Jesus' Presence that she forgot to eat and drink. "I do not know what I do there," she says, " but I feel a great desire to be consumed in His Divine Presence like a burning torch to render Him love for love. I cannot remain in the lower part of the church and, whatever confusion I may feel interiorly, I fail not to approach as near as possible to the Blessed Sacrament."

### THANKSGIVING.

When the God-Man instituted the Eucharist to replace His figurative by His personal Presence, to abide Body, Soul and Divinity in every tabernacle under the appearance of bread, thus concealing from us the magnificence of His glorified state, again in a very significant manner He calls attention to His Heart..

At the Last Supper, as soon as He had changed the bread into His own substance and given Himself as food to the Apostles, He attracted John to His breast and detained him there. He permitted him to lay his head on His bosom, to linger there, to give himself up to repose so peaceful and prolonged that the Gospel says " Now there was leaning on Jesus' bosom one of His disciples whom Jesus loved—*Erat ergo recumbens unus ex discipulis ejus in sinu Jesu, quem diligebat Jesus"* (1).

It is clear that what John, by an irresistible movement of divine love, sought on the bosom of Jesus and in His breast, was the Heart of His well-beloved Master, in which he understood that the loving thought of remaining among men under the form of a little bread had taken rise.   He saw that it was the Heart of Jesus which, in an excess of love, as inexplicable as incomprehensible. had impelled Him to give Himself as food to him, to his fellow-disciples, and through them to the whole world.   He felt, and Jesus seemed to say to him, that the reason for this ineffable institution could be found only in love, that is, in His Heart; that there alone would he comprehend the nature, the end, the spirit, all that it was necessary to know in order to gather the marvellous fruits It contains for the support, strength, and consolation of man here below.

It is a law of nature that the effect shows forth the qualities of the cause that produces it; that the thought of the workman appears in his work ; and that a child,

---

(1)   John xiii, 23.

for example, reproduces the moral dispositions of its parents as well as their features.
If the Eucharist is the masterpiece of the
love of the Saviour for men, and if the
heart is the instrument as well as the symbol *par excellence* of love, It must have all
the qualities, all the inclinations of the
Heart of Jesus. It will be sufficient for me
to recall this perfect Heart of the God-Man
to know the secret, the soul of the Eucharistic Mystery, though enveloped in impen-
etrable veils.

It was in this way that St. John penetrated into the depths of the Eucharist.
After having descended into the Heart of
Jesus, sounded Its hidden depths, and as-
similated It by plunging into It and cling-
ing to It by a close and prolonged embrace,
he set forth Its qualities and effects in his
Gospel.

Because Jesus has a true human Heart
like our own, He feels the necessity of dwelling with us. Forced to leave us in order
to return to His Father, He cannot resolve
to break the natural bond of consanguinity
and the moral bonds of labor accomplished,
of trials endured, and of dangers run in
common; and so, " having loved His own

who were in the world," and who were to remain in it after He should have left it, Christ was impelled by His Heart to substitute His Sacramental for His human Presence. This Presence was to be that of the Son of God made Man in order to dwell with man as long as there should be an earth for the place of his exile. There He was to remain until our entrance into the eternal country: *"Sciens Jesus quia venit hora ut transeat ex hoc mundo ad Patrem cum dilexisset suos qui erant in mundo"* (1).

Because Jesus has a true human Heart, sensible to the trials of his fellowmen, which, indeed, He shares with them, He was so much the more saddened at the thought of leaving us, as He read the grief of His disciples in the tears that filled their eyes. He could not witness such sorrow on His account without remaining to console them; therefore He instituted His abiding Presence to be the Consoler of every affliction: *"Vos nunc quidem tristitiam habetis; iterum autem vide vos et gaudebit cor vestrum*—You now indeed have sorrow,

---

(1) John xii, 1.

but I will see you again, and your heart shall rejoice " (1).

Because He brought forth His Apostles to the supernatural life and has for them as well as for us, their younger brethren, the true Heart of a father, Jesus cannot condemn them to the sad condition of orphans, exposed to the rapacity, the knavery, the iniquity of a world ranged against their inexperience, simplicity, and weakness. He remains with them, therefore. His Presence in the Sacrament will be that of the Father to guard, feed, and cherish His children, to defend the fireside against famine and violence: *" Filioli, non relinquam vos orphanos; veniam ad vos!*—My little children, I will not leave you orphans. I *will come to you!"* (2).

Because He has a Heart truly human, and because man fears solitude with its silence, its night, and its terrors, with the dangers there run in the absence of help, with the distress there endured from the want of succor, Jesus wishes not to abandon us in the sad loneliness in which every Chris-

---

(1) Ibid. xvi, 22,
(2) Ibid. xiv, 18.

tian must live in the midst of an indifferent
and hostile world.    He remains, therefore,
in the Sacrament to be with us wherever
we are    ' *Et si abiero, iterum venio, et ac-*
*cipiam vos ad meipsum, ut ibi sum ego, et*
*vos sitis*—And if I shall go         I shall
come again, and will take you to myself,
that where I am you also may be "(1).

Because Jesus has a human Heart, up-
right and loyal, He feels the responsibility
that He has taken upon Himself as well as
the obligations it imposes, and He desires
to satisfy them.    Having called His Apostles to follow Him, having compromised
them in the eyes of their nation, and then
cast them out into the world like lambs
among wolves, condemned to a merciless
war, He will not abandon them in so difficult a situation.    He will share their combats, preserve them from the blows aimed
at their souls, and help them to support and
even to draw advantage from those levelled
at their physical well-being.    He instituted,
therefore, His Presence as the palladium of
the Church and the source of that confidence
which rouses and inflames courage.    Every-

(1) Ibid. xiv, 3.

where does He present It to His followers in the thick of the fight, crying out to them *" Confidite, ego vici mundum!*—Have confidence! I have overcome the world!"(1).

### REPARATION.

Because He has the Heart of a true man, in all things like unto my own, and because He knows that nothing is more painful than unanswered prayer, a call unheeded, hope deceived, a vain endeavor, the heavens like brass, Divine Providence apparently deaf to our interests (small, doubtless, when compared with the government of the world, but very important for the tranquillity and prosperity of our life), Jesus has instituted His Presence in the Sacrament. He is there as our perpetual Mediator before God, as an infallible pledge of our being favorably heard. The only condition is that we abide in Him, that is, that we live in His grace by fidelity to the duties of our state of life. Because He knew that diffidence, discouragement, despair, and blasphemy might come upon us had we no visible refuge, might separate us from Him and ren-

(1) Ibid. xvi, 33.

der us irretrievably miserable both in time
and eternity, Jesus stays with us in the Holy
Eucharist. He said to His Apostles, and He
has never ceased to repeat " Amen,
amen, I say unto you : if you ask the Father
anything in My name, He will give it you.
Hitherto you have not asked anything in My
name. Ask, and you shall receive, that
your joy may be full—*Petite et accipietis,
ut gaudium vestrum sit plenum!"* (1).

Ah, yes! that we may here below be happy in a measure compatible with the necessity of purchasing eternal happiness by temporal trials, Jesus has instituted His Presence in the Sacrament as the never-failing
source of heavenly peace, of pure joy, which
sweetens all labors and trials, which above
all recognizes the truly human condition of
His Sacred Heart. He can not forget that
He created us for the unending joys of
heaven and that our nature was born to
happiness in the Garden of Eden, in which
there was no mingling of pain. He knows
how strongly in spite of our well-merited
exile, we are attracted by our first destiny
and how much the remembrance of what we

---

(1) Ibid. xvi, 20-24.

have lost inspires us with the desire to regain it. He knows how painful it is for us to live without joy, yes, not only painful, but impossible for long, and even dangerous to eternal salvation! On this account, therefore, Jesus remains in the Blessed Sacrament. There does He obtain from the Father peace and pardon for souls. He enlightens the peace of the mind with the serene joy of faith. He protects peace of conscience by confidence in His clemency. He maintains peace in the will by its perfect accord with the will of God. He pours into the heart the sweetest peace of filial piety so closely allied to perfect joy. Perfect joy is the presence, the sight, the possession of God and Jesus; and the Blessed Sacrament shows us and gives us truly Jesus and God! Jesus said: " Peace I leave with you. My peace I give unto you; not as the world giveth, do I give unto you," for My peace is assured and lasting. Again, He said " Amen, amen, I say to you, you shall lament and weep while the world shall glory in oppressing you. But I shall change your sadness into joy. You are now sad because I am about to go hence; but I shall return to you, and your heart shall rejoice and your joy no man shall take from you *Iterum videbo vos, et gaudium vestrum nemo tollet a vobis!* " (1).

PETITION.

In his contemplation of the Sacred Heart, against which his own was so closely pressed, the truth of the human nature of the Christ who had made Himself a Sacrament was revealed to St. John along with the power and splendor of His divine nature, of which He lost nothing by annihilating Himself in the sacramental state. He was shown the admirable union from all eternity of the Word with the Father and the Holy Ghost, into which the Sacred Humanity assumed by the Word entered victorious over the combats He had sustained for the reestablishment of His Father's kingdom.

By revealing Itself truly divine under the humble Species consumed in the beloved disciple's own breast, the Sacred Heart manifested to him Its sublime origin : *"Sciens quia a Deo exivit "*—and the divine end of the God-Man : *" Et quia ad Deum vadit."* It revealed to him His almighty

---

(1)   Ibid. xvi, 20-22.

power and His empire over all things: *"Sciens quia omnia dedit ei Pater in manus"*(1). It showed him His unalterable union with the Father, who never separates from Him, neither in the weakness of His mortal state, nor in His Eucharistic annihilation: *"Ego in Patre et Pater in me est; Ego et Pater unum sumus. Qui videt me videt et Patrem meum"*(2). Jesus again says: "My Divine Father, the Almighty Creator and Conservator of the world, who dwells in and with Me, who am one only God, does all the marvellous works by which I have manifested to the world My divine mission: *"Pater in me manens, ipse facit opera"*(3).

By an infinite word, the Divine Heart discovered to John the presence of His Divinity in the marvel of the Eucharist *In finem dilexit.* He loved to the end, He loved infinitely! He loved to the end of His power, for He could produce no greater marvel than the mystery of transubstantiation which renders Him present in the Eu-

---

(1) Ibid. xiii, 1-3.
(2) Ibid. xiv, 9.
(3) Ibid. xiv, 10.

charist. He loved to the end of time, since He will remain in It to close the ages after having secured the salvation of the last soul to be saved. He has loved to the end of space, since He is present at one and the same time all over the inhabited world. He has loved to the end of numbers, since He will be more abundantly multiplied than all men of all generations, in order to give Himself to every one. He has loved to the end of abasement, since He will live hidden in the dust of the Sacrament, the nearest approach to annihilation than that of any other living thing. He has loved even to the highest point of elevation, since He exalts to the glorious life of eternity all who cling to Him firmly: *In finem!*

To love to such an extent and to manifest His love by works so evidently divine, is to be truly God. It was His Divinity that remained integral in Jesus, in spite of His sudden annihilation in the particle of bread presented to His Apostles. It was that same Divinity which revealed to St. John the Sacred Heart upon which he was reposing, lost in wonder and gratitude: *In finem dilexit!*

These were the lights upon the nature,

the character and the effects of the Eucharist that fixed John's attention on the Heart of Jesus at the moment of the institution of the Sacrament. This is the model offered us. Whoever desires to penetrate beyond the Eucharistic clouds without being affrighted by Its profound night; whoever desires to comprehend as far as he can here below this incomprehensible Mystery, must look upon, must implore, must study the Eucharistic Heart of Jesus. The Sacrament, outwardly inert and lifeless, will suddenly become animated, will live, at one and the same time God and Man! The student of the Eucharist will love with the most sublime and tender of loves. He will be gentle and good, powerful and strong, helpful and faithful forever like Jesus Himself, the true Son of God and Son of Man.

Let us see how Blessed Margaret Mary comported herself before the Most Blessed Sacrament. She spent almost the whole of the various feasts before It, offering the homage of her interior and exterior love and respect to the Real Presence of the Sacred Humanity of Our Lord Jesus Christ. She loved Him as her God and Saviour, with her whole soul, her whole heart, and all her strength. She loved Him with a love of complacency, seeing in Him the Sovereign Good and the fruitful Source of all holy desires, alone sufficient for Himself. She loved Him with a love of benevolence, ardently longing to love Him as much as He deserves, and that all creatures should enter into her dispositions. She loved Him with a love of union with His will and His good pleasure, which she sought to bend to her own will, only that by sufferings, trials, and humiliations she might become more conformable to what He had been in His mortal life. Once she wrote: " When you make a genuflection before the Blessed Sacrament, say: May all things bow down before Thee, O Almighty Power! May all hearts love Thee, may every spirit adore Thee, and may every will be submissive to Thine ! "

Pray for resignation to the will of God.

Our Lady of the Cenacle, pray for us.
(50 *days' Indulgence.*)

# Twenty=ninth Day

REPARATION is one of the essential characteristics of the worship of the Sacred Heart. The Saviour declares it in express terms. There are three special sins against the Holy Eucharist which it is called upon to repair. On this subject we shall hear the repeated declarations of the Revelations of the Sacred Heart, and we shall see reasons that render such reparation urgent and necessary. What strength, what help, what means for its perfect accomplishment does the devotion of the Sacred Heart afford! We feel ourselves urged, as it were, to respond to the touching and pressing appeal made to Blessed Margaret Mary: "Do thou, at least, try to console Me by making Me some return!"

### ADORATION.

To be convinced that devotion to the Sacred Heart means reparation for sins against the Holy Eucharist, we need but

455

to listen to the clear and earnest words of the Saviour to Blessed Margaret Mary:

"One day, during the octave of Corpus Christi, I was praying before the Blessed Sacrament. I received from God some great graces of His love, and I felt moved by the desire to make to Him some return, and to render Him love for love. He said to me: 'Thou canst do nothing greater for Me than by doing what I have so often asked of thee.'

"Then showing me His Divine Heart, He said: 'Behold this Heart which has so loved men that It has spared nothing even to exhausting and consuming Itself in order to testify to them Its love. Instead of acknowledgment, I receive for the most part only ingratitude, irreverence, sacrilege, coldness and contempt in this Sacrament of Love. But what I feel much more deeply is that it is hearts consecrated to Me that treat Me so.

"'I ask, therefore, that the first Friday after the octave of Corpus Christi be devoted to a special festival in honor of My Heart, by communicating on that day and by making an act of reparation for the ingratitude It has received while exposed on the altars.'"

Nothing could be more formal. The Feast of the Sacred Heart sums up the whole devotion of the Sacred Heart. It was to be instituted in reparation " for the ingratitude, irreverence, sacrileges, coldness, and contempt which the majority of mankind exhibit for the Saviour in His Sacrament of Love."

### THANKSGIVING.

It might appear that, in this contemplation of the outrages committed against the Eucharist, there is little room for thanksgiving, for the mere thought of them fills the heart with sadness and calls loudly for reparation.

It is, however, a most precious gift from the Sacred Heart, and one that deserves earnest thanks, to recognize Its abasement, to be moved to pity It, and to be sensible of the necessity of offering some indemnification to It.

Our heart cannot fail to be overcome by the tenderest sentiments if we reflect on the incomprehensible love that led the Divine Saviour to institute the Eucharist, in spite of all the offences, humiliations, and ingratitude which He foresaw would result from so doing. We shall be still more moved when we think of the even more amazing love which leads Him to remain undaunted in the midst of a world which despises and rejects Him, which urges Him to give Himself to those that receive Him with the intention of outraging Him more cruelly, or to others that will profit nothing by His coming to them. Oh, what disgust the sweet Saviour must feel for such souls! What struggles He must endure!

Jesus was ignorant of nothing that He would be forced to encounter in the Eucharist. Long before Its institution, when looking upon Judas, the foresight filled His Heart with the sharp thorns of anxiety most sorrowful, dug in It an ever-increasing wound, and planted deeply in It a Cross that crushed and bruised It.

The first time that He manifested His Heart to Blessed Margaret Mary, it was " With the Wound He received upon the Cross, a crown of thorns around It, and surmounted by a Cross. And my Divine Saviour made me understand," she tells us, " that, from the first moment of His Incarnation, all His torments were present to Him, and from that first moment the Cross was, as it were, planted in His Heart. It was then that He accepted all the outrages to which His love for man exposed Him in the Blessed Sacrament till the end of time."

### REPARATION.

What renders sin grave and reparation necessary, is the injury done to Divine Majesty and the importance of the precept despised. Now, from each of these points of view, sins against the Eucharist take on a gravity unequalled by any other. They wound directly the sacred Person of the Christ, and go right to His Heart; they are the ungrateful response to His tenderest and most generous love; they despise His formal commandments, thus incurring eternal damnation; lastly, they audaciously put on the character of public apostasy. From all these considerations, they call for earnest and indefatigable reparation.

The Divine Master sorrowfully enumerates "ingratitude, contempt, irreverence, coldness, and sacrileges." On another occasion, He spoke of the "outrages to which His love had subjected Him by exposing Himself on our altars to the end of time." Finally, He bitterly complained of "meeting only coldness and rebuffs, despite His eagerness to do us good."

If we must complete and particularize this pitiful enumeration, passing over details of certain terrible profanations which, revealed from time to time, cast a sinister glare upon the profound Mystery in which, for our sake, resides our Saviour and our God, as well as upon the ferocious baseness of man's heart when filled with hatred, let us turn our attention to some grave infidelities toward the Eucharist, namely: the neglect to hear Mass on Sunday and to receive Holy Communion at Easter. These are real crimes, since they constitute a formal revolt against the manifest will of God and the positive precepts of the Church. They are real crimes of ingratitude and contempt of the Christ's death, which the Sacrifice renews, and against the unspeakable gift of His adorable Flesh as nourishment. They are true crimes of apostasy, since they who commit them refuse to join the public worship due to God. They are real crimes of hatred against God, since they refuse to unite themselves with Him, to His life here below and to His eternal life by participating in His Flesh, the only aliment of divine life in man.

In many places the churches are far from being filled at the Sunday Masses, and at Easter communicants are not numerous. If in some places we find crowded churches, yet even there the absentees far exceed those present. Can we say that the tenth part of baptized Christians render to God and to His Christ the primary duties of religion? Alas! with regard to God, universal apostasy, neglect of His authority, immense ingratitude toward Jesus Christ, who employs so much love, makes so many sacrifices, in order to immolate and give Himself, prevail everywhere. Mortal damage done to souls, loss to Christian society, the disappearance of Christ's beneficent action on the world, the liberty offered to Satan to establish his deadly empire—this is what everywhere confronts us.

Viewing it from the point of love, of which the Eucharist is the highest expression, as well as the tenderest manifestation, who can comprehend the bitter disappointment, the sharp sorrow experienced by the most loving Heart of Jesus, who finds His delights only in being with the children of men? To procure those delights He shrank not from embracing the abasement of the sacramental state and taking upon this miserable earth a new existence, just when His Father bade Him ascend to His glorious rest. Coldness, contempt, rebuffs, the obstinate turning away of the majority of men, are the only response, the only acknowledgment of His well-meaning Presence, that Presence so full of benevolence, of welcome, of courtesy to all. *" Tota die expandi manus meas ad populum nolentem et contradicentem!*—I have spread forth my hands all the day to an unbelieving people "* (1).

### PETITION.

The duty of reparation must now be evident and urgent to one who comprehends the gravity, the horror, and the number of sins against the Eucharist. But at the same time that reparation must appear difficult and altogether above the strength of one who sincerely recognizes his own weakness, the small value of his own good works, and the immense disproportion between them and their need.

Blessed Margaret Mary belonged to the class of the truly humble. Even when

---

(1)  Is. lxiv, 2.

pierced to the very soul by the groanings of the Sacred Heart, and inflamed by her own ardent desires for reparation, " she represented her utter inability to Our Lord, and He replied to her: ' Behold wherewith to supply all that is wanting to thee!' At the same moment the Divine Heart opened," she tells us, " and from It shot a flame so fiery that I thought I should be consumed. I was so penetrated by it that, unable to endure it, I begged Our Lord to have pity on my weakness. ' I will be thy strength. Fear not!' was His reply."

If we wish to repair worthily, we must earnestly, humbly, and perseveringly implore the Sacred Heart for the grace to do so. That dear Heart longs for nothing so much as to pour out such grace upon us. After having demanded of Blessed Margaret Mary the institution of Its feast, the Communion of reparation and the honorable amend of the Holy Hour, He said again to her: "I promise thee that My Heart will dilate to shed abundantly the influences of Its divine love upon those that will render to It this honor, and urge others to do the same."

The first grace necessary for reparation

is a compassionate love for Our Lord. This will make the soul attentive to the cruel and bloody wounds, to all that He endured in His mortal life, to all the mystical pains that He still undergoes in His sacramental life. This compassionate love will make the soul generous to enter into His sufferings, to endure them, to take upon herself the greater part of them, and to look upon such participation as the most precious joy.

The Divine Lover, the despised Lover, looks for one that will compassionate and console Him. "One day," says Blessed Margaret Mary, "Our Lord honored me with one of His visits, and said to me: 'My daughter, art thou really willing to give Me thy heart as a place of repose for My suffering love which all others despise?' 'My Lord, Thou knowest that I am all thine! Do with me as Thou dost desire.' Then He said to me: 'Knowest thou for what end I give thee My graces so abundantly? It is to make of thee, as it were, a sanctuary in which the fire of my love burns constantly. I have chosen thy heart as a sacred altar upon which to offer to My Eternal Father holocausts to appease His justice, and to render Him infinite glory by the offering that thou wilt make to Him of thyself, uniting thereto the sacrifice of thy being in order to honor Mine.'"

The second grace to be asked for reparation, is a very compassionate, a very devoted charity for the misfortune of souls who, by their sins injure the Sacred Heart. To pray for them, to offer one's self for them, to humble one's self, to chastise one's self in expiation of their sins and to obtain their conversion, to persevere in this devotedness till the end has been obtained—this is reparation sincere and efficacious. This is the reparation so much desired by that Heart which never ceases to love those that tear It to pieces, patiently to endure all their blows to win for them by Its patience pardon and conversion. What does St. Paul say? " For I wished myself to be an anathema from Christ for my brethren who are kinsmen according to the flesh "(1). " One day, when Our Lord had shown Blessed Margaret Mary the bad treatment He had received in a soul who had communicated with affection to sin, seized with fear and sorrow, she cast herself at His

---

(1)   Rom. ix, 3.

feet, watered them with the tears she could not restrain, and said to Him: 'My Lord and my God, if my life will be of any use to repair these injuries, although what Thou dost receive from me is a thousand times greater, yet behold me! I am Thy slave. Do with me whatever Thou pleasest.' He replied: 'Whenever I make known to thee the bad treatment I receive from that soul, I wish thee to prostrate at My feet after Communion and make honorable atonement to My Heart. Offer to the Father for the same end the bloody sacrifice of the Cross, along with thy own being, to pay homage to Mine and to repair the indignities I receive in this Heart.' At these words, I suffered great pains, and I repeatedly begged for mercy. After I had received Him one Easter Day, He said to me: 'I have heard thy groaning, and I have shed My mercy on that soul.'"

Make a visit to the Blessed Sacrament in reparation for those who visit It not.

May the Eucharistic Heart of Jesus be blessed!

(*50 days' Indulgence.*)

THE EUCHARISTIC HEART PLEADING FOR REPARATION.

ADORATION.

THE octave of Corpus Christi, with the Solemn Masses and processions that open and close it, the uninterrupted Exposition of the Adorable Sacrament, is the culminating point of Eucharistic worship. And yet "the indignities committed against Him during it," as the Saviour says, lead Him to demand "Communion and an Act of Reparation to repair the indignity offered Him during the time of Exposition on our altars." Now it is clear why the Friday after the octave of Corpus Christi has been chosen by the Saviour for the celebrating of the Feast of His Heart.

This very distinctly marks the reparative character of devotion to the Sacred Heart for the sins committed against the Eucharist. "Corpus Christi," as St. Thomas declares, "is intended, by solemn and prolonged homage, to repair the indifference of

467

the preceding year in the daily celebration and reception of the Holy Mysteries." The Feast of the Sacred Heart will repair the faults that shall have glided even into the solemn celebration of the eight days of the octave just completed. Devotion to the Sacred Heart will be not only an expression of gratitude for the infinite love and the incomparable benefits which Jesus has centred in the gift of His Eucharist, but an honorable reparation for that love despised, for those benefits profaned or rendered useless.

It is the Heart of Jesus, the " Victim of Its own too great love," that there is question of adoring, consoling, and exalting in the Sacrament in which It is offered: *" Cor Jesu, charitatis victimam, venite adoremus!* Come, let us adore the Heart of Jesus, Victim of love."

### THANKSGIVING.

For twenty centuries Jesus has been despised, repulsed, hated. The uncalled-for, multiplied, and obstinate rebuffs that He meets; the icy coldness upon which His ardent love has no effect; the profanations that outrage His Majesty, violate His sanctity, and abuse the weakness of His Humanity, ought to have been able to tire Him out, to make Him abandon this ungrateful earth, or, at least, to give rein to His just anger for the avenging of His discarded love. But no! He acknowledged the inconvertible weakness of His Heart for us when He confided to Blessed Margaret Mary the following: " To receive from men only ingratitude after having loved them to so inexplicable an excess, is more painful to Me than all that I suffered in My Passion." " But," He added, in an adorable disclosing of the secret sentiments of His Heart, " if they would give Me some return for My love, I should esteem all that I have done for them as little, and I should wish, if it were possible, to endure still more."

Far from being worn out with loving this ungrateful world, Jesus desires to redouble His love and overcome hatred by kindness. It was for this end that He revealed His Heart. Let us hearken again to a love which cannot contain itself, and which, instead of being extinguished by the waves of hatred that It meets, is, on the contrary, increased, and breaks out in a paroxysm like the following: " My Divine Heart is so passionately in love with men that, unable to restrain the flames of Its ardor, It is forced to allow them to escape, It manifests them in order to enrich men with Its precious treasures." "He told me," says Blessed Margaret Mary, "that the intense desire He has of being loved by men led Him to form the design of manifesting His Heart to them, and in these latter ages of giving to them a last effort of His love, by proposing to them an object and a means so proper to win them to love Him and to love Him truly. He opens to them all the treasures of love, grace, and mercy, of sanctification and salvation that It contains. This He does that they who wish to render and procure for Him all the honor and love possible may be enriched with a profusion of the divine treasures of which It is the faithful and inexhaustible source!"

Shall not our hearts overflow in thanksgiving to this Heart which loves us to Its own detriment, and which opposes to our ingratitude only new acts of love? "*Nos ergo diligamus Deum, quoniam Deus prior dilexit nos!*—Let us therefore love God, because God first loved us" (1).

---

(1) I John iv, 19.

### REPARATION.

If there is question of sacrilegious Communion, " the sorrowful trembling of the Heart of Jesus at the Last Supper and the indignant protests of the Saviour against Judas "(1), tell of the horrible violence, the outrageous treatment, the cruel punishment that He endures from it! He feels the claw of sacrilege fastening upon Him, and He declares that it would have been better for the traitor never to have been born than to commit such a crime!(2)

The Saviour's communications to His faithful confidante, Blessed Margaret Mary, may give an idea of the suffering inflicted on His Heart, not only by those that communicate in the state of mortal sin, but by those that entertain an affection to venial sin, voluntary tepidity and, above all, to sins of pride.

" After Holy Communion," she tells us, " my Divine Saviour presented Himself to me as the *Ecce Homo,* all torn and disfigured. He said to me : ' If thou didst but know who it is that has reduced Me to this

---

(1) John xiii.
(2) Mark xiv, 22.

state!　.　　　　Five souls consecrated to
My service have treated Me thus, for I have
been forcibly dragged with ropes into very
narrow places that were filled with all sorts
of sharp spikes, nails, and thorns, and they
have reduced me to what you see.'

" I was desirous for an explanation of
these words.　Then Our Lord gave me to
understand that the rope was the promise
that He has made to give Himself to us; the
force used against Him was His own love;
the narrow places were ill-disposed hearts;
the spikes, the spirit of pride.　I offered
Him as a place of rest the Heart He had
given me.　In His weariness He presented
Himself to me as soon as I had a moment,
telling me to kiss His Wounds, and thus alleviate His suffering.

" On another occasion, when preparing
for Holy Communion, I heard a voice saying to me:　' Look, My daughter, at the bad
treatment that I meet in the soul that has received Me!　She has renewed all the pains
of My Passion.'　I was filled with surprise
at hearing such words of a soul that had
bathed in the Precious Blood of Jesus Christ.
But the same voice continued:　' It is not
that she is actually in sin, but the will to sin

has not left her heart. I hold this more in horror than even the sinful act itself, for it is contemptuously applying My Blood to a corrupt heart, since the will to sin is the root of all corruption.'"

Wounds, dishonor, sorrow, the renewal of His whole Passion—it is thus that the Saviour depicts the punishment inflicted on His Heart by sins against the Holy Eucharist, and of which He even says: "It pains Me more than all that I endured in My Passion." Is not this sufficient to make us understand the gravity of such sin? Is it not sufficient to impress every faithful soul with the urgent duty of reparation? to make her earnest and compassionate toward the wounded Heart, generous and energetic in winning pardon for those that offend It?

### PETITION.

"On another occasion, Our Lord said to me: 'Dost thou wish to bear the weight of My sanctity of justice? I am about to let it fall upon that religious in name, whom behold!' And He showed her to me. Instantly I fell at His feet, exclaiming: 'Rather consume me to the marrow of my

bones than destroy this soul that has cost
Thee so dear! Do not spare my life. I
sacrifice it to Thy interests!' As I rose
from the ground, I felt burdened with so
great a weight that I could not drag myself
along. I was at the same time attacked by
so violent a fever that it penetrated even to
the marrow of my bones, and shortly obliged
me to keep my bed. I was exceedingly ill.
I would have desired to see myself forsaken,
abandoned by all creatures, thus to be more
conformed to Jesus' suffering. I felt in myself so great a hunger to receive Him that I
knew not what to do, except to seize Him
with my eyes by their tears. My agony was
like that of the souls in purgatory, who
suffer from the privation of the Sovereign
Good; for, notwithstanding the ardent desire that consumed me, my Divine Master
made me see that I was too unworthy to
lodge Him in my heart. This was a suffering not less than the first, which urged
me to approach Him."

If love so consuming for the adorable
Victim of the Eucharist, if such sufferings
embraced for the conversion of His unfortu-
nate scorners are above our courage and
even our desires, it remains for us to employ

for Eucharistic reparation the means that are in the reach of every soul of good will, namely, frequent attendance at Holy Mass, with closer attention to the Passion, which it renews in so real a manner; more frequent Communions, with better preparation, more purity, recollection, and fidelity to all our duties, more fervent and assiduous visits to the Blessed Sacrament, and more faithful participation in daily and nocturnal adoration. We may add to this the more patient and humble acceptance of the privations entailed upon us by our condition in life, more perfect resignation to our sufferings, whatever they may be, and more filial and lasting abandonment to the holy will of God in all kinds of trials, whencesoever they proceed. The generous choice of some mortifications, fasts, disciplines, and humiliations, suited to our state of life and physical ability, will be, also, a proper and very laudable means of reparation. United to the sufferings, humiliations, and perpetual sacrifice of the annihiliated and immolated Heart of the Eucharistic Christ, purified and inflamed by His love, they will be most powerful to console Him, and to obtain from Him the conversion of all those who crucify anew to themselves the Christ, who profane or who neglect the " Heavenly Gift "(1).

Pray for true humility of heart.

Jesus, meek and humble of Heart, make my heart like unto Thine.

(300 *days' Indulgence.*)

_____

(1)   Heb. vi, 4.

Made in United States
North Haven, CT
11 June 2023

37601357R00271